IS REALITY BEYOND GOOD AND EVIL?

TRADITIONS AND TRANSFORMATIONS IN TIBETAN BUDDHISM

David Germano and Michael Sheehy, Editors

Is Reality beyond Good and Evil?

Tibetan Buddhist Inquiry into the Ultimate Virtue

Yaroslav Komarovski

University of Virginia Press | Charlottesville and London

The University of Virginia Press is situated on the traditional lands of the Monacan Nation, and the Commonwealth of Virginia was and is home to many other Indigenous people. We pay our respect to all of them, past and present. We also honor the enslaved African and African American people who built the University of Virginia, and we recognize their descendants. We commit to fostering voices from these communities through our publications and to deepening our collective understanding of their histories and contributions.

University of Virginia Press

Printed in the United States of America on acid-free paper

First published 2024

9 8 7 6 5 4 3 2 1

LIBRARY OF CONGRESS CATALOGING-IN-PUBLICATION DATA

Names: Komarovski, Yaroslav, author.
Title: Is reality beyond good and evil? : Tibetan Buddhist inquiry into the ultimate virtue / Yaroslav Komarovski.
Description: Charlottesville : University of Virginia Press, 2024. | Series: Traditions and transformations in Tibetan Buddhism | Includes bibliographical references and index.
Identifiers: LCCN 2024010133 (print) | LCCN 2024010134 (ebook) | ISBN 9780813952154 (hardcover) | ISBN 9780813952161 (paperback) | ISBN 9780813952178 (ebook)
Subjects: LCSH: Good and evil—Religious aspects—Buddhism. | Virtue. | Buddhism—Doctrines.
Classification: LCC BQ4570.G66 K66 2024 (print) | LCC BQ4570.G66 (ebook) | DDC 294.3/42—dc23/eng/20240312
LC record available at https://lccn.loc.gov/2024010133
LC ebook record available at https://lccn.loc.gov/2024010134

Cover photo: Gilded statue of Rinchen Zangpo, Sakya Tangyud monastery, Kaza, Spiti, Himachal Pradesh, India. (Neil McAllister / Alamy Stock Photo)
Cover design: Susan Zucker

CONTENTS

Acknowledgments *vii*

An Introduction: Ultimate, Virtue, Ultimate Virtue 1

1. Tibetan Virtuosi Positions Compared: Four Approaches to the Ultimate Virtue 5

2. Virtual Ambivalence: Indian Textual Background 13

3. The Ultimate Is a Virtue Worth Dedicating: Dorjé Sherap on Jikten Gönpo's Teachings 21

4. The Ultimate Is Not a Virtue Unless You Do Not Mean It: Sakya Pandita's Objections 31

5. Admiring Your Virtues, I Have Questions to Ask: Shakya Chokden's Inquiry 47

6. What Colors Are Virtues? Gorampa vs. Shakya Chokden on Karmic Causes and Results 53

7. Is the Ultimate an Actual Virtue? Gorampa vs. Shakya Chokden on the Dharma-Sphere 74

8. Who Owns the Highest Virtue? Gorampa vs. Shakya Chokden on the Buddha-Essence 125

Final Remarks: The Virtue of Contesting the Ultimate Virtue 151

Notes *157*
Bibliography *193*
Index *201*

ACKNOWLEDGMENTS

I am grateful to all the people who directly or indirectly contributed to my work on this manuscript and helped bring it to completion: the late Khenchen Künga Wangchuk and other Tibetan teachers with whom I studied Sakya scholastic writings at the Dzongsar Institute in Bir, India; Professor Jan-Ulrich Sobisch, who generously shared with me his knowledge of the Kagyü writings explored in the book; Professor Dominic Sur, who carefully read the manuscript and provided numerous insightful suggestions for improving it; anonymous readers of the manuscript, who made valuable critical comments on how to further modify and improve it; the editors of the Traditions and Transformations in Tibetan Buddhism series, Professor David Germano and Professor Michael Sheehy; UVA Press director Eric Brandt, managing editor Ellen Satrom, copyeditor Joanne Allen, and other members of the UVA Press editorial team who helped to smoothly move the manuscript through the editorial process; L. S. Summer, for her thorough indexing of the book; and last but not least, my dear wife, Trang Nguyen, for her invaluable support and kindness throughout my work on this book.

While the virtue of writing this book is not ultimate and might ultimately result in raising more questions than clear-cut answers, I hope that my inquiry into the intricate Tibetan polemics on the ultimate virtue will contribute to further exploration of the rich network of ideas surrounding the topics of virtue, the ultimate, and their relationship, deepening our insights into the key categories of Buddhist philosophy and practice.

IS REALITY BEYOND GOOD AND EVIL?

An Introduction

Ultimate, Virtue, Ultimate Virtue

Is the ultimate nature of our being a virtue? Is it dynamic or static? Does it share with other virtues such qualities as momentariness and ability to function and produce results? Or is it a unique phenomenon in a separate category of its own? Do we already possess the ultimate virtue in the form of the buddha-nature? Will we have it only when we become buddhas? Or will we acquire it at a certain point along the path to buddhahood? Is the ultimate a part of the eight types of consciousness or does it transcend them all? What can we do with or about it? Can we focus on, contemplate, nourish, dedicate it? Is it helpful to compartmentalize interpretations of reality and virtue into schools, systems, and dharmacakras? Are those interpretations reconcilable, or do they come down differently on the same point? Should interpretations of the ultimate virtue by Niḥsvabhāvavāda Madhyamaka be preferred to those by Yogācāra, or vice versa? Alternatively, should we focus on clarifying interpretive approaches followed in specific texts without passing definitive judgments about which ones are "correct"? Does our choice of one interpretation over another make a difference on the practical level, such as in the cultivation of virtuous actions? If so, why and what is that difference? As this study demonstrates, none of these questions has a definitive answer. Answers depend on the context, the thinker, the text, the intention, the purpose, the interpretation, the system of thought, and the way of practice.

From the early stages of development of Buddhism to the present day, Buddhist thinkers have been developing diverse, often conflicting models of the nature of living beings, their potential for achieving awakening, and the ways of developing that potential. Buddhists clash on such questions as whether at the core of our being we are in need of perfection or already perfect, whether the ultimate nature of our mind is virtuous or transcends both virtues and nonvirtues, and whether the qualities of buddhahood are already present within us or have to be developed anew. These questions often lie at the intersection of two forms of discourse, ontological and ethical. Among other issues, the former explores the nature of reality, mind, and being, while the latter explores goodness, virtues, and positive qualities that may or may not pertain to that nature.

A prominent feature shared by Indian and Tibetan Mahāyāna approaches to human nature, and to the nature of sentient beings more generally, is the unwillingness to treat it as evil or impure. Indian and Tibetan Mahāyāna thinkers are in agreement that on the most fundamental or ultimate level our nature is always pure, while afflictions and other obscurations are only adventitious.[1] Nevertheless, what exactly that ultimate nature is, whether it is virtuous/good or neutral,[2] and what the relationship is between it and virtue are subjects of continuing debates. Focusing on these issues, this book addresses conflicting positions of Tibetan thinkers on the question whether our ultimate nature is a virtue / virtuous, appraising how different understandings of the ultimate nature affect their perspectives on what can or cannot be treated as a virtue. It thereby assesses the vital interplay between ontology and ethics in Buddhism.

Tibetan Buddhist thinkers generally adopt one of two contradictory models of the ultimate nature of living beings. According to one model, our ultimate nature is neutral and/or transcends all notions of virtue and evil. Consequently, it is argued that although we have a potential to develop positive qualities and virtues, our ultimate nature is not good or virtuous. According to another model, our ultimate nature has positive, virtuous qualities, even though it transcends dualistic concepts of goodness and badness. Thus, it is argued that it is good and virtuous / a virtue. While both positions are articulated in Indian texts taken by Tibetans as authoritative, Tibetan scholars usually treat only one of the two as definitive, issuing dramatically different interpretations of such categories as "ultimate virtue" (*don dam dge ba*) or "virtue in terms of the ultimate" (*don dam pas dge ba*) stemming from, among other sources, Asaṅga's *Summary of Abhidharma,*[3] which states, "What is virtue in terms of the ultimate? It is suchness [*de bzhin nyid*]."[4]

A closely related topic that is also given highly diverse interpretations is the nature of mind (not necessarily in the ultimate sense). Greatly simplifying, we can point to two approaches to mind or consciousness in Buddhism. According to one, mind is a network or series of constantly changing mental events without any underlying subliminal type of mentality. According to the other, there is indeed such subliminal mentality, and it can also be understood as the ultimate nature of mind. While both accept the natural purity, or luminosity (*'od gsal, prabhāsvara*), of consciousness in general, they disagree on whether a particular subliminal type of mind separate from all others can exist regardless of the presence or absence of other minds. The question of the existence of this subliminal mind plays an important role in polemics on the ultimate virtue. When accepted, it can be treated as either neutral or virtuous and identified as the universal basis (*kun gzhi, ālaya*), primordial mind (*ye shes, jñāna*), or tathāgata-essence (*de bzhin gshegs pa'i snying po, tathāgatagarbha*) / sugata-essence (*bde bar gshegs pa' snying po, sugatagarbha*).

Overall, when debating the question of the virtuous ultimate reality, Tibetan thinkers are occupied not so much with the nature of virtue or goodness per se as with what the nature of ultimate reality is and how it is related to such categories as virtue and the innate potential for awakening. Their positions on ultimate reality vary significantly, and they hold highly diverse opinions on the relationship between it and virtue.

This book discusses positions of several rival Tibetan thinkers regarding the ultimate virtue. What primarily interests me is the insightful polemics. In particular, we look at how a particular position on the nature of ultimate reality shapes their philosophical approach to virtue. Chapter 1 introduces several conflicting approaches to the ultimate virtue that are explored in further detail in the following chapters. Chapter 2 traces the origins of the polemics on the ultimate virtue back to the Indian canonical texts and commentarial works, providing a general background and addressing sources relevant to the subsequent discussion. Chapter 3 discusses the position embraced by Dorjé Sherap (*rdo rje shes rab*, n.d.), a disciple of the seminal Drigung Kagyü (*'bri gung bka' brgyud*) thinker Drigung Kyoppa Jikten Gönpo (*'bri gung skyobs pa 'jig rten mgon po*, 1143–1217), articulated in his commentary on Jikten Gönpo's teachings. That position became a target of criticisms by the thinkers of the Sakya (*sa skya*) tradition. Chapter 4 outlines the refutation of the key elements of that position by the towering figure of the Sakya tradition Sakya Pandita Künga Gyeltsen (*sa skya paṇḍita kun dga' rgyal mtshan*, 1182–1251). Chapter 5 lists questions regarding Sakya Pandita's stance by the controversial Sakya thinker Serdok Penchen Shakya Chokden (*gser mdog paṇ chen shākya mchog ldan*, 1428–1507). Chapters 6–8 juxtapose Shakya Chokden's own answers to the critical responses to those questions by his contemporary and rival Gowo Rapjampa Sönam Senggé (*go bo rab 'byams pa bsod nams seng ge*, also known as Gorampa, *go rams pa*, 1429–1489), whose position is held as the mainstream in the Sakya tradition. Chapter 6 outlines the two thinkers' positions on the working of karmas and their effects. Chapter 7 explores in detail their conflicting approaches to the ultimate as a virtue. Chapter 8 provides additional details of the buddha-essence involved in the discussion of the ultimate virtue.

As is clear from this outline, in addressing conflicting positions on the ultimate virtue I treat some more extensively than others. There are several reasons for this. In order not to make the discussion of the ultimate virtue overly broad, this book is mainly concerned with representative positions of the leading thinkers of only one Tibetan tradition, Sakya. Consequently, Jikten Gönpo's position in Dorjé Sherap's interpretation, though discussed in some detail, serves primarily as a starting point for the discussion of polemical responses, questions motivated by the responses, and responses to those questions by seminal Sakya thinkers. My focus is on the ingenious position of Shakya Chokden, who applies the widespread understanding of virtue as a phenomenon producing positive results to the everlasting and transcendent ultimate reality, providing in the process intriguing perspectives on the nature of mind, the potential for awakening, and more.

1 | Tibetan Virtuosi Positions Compared

Four Approaches to the Ultimate Virtue

Dorjé Sherap's Position

Dorjé Sherap argues that the naturally pure element is the tathāgata-essence, the dharma-sphere, and the dharma-body. As such, it is permanent, virtuous, and unchangeable. It is permanent not with regard to one of the eight extremes but with regard to its never-ending continuity. Being a virtue, the dharma-sphere qua tathāgata-essence comprises two factors, unafflicted wisdom and extensive positive qualities. It is not impermanent and does not undergo change, but on the conventional level, until the defilements of mistaken appearances have been purified, it can be interpreted in terms of the change of state: on the causal level of sentient beings, it is not yet purified of defilements; on the resultant level of buddhahood, it is free of them.

The ultimate, existent virtue is analogized to conventional, accumulated virtues as an ocean is to its waves. This connection plays an important role on the practical level as well: with the tathāgata-essence's being inconceivable and immeasurable, the roots of dedicated conventional virtues also become inconceivable and immeasurable when blessed by it. The dedication of the ultimate virtue is not only effective in its own right; it also increases the effectiveness or power of other dedicated virtues.

The category of the ultimate virtue is also connected with that of mahāmudrā, which for Dorjé Sherap is synonymous with the naturally pure element, perfection of wisdom, freedom from extremes, and the ultimate reality qua luminosity. As such, mahāmudrā primordially abides as the nature of all positive qualities throughout the basis, path, and result, with nothing to eliminate or establish. All happiness and goodness of saṃsāra and nirvāṇa, not unlike the ray-like qualities of mahāmudrā, emerge from within the sun-like mahāmudrā. As the basis, mahāmudrā is the naturally pure element. Whatever virtuous thoughts arise owing to its power are all its stirring. Familiarization with it is the path. Whatever roots of virtues are created, they become immeasurable through mahāmudrā's power. On the resultant level, the final mahāmudrā spontaneously and ceaselessly emerges as the dharma-body endowed with positive qualities. Thus, mahāmudrā serves as both the nature and the source of virtues and itself is a virtue.

Sakya Pandita's Position

In contrast to this position, Sakya Pandita argues that there is no primordially existent virtue, the ultimate reality is not a virtue, and the dharma-sphere cannot be dedicated because it is unchanging. Virtues are necessarily functional phenomena producing happiness as their fruition. Unless something functions as a productive cause of happiness and therefore is impermanent, compounded, and on account of that falling outside the scope of ultimate reality, it cannot be an actual virtue—only an imagined one. The dharma-sphere is uncompounded and thus is neither a virtue nor an evil.

Teachings that the dharma-sphere is a virtue refer either to virtues or to the ultimate, never to something that is both. The *ultimate* in the *ultimate virtue* taught in such texts as the *Summary of Abhidharma* refers to the ultimate reality that is never a virtue. Similar to the *ultimate evil* and the *ultimate unspecified phenomena,* the *ultimate virtue* should not be taken literally. The dharma-sphere is called *virtue* simply to mean the absence of evil. Because there are no phenomena apart from the dharma-sphere, were it an actual virtue, rebirth in the low transmigrations would be impossible since nonvirtues too, not existing apart from the dharma-sphere, would turn out to be virtues.

Not being impermanent, the dharma-sphere transcends existence itself (although it is not nonexistent either). What is termed *mere existence* is a phenomenon able to function; the dharma-sphere, being free from proliferations, is beyond functioning. Were the dharma-sphere existent, it would also have to be treated as accomplished and for that reason produced and impermanent, which contradicts its being described as uncreated.

Within the two types of dedication—realistic and unrealistic—dedication of reality belongs to the latter type and thus cannot be accomplished. Furthermore, dedication of virtues that have not been produced is impossible: only the virtues that have been created are dedicatable; what is uncreated transcends virtue or evil. Were the dharma-sphere, or reality, a dedicatable virtue, the reality of all phenomena would be suitable for dedication because there is no difference between the reality of sentient beings and that of the rest of phenomena. Since the dharma-sphere has no divisions, it is also wrong to claim that the dharma-sphere of sentient beings is the sugata-essence and that of inanimate matter is not.

Because the sugata-essence is the unchangeable dharma-sphere, it transcends virtue and evil and cannot be dedicated. If the dharma-sphere were a virtue suitable for dedication, dedication would have to transform it and thus render it a functional thing. Otherwise, dedication that does not involve transformation or change is meaningless. Accepting that the dharma-sphere can undergo transformation or change would contradict the Buddha's teaching that it is unchangeable.

Dedication of the dharma-sphere negatively affects Buddhist practice; it is unacceptable even as a form of mind training since such dedication involves conceptual discrimination, thereby spoiling other dedications. The actual mind training consists in dedicating to others all virtues from within the state of the dharma-sphere free from proliferations. Treating the dharma-sphere free from proliferations as a virtue will render it an observable object.

Nor is it true that *sugata-essence* refers not to the dharma-sphere per se but exclusively to the element of sentient beings. *Element* can refer to things, nonthings, or freedom from proliferations. Not being either of the first two, the sugata-essence is freedom from proliferations and thus is none other than the dharma-sphere. Also, the virtuous sugata-essence cannot be identified as the stainless mental continuum, the clarity aspect of the universal basis consciousness, which, being an unobscured unspecified phenomenon, cannot be a virtue. Excluding the stainless mental continuum from the eight types of consciousness is not an option either because it would wrongly entail nine consciousnesses.

Although the tathāgata-essence transcends virtue and evil, it is not unrelated to them: being freedom from proliferations, it allows for emergence of both buddhahood and saṃsāra. Yet it is not some sort of a virtuous source or, worse, the buddha-essence already existent within sentient beings. The teachings on the existence of the buddha-essence within sentient beings should not be taken literally.

Gorampa's Position

Defending and elaborating on Sakya Pandita's position, Gorampa argues that all interpretations of the dharma-sphere as a virtue refer exclusively to an imputed virtue. It is pointless to keep asking questions about such texts as the

Sublime Continuum teaching the dharma-sphere as a virtue after such a virtue has already been determined by Sakya Pandita as imputed. Sakya Pandita explained that the mere absence of evil was intended when calling the dharma-sphere *virtue.*

The dharma-sphere is not a functional phenomenon capable of producing results. There are two types of causes, productive causes and nature-causes. Only the former undergo change or transformation; the latter do not. When the dharma-sphere is posited as the causal lineage, it is with reference to the nature-cause; it does not undergo changes apart from its being or not being separated from adventitious defilements. The same applies to its being called the *cause of ārya dharmas.* Were the dharma-sphere the productive cause of ārya dharmas, it would be compounded. Because it cannot function as a productive cause, it cannot be a virtue capable of producing positive results. Were it able to do so, it would fall under the category of compounded—and thus not ultimate—phenomena.

When criticizing the notion of the ultimate virtue in the context of there being no phenomena apart from the dharma-sphere, Sakya Pandita argued that all evils and unspecified phenomena will turn out to have virtue because they all have the dharma-sphere. If this position is accepted, then it will follow that it is impossible to be reborn in low realms; whether one has created virtuous, nonvirtuous, or unspecified actions, in each case one will have created virtues.

There are two types of meaningless dedication: that which pertains to the roots of virtues being dedicated not being transformed and that which pertains to the results of dedication not being accomplished. The dedication illustrated by the story of Maitrakanyaka is not meaningless in the former sense because it results in the transformation of the roots of virtues. The dedication of the dharma-sphere, by contrast, is not just meaningless in both respects but harmful too. The *Jewel Heap Sūtra*'s statement that "the reality of dharmas cannot be transformed by the power of aspirational resolve" refers not to the reality in the sense of freedom from proliferations but to the reality in the sense of dependent origination; *cannot be transformed* refers to the result of dedication. While that result cannot be accomplished, the cause dedicated is transformed in the process of dedication: the virtue of aspiration undergoes transformation with respect to bringing about positive results.

If there were both virtues and unspecified phenomena among the seeds of one and the same universal basis, it would follow that the seeds and the universal basis that possesses them have discordant entities. If the stainless seeds on the universal basis were virtues, because its entity was concordant with them, it would follow that the universal basis is not an unspecified phenomenon. The stainless seeds do become antidotes of the universal basis when they become the truth of the path, which itself is stainless. The seeds themselves are not the antidotes of the universal basis.

The naturally abiding lineage, the sugata-essence, the ultimate reality, and the dharma-sphere are directly perceived by the individually self-cognizing primordial mind of āryas. Thus, their own entity is not a relative reality, and their teachings are definitive, not interpretive. Interpretive are the teachings that they exist in the mental continua of sentient beings by way of the support and supported or as being accomplished, as demonstrated by the examples given in the *Tathāgata-Essence Sūtra* and the *Sublime Continuum*. Other than being free from proliferations, the nature of mind does not exist at all in the way illustrated by those examples. This interpretation is based on the *Sublime Continuum,* which teaches that the reality characterized as the thorough pacification of proliferations of the two types of self is the ultimate reality, while that reality's existence in the mental continua of migrators is a relative reality.

Shakya Chokden's Position

Shakya Chokden interprets Sakya Pandita's position in a way that fits his own approach, which in many respects differs from that of Sakya Pandita. Distinguishing between the self- and other-emptiness positions, he argues that Sakya Pandita advanced the position of the self-emptiness. According to that presentation, the dharma-sphere, transcending existence, nonexistence, and so on, is not a virtue and cannot be dedicated. The other-emptiness approach was determined by him as a provisional position at best. This does not undermine the validity of the other-emptiness approach, according to which the dharma-sphere—the ultimately real nondual primordial mind—does exist, functions, and is a virtue, though it cannot be dedicated. It is impermanent, momentary, and a cause of ārya dharmas. While it is permanent with respect to its everlasting continuity, it is compounded since it is produced and disintegrates. That nondual primordial mind is incorporated into the very heart of tantric contemplative practice. If it is not treated as a virtue, the tantric way of accumulating the two collections of merits and wisdom will be impossible.

That primordial mind is also a projecting cause, a causal condition, a stainless knowing, and the naturally abiding lineage. As the clarity and cognition factor of experience on the universal basis, it coexists with but is not subsumed under it; it is the antidote to the universal basis and persists all the way through to buddhahood. It is also characterized as stainless seeds (thus, both stained and stainless seeds can be virtues). Among stainless seeds, the ones obtained by nature are the naturally abiding lineage; the ones appropriated anew are the developmental lineage. Although similar to the latter, the former also undergo momentary disintegration; they are posited as permanent with regard to their continuity. Those stainless seeds are virtues because when meeting with nourishing conditions their entity turns into virtues. Being the primary causes of fruitions, the seeds of both stained and stainless virtues are the actual virtues. When virtues are dedicated, the seeds of virtues—not the manifest virtues themselves—are directly dedicated.

There are two different approaches to there being no dharmas apart from the dharma-sphere. They stem, respectively, from the second and third dharmacakras with works based on them. In the former context, all phenomena are said to have two entities—of the mode of appearance and of the mode of being—which appear, respectively, to unreal ideation and primordial mind. The former is the dualistic appearance as the apprehended and apprehender to consciousness; the latter refers to not appearing as anything at all to the nondual primordial mind in the meditative equipoise of āryas. There are no dharmas apart from the dharma-sphere because the mode of being of all knowables is the dharma-sphere. Not only do relative phenomena not exist but what is imputed as their mode of being is the lack of the mode of being. That said, relative phenomena are not the dharma-sphere; otherwise they would be the ultimate reality. In the latter context, there are no dharmas apart from the dharma-sphere because nothing but the dharma-sphere—the ultimate virtue—exists. No existence is admitted to anything subsumed under the apprehended and the apprehender, be it a nonvirtue, a relative virtue, or an unspecified phenomenon. With respect to Sakya Pandita's approach, having assumed the position of Niḥsvabhāvavāda stemming from the second dharmacakra, he was refuting the Yogācāra claim that on the one hand the dharma-sphere is a virtue, while on the other hand if something exists, it has to be the dharma-sphere.

The main reason why the dharma-sphere is not dedicatable is that dedication is structured by transformation. The dharma-sphere, by contrast, persists into buddhahood without changes to its entity. While the dharma-sphere, as the ultimate virtue, cannot be meaningfully dedicated, dedication of other virtues to awakening does benefit it: nourishing the dharma-sphere, that dedication makes it give rise to the sprouts of awakening, which in turn give rise to awakening itself. Furthermore, distinctions should be made between dedication and aspirational resolve. Although it is impossible to dedicate what is not liable to change, it is still acceptable to make an aspirational resolve that cannot be realized. Dedication, which, in contrast to aspirational resolve, requires a substance to dedicate, pertains only to virtues created by the person who makes that dedication and thus excludes the ultimate virtue. As for the aspirational resolve in connection to the dharma-sphere, when one aspires to attain awakening, that resolve can be realized. Such resolve is one of the two types of aspirational resolve, that which will be accomplished if made, in contrast to that which will not be accomplished. Dedication is exclusively the realistic aspirational resolve because the substance being dedicated necessarily has to be suitable for transformation or change into that to which it is dedicated. Consequently, the virtuous dharma-sphere is not suitable for either of the two types of dedication, realistic and unrealistic.

Regarding the ultimate virtue qua the buddha-essence, Sakya Pandita treated the buddha-essence and the buddha as the same and thus existent only in the state of buddhahood. He explicitly rejected the claim that the lineage and the dharma-sphere are the actual buddha-essence; he implicitly suggested that only the dharma-body is the essence. The *Sublime Continuum*—which posits the buddha-essence primarily with respect to the positive qualities' inseparability from it—did not teach that all sentient beings are possessors of the buddha-essence ornamented with the buddha-qualities; Sakya Pandita did not interpret it as such either. The *Sublime Continuum* interpreted such teachings as having a special intent; Sakya Pandita agreed. That said, when Sakya Pandita argued that the sugata-essence is uncompounded, he meant that it is uncompounded by karmas and afflictions, not that it is free from production and disintegration. Both the actual essence, which according to Sakya Pandita is the dharma-body in the state of buddhahood, and the basis of the intent behind teaching it, which is the primordial mind of emptiness, are compounded in the sense of undergoing production and disintegration.

Of multiple issues mentioned above, some were explicitly addressed only by some—not all—of the four thinkers. That said, we can justifiably put side by side five contested points regarding the ultimate virtue and look at how they are dealt with by Dorjé Sherap, Sakya Pandita, Gorampa, and Shakya Chokden. In the table below I list only those issues that are explicitly addressed by all four thinkers and demonstrate their respective positions. Consequently, I do not address such categories as the stainless seeds or the buddha-essence: the former is not explicitly discussed by Dorjé Sherap or Sakya Pandita, and while the latter is discussed by all four thinkers, including Shakya Chokden, his interpretation expresses not his own position but that of Sakya Pandita as

THE FOUR ARGUMENTS on the five key points regarding the ultimate virtue

	DORJÉ SHERAP	SAKYA PANDITA	GORAMPA	SHAKYA CHOKDEN
1. Primordial virtue exists	+	–	–	+
2. The ultimate is a virtue	+	–	–	+
3. The ultimate is primordial mind	+	–	–	+
4. The ultimate is momentary	–	–	–	+
5. The ultimate is dedicatable	+	–	–	–

Note: + indicates acceptance; – indicates rejection.

he understands it. We should also note that Shakya Chokden's position pertains specifically to what he understands as the other-emptiness approach followed in Alīkākāravāda and Tantra. According to him, in the self-emptiness system of Niḥsvabhāvavāda neither actual ultimate reality nor ultimate virtue was taught.

It is striking that although Shakya Chokden allegedly clarifies the views of Sakya Pandita, with the exception of the question of dedicatability (5), the first four categories listed in the table (1–4) are addressed by the two thinkers differently. Even when addressing the last issue, Shakya Chokden does not follow Sakya Pandita's take on it unequivocally; he attempts to "update" it. On the other hand, while on the surface Shakya Chokden and Dorjé Sherap appear to agree on several issues, the way they understand them is vastly different. For example, both thinkers treat the ultimate as primordial mind, but they hold conflicting views on its nature: according to Shakya Chokden, it is momentary, while according to Dorjé Sherap, it is not. As for Gorampa, he faithfully follows Sakya Pandita on the five points, elaborating on the latter's position and defending it from what he sees as unjustified attacks by Shakya Chokden.

2 | Virtual Ambivalence

Indian Textual Background

Buddhist vocabulary contains many terms whose meanings and applications vary depending on context, tradition, and thinker. Commentarial literature lists and elaborates upon multilayered meanings of such terms.[1] This context-dependent variety is not seen by Buddhist thinkers as problematic. After all, what is surprising in one and the same term having different referents?

When we turn to the Tibetan and Sanskrit terms translated as "virtue" or "goodness"—*dge ba* and *kuśala*[2]—which figure prominently throughout this book, the situation initially appears to be the same. Indian and Tibetan thinkers provide lists of phenomena subsumed under the category of virtue, explain why each of them is termed so, and do not necessarily raise questions about which of these phenomena are actual virtues and which are only imputed as such. Depending on context, those thinkers might use the term *virtue* narrowly, for example, when identifying a specific mental state as a virtue, or broadly, when calling all teachings of the Buddha "virtue at the beginning, middle, and end." They can apply the term to the Buddhist practice with its results, contents of Buddhist texts, and much more.[3]

A good example of this broad and inclusive treatment is Asaṅga's *Summary of Abhidharma.* The text addresses thirteen types of "virtues."[4] Addressing them, Asaṅga does not ask which virtues are "real" and which are not. On the surface, the usage of *kuśala* in the broader sense does not appear to be more problematic than the usage of *dharma.*[5] The same text also provides lists of nonvirtues and unspecified phenomena without raising the issue of which are actual and which are only imputed. Of particular importance for the polemics regarding the ultimate virtue explored in later chapters is what it treats as the ultimate nonvirtues and the ultimate unspecified phenomena. Regarding the former, the text states, "What is nonvirtue in terms of the ultimate? It is the whole saṃsāra."[6] About the latter it states, "What is the unspecified in terms of the ultimate? Space and the nonanalytical cessation."[7]

Another example is Vasubandhu's *Explanation of the "Treasury of Abhidharma,"* the autocommentary on his *Treasury of Abhidharma.* It explicitly argues against treating phenomena as virtues or evils only in terms of motivation (*kun nas slong ba, samutthāna*)[8] and posits four types of virtues (and nonvirtues), in terms of (1) the ultimate (*don dam pa, paramārtha*), (2) entity (*ngo bo, svabhāva*), (3) concordance (*mtshungs par ldan pa, saṃprayoga*), and (4) motivation.[9] Vasubandhu does raise the question whether such broad treatment of virtues would entail internal contradictions.[10] That discussion notwithstanding, Vasubandhu uses the term *kuśala* in this context rather broadly, without concern for which virtues are real and which are merely imputed.

Yet the question whether ultimate reality is a virtue—or to put it differently, whether it is a real or an imputed virtue—became an important polemical issue in Tibet. Why so? To start with, we should note that despite the diversity of phenomena subsumed under the category of virtue, all of them share one specific feature in common: *engaging them explicitly or implicitly, directly or indirectly, is believed to bring about positive results.* This approach is closely connected with the widely used interpretation of virtues as *phenomena that produce happiness as their main result.* Contributing to this take on virtues as positively functioning phenomena is the fact that virtues are given the most exhaustive treatment in the discussion of karmas (intentional actions), such as the ten virtuous and ten nonvirtuous karmas. In that context, characteristic features of the narrow category of virtuous karmas are applied to the broader category of virtues in general. Sakya Pandita, whose views on the ultimate virtue are analyzed in chapter 4, did precisely that when in the context of discussing karmas he wrote: "Virtue is what is well performed, / Producing happiness as its fruition."[11]

Karmas play a crucial role in the Buddhist world, being viewed as among the major forces driving the universe of saṃsāra and also contributing to its transcendence. That is, on the one hand, we experience results of, and our rebirths are determined by, previously accumulated good and bad karmic potentials; on the other, we can eliminate all karmic potentials binding us to saṃsāra and become completely free from experiencing their results. This objective is achieved through the cultivation of such antidotes as karmas that are not associated with or caused by the afflictions of ignorance, desire, and so on. Such karmas are necessarily good or virtuous because they bring about the positive result of freedom from saṃsāra. We will return to different ways of classifying karmas and their results starting in chapter 4.

Besides virtuous karmas, the category of virtue includes numerous other phenomena, such as virtuous mental states of faith, and so on.[12] It also includes such worldly and world-transcending states and phenomena as meditative absorptions, compassion, the eightfold path, and the six perfections (*pha rol tu phyin pa, pāramitā*). Practice of the Buddhist path, for example, is often described in terms of accumulating the two collections (*tshogs, saṃbhāra*) of merits (*bsod nams, puṇya*) and wisdom (*shes rab, prajñā*), wherein cultivation of such virtues as compassion and patience is subsumed under the former while realization of reality is subsumed under the latter. That realization of reality itself, as well as most of what is covered by the category of the path, is also understood as a virtue.[13] Not only that but such resultant qualities of buddhahood as omniscience are understood as virtues too. The list can go on.

The diversity of those virtues notwithstanding, we can easily recognize the aforementioned common feature they share: the capacity to *function,* bringing about positive results. This explains why virtues (together with nonvirtues and unspecified phenomena) are often addressed in the broader discussion of different types of causes and results, in particular six types of causes and five types of results that will be referred to in the polemics regarding the ultimate virtue.[14] Partly because of the emphasis on the functional, dynamic, causal quality of virtues, when focusing on the analysis of virtues, Tibetan thinkers seldom address phenomena that do not have this functioning quality. Because ultimate reality is often seen as one such phenomenon, in the context of discussing virtues it is usually addressed merely as a static object of wisdom or insight, with no deeper connection—much less overlap—between the categories of virtue and ultimate reality. From such a perspective, ultimate reality can at best be an imputed virtue, while treating it as a real virtue entails numerous unwelcome consequences. Little wonder, then, that the virtues in terms of thorough pacification or in terms of the ultimate on Asaṅga's list would not be treated as actual virtues by leading Tibetan thinkers.[15]

Yet even Asaṅga's *Summary of Abhidharma,* which puts ultimate reality in the category of uncompounded (*'dus ma byas, asaṃskṛta*) phenomena and thereby denies, on the surface at least, its ability to function, provides room for alternative interpretations. The text discusses eight types of uncompounded phenomena, including the suchness of virtuous phenomena (*chos dge ba rnams kyi de bzhin nyid, kuśaladharmatathatā*), the suchness of nonvirtuous phenomena (*chos mi dge ba rnams kyi de bzhin nyid, akuśaladharmatathatā*), and the suchness of unspecified phenomena (*chos lung du ma bstan pa rnams kyi de bzhin nyid, avyākṛtadharmatathatā*).[16] Asaṅga identifies the suchness (*de bzhin nyid, tathatā*) of virtuous, nonvirtuous, and unspecified phenomena as the two types of selflessness (*bdag med pa, nairātmya*), emptiness (*stong pa nyid, śūnyatā*), signlessness (*mtshan ma med pa, animitta*), reality-limit (*yang dag pa'i mtha', bhūtakoṭi*), the ultimate (*don dam pa, paramārtha*), and the dharma-sphere (*chos kyi dbyings, dharmadhātu*).[17] Unpacking the meaning of these terms, he writes that *suchness* is called so because it cannot change into something else; *emptiness*, because of the nonfunctioning of afflictions; *signlessness*, because of the pacification of characteristics; *reality-limit*, because of being an object of observation devoid of errors; *the ultimate*, because of being an object of functioning of the ultimate primordial mind of āryas; and *the dharma-sphere*, because of being the cause of all dharmas of śrāvakas, pratyekabuddhas, and buddhas.[18]

While other terms do not seem to be problematic in this context, Asaṅga's treatment of the dharma-sphere as the *cause* of dharmas connected to the three types of awakening may be—and, as we will see, has been—taken literally. While this approach may raise the objection that such an uncompounded phenomenon will turn out to be impermanent, it does allow one to treat the ultimate as an actual virtue capable of producing positive results. The possibility of such a take on the ultimate can in part explain why, although the static version of ultimate reality and its exclusion from the category of the actual virtue are quite widespread in Tibet, some thinkers do treat their particular version of ultimate reality as an actual virtue, raising in the process important philosophical, ethical, and practical questions. (We return to this point below.) Those questions are raised primarily in the context of analysis of ultimate reality and, in particular, the ultimate nature of living beings.

When virtue and ultimate reality are treated together and the latter is viewed as a type of the former (whether in the actual or metaphorical sense), Mahāyāna thinkers face further complications because opinions differ on what reality is. It is true that, in contrast to *virtue*, fewer phenomena are called *ultimate reality* by Mahāyāna thinkers. It is also true that the latter term usually refers to very specific and closely related categories, such as emptiness or nirvāṇa. Yet what is read into the meaning of the term and related phenomena is highly diverse and varies significantly from thinker to thinker. As a result of this diversity of perspectives on ultimate reality on the one hand and diverse applications of the category of virtue on the other, we are faced with a rich variety of approaches to the relationship between virtue and reality.

We can look at four different approaches. According to one approach, when ultimate reality is treated as a permanent, unchangeable phenomenon or as transcending all phenomena, it cannot be treated as a virtue in the sense of a cause producing positive results or even as having a potential for developing virtues. The best it can "do" is to "provide space" for functional virtues to arise. It can also be accessed or "connected with" by minds realizing it. Those minds are necessarily virtuous because they serve as antidotes to obscurations, transforming generosity, patience, and other virtues into the means of achieving awakening. According to a second approach, wisdom realizing ultimate reality can be treated as the ultimate reality itself. Consequently, if such wisdom is understood as a virtue producing positive results, the same applies to ultimate reality too. A third possible approach is to treat the tathāgata-essence, or buddha-nature, as the ultimate reality within living beings (if not the whole universe) and treat that reality as being imbued with virtuous qualities and therefore as virtuous by nature. In these first three approaches ultimate reality is understood differently, while virtue is treated as a functional phenomenon producing happiness. But in a fourth approach, as we have already seen, the category of virtue itself can be expanded to include phenomena that are usually understood as *not* functional, with further combinations of virtue and ultimate reality emerging as a result. For example, the category of virtue can include nirvāṇa, emptiness, and dharma-sphere, all of which can also be treated as permanent and seen not just as objects of virtuous minds but as actual virtues in their own right.

There are other possible combinations of virtue and reality. But were we to limit our analysis to the issue of whether virtue should be an impermanent, functional phenomenon producing happiness as its main result or also include such static things as ultimate reality because they also contribute to happiness, we would mostly be dealing with the question of terminology, with how restrictive we should be in using the term *virtue*. Whichever stance on this issue we chose, it would not affect our understanding of ultimate reality. But we may choose a different approach: to retain the "standard" definition of virtue as a phenomenon producing positive results and explore how and why such an unchanging, inexpressible, transcendent phenomenon as ultimate reality can be interpreted as fulfilling that very definition. It is this approach that will primarily interest us here because it largely informs the polemics explored in this book. As will be demonstrated below, far from being limited to the question of terminology, it has a potential heuristic value, extending beyond the question of the goodness of ultimate reality and addressing important issues in Buddhist ethics, philosophy, and practice.

We should note that the choice of terms used in translating *kuśala* as *dge ba* did contribute to polemicizing the issue of the ultimate virtue in Tibet. *Kuśala* has a wide range of meanings that are not limited to what Tibetans translate as *dge ba.* In general, *kuśala* can mean "right," "proper," "good," "auspicious," "happy," "prosperous," "able," "skillful," "welfare," "happiness," "virtue," and more.[19] In the Buddhist context, it is used in a narrower sense, such as "good in a moral sense," "merit," or "righteous action,"[20] and it is this narrower sense that is conveyed by the Tibetan *dge ba.* After all, Tibetan translators of Sanskrit texts were interested in adopting and devising Tibetan words that would express specific Buddhist ideas most precisely, excluding in the process those meanings that did not apply to those ideas. As a result, Tibetans were apparently more constrained in their usage of *dge ba* than such Indian scholars as Asaṅga, who, writing in Sanskrit, could apply *kuśala* to a much broader range of phenomena.[21] When translating terms that included *kuśala* as their part, Tibetans still used *dge ba,* but over time questions arose as to whether and why some phenomena indicated by those terms could be treated as an actual *dge ba* (or *kuśala* in the narrower sense). This development contributed to polemics about whether the ultimate can be a virtue. This terminological issue, while not necessarily the cause of those polemics, lurks behind the debates on the ultimate virtue addressed below.

In contrast to the murkier issue of terminology, the nature of ultimate reality is clearly at the forefront of the polemics on the nature of the ultimate virtue.[22] Polemics on the ultimate virtue also target other issues related to the question of ultimate reality. One such issue is the status of the tathāgata-essence, which can be roughly identified (as one among many possible identifications) as the ultimate reality of minds of living beings. It too became a highly polemicized issue in Tibet, where interpretations of the tathāgata-essence vary from just a negation of inherent existence of mind to the innate state of buddhahood imbued with various virtuous qualities inherent in our minds.[23] These and related issues are discussed in subsequent chapters.

Some Indian Buddhist writings describe ultimate reality as a virtue; others explicitly deny that interpretation. Many Buddhist texts treat virtues and nonvirtues alike as concepts and present ultimate reality as transcending all conceptuality. Sometimes it is said that ultimate reality is beyond virtues and nonvirtues precisely because it is beyond concepts. While it is tempting—and to a certain extent helpful—to trace these conflicting approaches to different philosophical systems, texts, and thinkers, the overall picture is not straightforward for a good reason: virtually built into the fabric of Mahāyāna philosophy is the tension between the claim that ultimate reality transcends all concepts, including those of ultimate reality, virtue, existence, and nonexistence, and attempts to classify or approach ultimate reality by using those very concepts.[24] Consequently, those same authoritative Indian texts that call ultimate reality *virtue* can also either explicitly or implicitly present it as transcending both virtue and evil.

When exploring Tibetan polemics, we should also take into account different types of Indian texts resorted to in those polemics. Greatly simplifying, and keeping in mind significant overlaps between them, we can point out three types of texts: classificatory, deconstructive, and positively articulating innate awakening. Examples of the first type are the Abhidharma texts, such as Asaṅga's *Summary of Abhidharma* and Vasubandhu's *Treasury of Abhidharma.* Those texts are concerned with defining and classifying phenomena into different categories and exploring connections between those categories as the means of organizing and coherently presenting diverse sets of Buddhist teachings. It is little wonder that those texts include even such phenomena as ultimate reality in lists of different categories. Examples of the second type are the Niḥsvabhāvavāda Madhyamaka writings, such as Nāgārjuna's *Wisdom: Root Stanzas on Madhyamaka.*[25] Those writings are largely concerned with deconstructing conceptual proliferations and with presenting reality and its realization as completely transcending all concepts, including that of virtue. Examples of the third type are the texts on the tathāgata-essence, such as Maitreya's *Sublime Continuum of Mahāyāna.*[26] That literature is concerned with describing an innate reality within beings that is not qualitatively different from that of buddhas. That reality, similar to the awakened mind of a buddha, might be treated as virtuous or, when the transcendent dimension of buddhahood is emphasized, as transcending virtues.

Seminal Tibetan thinkers of the first half of the second millennium—including the ones whose writings are addressed in this book—engaged in the common work of organizing and systematizing heterogeneous Buddhist works inherited from India, such as the ones just mentioned. Owing to their individual perspectives, preferences, and traditions, they classified and interpreted those works very differently. As we will see below, some gave preference to the views stemming from what is known as the third dharmacakra (*chos 'khor*), others to those stemming from the second. Some based their views on the works of Niḥsvabhāvavāda thinkers such as Nāgārjuna and his followers, others on the works of Yogācāra thinkers such as Maitreya and Asaṅga. Those preferences affected their specific perspectives on the ultimate virtue, further contributing to the Tibetan polemics on the issue.

Before we proceed to the analysis of those polemics, it should be mentioned that this book focuses primarily on epistemological and ontological issues involved in different interpretations of the ultimate virtue, and much less on ethical conclusions that might be drawn from different positions on the nature of virtue and the ultimate. This is largely owing to the positions of the authors I am addressing; while offering radically different perspectives on the nature of the relationship between ultimate reality and virtue, overall they do not seem to be too concerned with how those positions might entail changes in the ethical dimension. That said, different perspectives on the ultimate virtue can be relevant to Buddhist practice, and as we will see, Tibetan thinkers debating the issue were also concerned with practical outcomes of their interpretive positions.

A good example of one such practical outcome is related to the question of dedicating ultimate reality to awakening (on which more will be said in later chapters).[27] The Buddhist emphasis on producing, accumulating, and channeling virtues toward awakening through dedication is well known. It can be argued, then, that if one asserts that the very core of our being is imbued with virtuous qualities of awakening; and if one claims that this virtually inexhaustible virtue can be dedicated, that can affect one's understanding of which virtues, how, and how fast, can bring one to buddhahood. This in turn can influence one's understanding of which virtues to cultivate in practice.

Another example is related to two conflicting positions on primordial mind held by Tibetan thinkers and contemplatives. According to one, primordial mind is ultimate reality, a virtue, and is imbued with the potential to develop other virtues, such as the six perfections. Meditation on primordial mind in this case can be understood as a simultaneous cultivation of all those perfections. According to the other position, primordial mind is not ultimate reality because ultimate reality is a sheer negation—or even transcends existence as such—and is not a functional thing. Meditation on it can then be understood as very different from the cultivation of other perfections, and its realization can be treated as not necessarily entailing the development of such virtues as great compassion (*snying rje chen po, mahākaruṇā*), for example. Consequently, followers of the former approach can feel justified in putting more practical emphasis on the cultivation of primordial mind per se than followers of the latter who emphasize the importance of a separate cultivation of perfections and other virtues.[28]

3 | The Ultimate Is a Virtue Worth Dedicating

Dorjé Sherap on Jikten Gönpo's Teachings

This chapter focuses on the *Illuminating Lamp of Primordial Mind: Great Commentary on the Single Intent,*[1] one of the earliest commentaries on Jikten Gönpo's *Single Intent.* That commentary was written in 1267 by Dorjé Sherap, a disciple of both Jikten Gönpo and his nephew and close disciple Sherap Jungné (*shes rab 'byung gnas,* 1187–1241), who was responsible for recording and organizing Jikten Gönpo's teachings, including the *Single Intent.*[2]

The part of the *Illuminating Lamp* that will be the main focus of our discussion is the part in which Dorjé Sherap explains and comments on Jikten Gönpo's teachings related to the following line from the *Single Intent:* "Roots of virtues of all saṃsāra and nirvāṇa are to be dedicated."[3] Before elaborating on Jikten Gönpo's own position, Dorjé Sherap explains that usually it is taught that when one engages in the threefold practice of the Buddhist teachings—generation of the mind striving for supreme awakening (*byang chub mchog tu sems bskyed pa*) on the preparatory stage, cultivation of the six perfections as the main part of practice, and dedication to the goal of unsurpassed buddhahood at the conclusion—one can only dedicate the roots of virtues that have been created and accumulated by oneself, and nothing else. He clarifies this widespread position by referring to, among others, the dedication lines composed by Atiśa (982–1054): "Due to these merits of generosity, etc., that I have created, / Let me attain buddhahood for the benefit of migrators."[4]

Next, Dorjé Sherap unpacks Jikten Gönpo's distinctive approach. He first focuses on the created and accumulated virtues (*byas bsags kyi dge ba*), which he also calls "roots of created and accumulated virtues" (*byas shing bsags pa'i dge ba'i rtsa ba*). Then he explains the meaning of the "existent virtue" (*yod *pa'i dge ba*), which he also calls the "root of existent virtue" (*yod pa'i dge ba'i rtsa ba*).

In the former case, he points out that in the aforementioned *Single Intent* passage, Jikten Gönpo proposes to "appropriate" or "own" (*bdag tu bzung*) *all* roots of virtues in *all* of saṃsāra and nirvāṇa, collect them in the single mind-maṇḍala (*sems kyi dkyil 'khor;* i.e., mentally put them together), and dedicate them to awakening.[5] According to Dorjé Sherap, this process can be accomplished for four reasons. First, sūtras of the definitive meaning (*nges don gyi mdo*) teach that because all dharmas of saṃsāra and nirvāṇa boil down to one's own mind, they appear in accordance with how they are established by that mind. Second, Buddhist sūtras teach that the dharma-sphere, or suchness, does not have divisions. Third, the *Pronouncement of the Basis of [Reconciliation of] Schisms*[6] teaches that generation of the mind of awakening (*sems bskyed*) is the "owner" or "appropriator" (*bdag po*) of the whole saṃsāra and nirvāṇa. And fourth, according to most of the Buddha's teachings, from the initial generation of the mind of awakening until the final disappearance of the Dharma from this world, buddhas and bodhisattvas accumulate all roots of virtues for the sake of sentient beings. He adds that because all beings are one's parents (i.e., they have been one's parents in numerous previous lives), such dedication is like a son's using his father's wealth.[7]

Dorjé Sherap does not focus on the first two reasons; in his opinion, they are easy to understand. He appears to suggest that not only one's own virtues but others' virtues too can be dedicated because these two types of virtues do not differ in two respects: They do not differ in the nature of their appearance, because both are reduced to appearances or manifestations of one's mind. They also do not differ in their ultimate nature (which is also the nature of one's mind), because that nature is indivisible. (The view that phenomena can be reduced to mental appearances is shared by Yogācāra and some Niḥsvabhāvavāda Madhyamaka thinkers and utilized in Tibetan contemplative instructions. The view that ultimate reality has no divisions is the mainstream Mahāyāna view.)

Proceeding to the third reason, Dorjé Sherap points out that in order to liberate all motherly sentient beings from saṃsāra, one has to attain awakening, which requires putting together and dedicating to the goal of awakening all of one's own and others' virtues accumulated in the three times. All those virtues can be dedicated, he insists, because a person who undertakes that dedication is the "owner" of sentient beings (the reason apparently being that such a person "appropriating" them intends on eventually bringing them to awakening). Regarding the fourth reason, Dorjé Sherap writes that all virtues of ārya beings can be dedicated because it is for the sake of sentient beings that buddhas initially generated the mind of awakening, accumulated collections of positive qualities, etc., became buddhas, turned dharmacakras, passed away, and left their teachings for posterity. Since āryas established the roots of virtues for the sake of sentient beings, we should "appropriate" those roots and dedicate them, which is like a son's using wealth accumulated by his father because he owns (*dbang ba*) it.[8]

Although these four arguments may raise objections and require additional clarification, I leave them without further comment because it is not them per se but Dorjé Sherap's interpretation of the existent virtue that became a target of the polemical attacks and rebuttals we are concerned with in this book.

Regarding the root of existent virtue, Dorjé Sherap writes that it is the naturally pure element (*khams rang bzhin gyis rnam par dag pa*), which is none other than the tathāgata-essence. Arguing in favor of dedicating this virtue, he first refers to objections raised by a nameless opponent that partly resemble, if they do not actually acknowledge, those of Sakya Pandita discussed in the next chapter. Treating dedication as a type of wish or aspiration (*'dod pa*),[9] this opponent argues that because wishes are necessarily impermanent (*mi rtag pa*), were the tathāgata-essence dedicatable, it would turn out to be impermanent too. But that would contradict Maitreya's *Differentiation of the Middle and Extremes*,[10] which treats emptiness as synonymous with suchness (*de bzhin nyid*), reality-limit (*yang dag mtha'*), signlessness (*mtshan ma med*), the ultimate (*don dam*), and the dharma-sphere. Consequently, this empty dharma-sphere, or suchness, cannot be posited as a virtue. Nor can suchness be dedicated, because dedication implies change or transformation (*'gyur ba*), while suchness is changeless (*'gyur ba med pa*).[11]

The opponent thus raises two objections. First, he argues that because such authoritative texts as the *Differentiation of the Middle and Extremes* equate the dharma-sphere with ultimate reality or emptiness, and because emptiness, as he understands it, cannot be a virtue, the dharma-sphere cannot be a virtue either. Second, he argues that because the dedication of virtues consists in *wishing* to achieve awakening for the benefit of others, were such a wish accomplishable by directing a virtue—in this case the dharma-sphere, suchness, ultimate reality—toward awakening through dedication, it would entail that the dharma-sphere be changeable and impermanent. That would contradict the same source that treats it as suchness, ultimate reality, and so on, none of which, in the opponent's opinion, is subject to change. Thus, the dharma-sphere is not a virtue, nor can it be dedicated.

In response, Dorjé Sherap cites scriptural passages that outline three characteristics of the tathāgata-essence that he himself accepts: permanence (*rtag pa*), virtuousness (*dge ba*), and unchangeability (*mi 'gyur ba*). He clearly agrees with the opponent that the dharma-sphere—here synonymous with the tathāgata-essence—is permanent and not liable to change. Nevertheless, unlike his opponent, he does not think that these two features cancel out the possibility that ultimate reality is a virtue.

Discussing the three characteristics in the abovementioned order, Dorjé Sherap starts with permanence. He points out that the Buddha himself taught the tathāgata-essence to be permanent in such sūtras as the *Tathāgata-Essence Sūtra*[12] and the *Sūtra Benefiting Aṅgulimāla.*[13] The latter says: "Mañjuśrī, even if all buddhas emphatically labeled [it impermanent], the tathāgata-essence would not be found impermanent. All sentient beings have the permanent sphere, the dharma-sphere—the dharma-sphere ornamented with good primary and secondary marks."[14] Also: "If the tathāgata-essence were nonexistent, then putting efforts into moral conduct [*tshul khrims*] and observances [*brtul zhugs*] would also become meaningless. For example, no butter will emerge from churning water."[15]

Dorjé Sherap also argues that while the tathāgata-essence is existent, it is not characterized by the permanence advocated by non-Buddhists. This is because, he writes, it does not exist in terms of the existence that is one of the eight extremes. This is also because the permanent dharma-body (*chos sku*) of a buddha consists in the abandonment of errors regarding reality (*chos nyid la ltos pa'i phyin ci log spangs pa*). In other words, he argues that although the tathāgata-essence is not impermanent, it is not subsumed under the category of nonexistence; and although it falls under the category of existence and thus permanence (since what exists is either permanent or impermanent), it is not characterized by the extreme of permanence within the eight extremes of proliferations (*spros pa'i mtha' brgyad*).[16] He further equates the tathāgata-essence/dharma-sphere with the dharma-body, treating the latter as permanent in being forever free of errors. It has never been stained by any errors and thus always exists as the never-ending purity, regardless of whether adventitious errors have or have not been abandoned.

It is clear that Dorjé Sherap addresses the permanence of the sugata-essence not as its lack of change (in which case he would not need to discuss its nonchangeability separately) but as its never-ending continuity. He also understands its existence not as simply existing but rather as existing permanently, forever. This explains why he writes that it is "existent, but without becoming [permanent] in terms of the permanence of non-Buddhists."[17]

Next, Dorjé Sherap discusses the sugata-essence's interpretation as a virtue. Treating the element of the sugata-essence as the sugata-essence itself, he resorts to the following quotations from the *Dense Array Sūtra:*

> For example, when a crystal or
> A sunstone with pure characteristics
> Is hit by the sun's rays,
> It emits its own rays of light.
>
> The same is also [true for] the universal basis consciousness [*kun gzhi'i rnam shes*]:
> Results will ripen if one dedicates
> That virtuous element of the sugata-essence [*bde gshegs snying po khams dge ba*]
> Which has stainless positive qualities.[18]

and

> Grounds are the bases of all varieties [of things].
> The virtuous sugata-essence is also [like] that.[19]

He further adds that the sugata-essence is taught as a virtue in the tenth Vajradhvaja dedication: "As many virtues of migrators as there exist,"[20] a passage to which he (and we) will soon return. Dorjé Sherap clearly reads such passages literally and takes them as supporting the claims not only that the (element of) sugata-essence is a virtue but also that it is suitable for dedication.[21]

Explaining why the sugata-essence is taught as a virtue in these three passages, Dorjé Sherap turns to yet another source, the *Lion's Roar of Śrīmālādevī.*[22] He writes that according to that text, the sugata-essence is a virtue because it is both the factor of wisdom (*shes rab kyi cha*) with regard to its lack of afflictions and the factor of method (*thabs kyi cha*) with regard to its extensive positive qualities. This clearly indicates that for Dorjé Sherap, the dharmasphere/tathāgata-essence is a virtue not just because it provides support for virtues to function or positive results to ripen but also because it is a "combination" of two factors, nonafflicted wisdom and positive qualities.[23]

Dorjé Sherap now turns to the unchangeability of the tathāgata-essence, which is quite timely. After all, his treatment of the tathāgata-essence as a virtue for having the two dimensions of wisdom and positive qualities might suggest that he understands it as an impermanent, changeable phenomenon producing positive results. He again resorts to scripture, this time to the extensive *Perfection of Wisdom Sūtra.*[24] The text teaches, he writes, that in the same way that mind is changeless and conceptless (*sems 'gyur ba med cing rnam par rtog pa med pa*), all phenomena are free from change. Treating the statement as referring to the changeless ultimate reality, or suchness, he argues that all phenomena are likewise changeless. Yet sentient beings do not recognize them as such. Therefore, there is no contradiction in positing the tathāgata-essence as the cause-effect qua the change of state (*gnas gyur gyi rgyu 'bras*), based on the purification of the erroneous defilements.[25]

In other words, Dorjé Sherap argues that regarding reality or the dharma-sphere itself, there is no change in either reality or phenomena it underlies. Nevertheless, on the conventional level, until the defilements of mistaken appearances of sentient beings have been purified, the dharma-sphere can be posited in terms of cause and result. Yet in that context, it should be posited in terms not of productive causes (*skyed byed kyi rgyu*) and their results but of the change of state: on the causal level of sentient beings, it is not purified of erroneous defilements; on the resultant level of buddhahood, it is free of them. Although with regard to this "change of state" it might *appear* to be undergoing changes, in fact it does not. This makes clear that he does not view the dharma-sphere as impermanent, as a virtue qua a functional phenomenon producing positive results.

Having discussed the dharma-sphere's permanence, virtue, and changelessness, Dorjé Sherap returns to the twofold division of virtues into accumulated and existent. Addressing their connection, he writes that the primordially existent virtue (*gdod nas yod pa'i dge ba*) is like a great ocean, while the created and accumulated virtues are like the ocean waves. As support he quotes from Sherap Jungné's *Refined Gold: Answers to the Questions about Skillful Means:*[26] "The ocean-like virtuous element [*khams dge ba*] / [Ornamented] with the great weaves of the created and accumulated [virtues]."[27] Arguing that the dedication of both types of virtues to the unsurpassed awakening was taught in the sūtras of the dharmacakra of definitive meaning (*nges don chos kyi 'khor lo'i mdo sde*), he returns to the tenth Vajradhvaja dedication, this time quoting the text more extensively:

> As many virtues of migrators as there exist,
> Created, to be created, and likewise being created,
> In such grounds that accord with good,
> Let in all ways everything come in contact with good![28]

and

> The Victor's sons are also to train in the following:
> Having completely gathered as much as and whatever exists—
> Everything without exception, and all elements too—
> By all [means they] are to dedicate [those] to engaging in the sugata-powers.

> In the same way as the Transcendent Conqueror
> Made previous dedications,
> [They] are to likewise dedicate virtues arisen from yoga.
> By the bodhisattva might,
> [They] are to dedicate [their] own minds as well.
> As with the nature of suchness,
> As with the characteristics of suchness,
> As with the mode of being of suchness—
> All such karmas too are to be completely dedicated.[29]

And he refers to the *Summary of Abhidharma* passage that we have already encountered: "What is virtue in terms of the ultimate? It is suchness."[30]

It is clear from the context that Dorjé Sherap reads the first passage from the tenth Vajradhvaja dedication as referring to the existent and accumulated virtues, the former being the tathāgata-essence. The thrust of the second passage is that everything virtuous or connected with virtue is to be dedicated to the attainment of buddhahood. The last four lines of the passage also allude to parallels or connections between reality and virtue in the context of dedication. While it is not specified what those are exactly, we have already encountered Dorjé Sherap's claim that all virtues of saṃsāra and nirvāṇa can be dedicated because the dharma-sphere has no divisions. These lines too can be read as indicating a similar connection.

On the basis of the above quotations, Dorjé Sherap writes that with the tathāgata-essence being inconceivable and immeasurable, the roots of dedicated virtues[31] will also become inconceivable and immeasurable when "blessed" (i.e., positively affected) by that sphere. He argues that this position is articulated in the *Tathāgata-Essence Sūtra,* which teaches that if virtues are dedicated to awakening, they become inconceivable, and that there are limitless benefits of dedication to awakening by the blessings and power of the virtuous element (*khams dge ba*). It was therefore taught, he continues, that it is important to dedicate to the unsurpassed awakening all our virtues accumulated and existent in the three times.[32] Thus, Dorjé Sherap not only accepts the effectiveness of dedicating the ultimate virtue in its own right but also believes that such dedication increases the effectiveness or power of other dedicated virtues.

At this point, it is worth looking at other places in the same text where Dorjé Sherap's interpretation of Jikten Gönpo's position is illuminated. One such place is where Dorjé Sherap comments on the root text's line "Mahāmudrā [*phyag rgya chen po*] is the selfness [*bdag nyid,* i.e., nature] of all positive qualities."[33] Here, he explicitly objects to the view that mahāmudrā is just emptiness transcending virtues and nonvirtues, abandonment of faults, and accomplishment of positive qualities. He writes that in contrast to that, Jikten Gönpo taught that mahāmudrā abides as the nature of positive qualities throughout the basis, path, and result. On the level of the basis, it is the naturally pure element (*khams rang bzhin gyis rnam par dag pa*). Dorjé Sherap quotes the *Sublime Continuum*'s passage

> If the buddha-element did not exist,
> No weariness of sufferings would arise, and
> No striving for, interest in, and
> Aspiration toward nirvāṇa would arise either.[34]

He explains that whatever virtuous thoughts arise due to its power (*mthu*), such as weariness of the sufferings of saṃsāra and aspiration and striving for nirvāṇa, they are all its stirring (*g.yos*, i.e., display). Arguing that because of that, mahāmudrā is the nature of positive qualities even on the level of the basis, he clearly understands nature here not just as what underlies virtues but also as what serves as their active source and itself is a virtue.

When that very basis has been introduced (*ngo sprod*) by a lama, familiarization with it is called *path*. The path also serves as the nature of positive qualities. Dorjé Sherap proceeds to connect the category of mahāmudrā with terms for ultimate reality, treating it as synonymous with the naturally pure element, perfection of wisdom (*shes rab kyi pha rol tu phyin pa*), freedom from extremes of all proliferations (*spros pa thams cad kyi mtha' dang bral ba*), and the ultimate reality as luminosity (*'od gsal don dam pa'i bden pa*). He writes that whatever roots of virtues are created, they become immeasurable (*dpag tu med pa*) through mahāmudrā's power, citing in support such texts as the *Abbreviated Perfection of Wisdom Sūtra:* "Whatever positive qualities of the five perfections and awakening there are—/ All of them too are born from the perfection of wisdom."[35] Mahāmudrā is the nature of all positive qualities on the resultant level too. On that level, the final mahāmudrā (*phyag rgya chen po mthar thug pa*)—the dharma-body with positive qualities and activities—spontaneously and ceaselessly emerges as the inexhaustible ornamental wheels of the buddha body, speech, and mind (*sku gsung thugs mi zad pa rgyan gyi 'khor lo*). We can see that on all three levels—basis, path, and result—he presents mahāmudrā as an active and dynamic force that serves as a source of various positive qualities rather than simply pervading or underlying them as their nature.

Summarizing his points, Dorjé Sherap writes that mahāmudrā primordially abides as the nature of all positive qualities throughout the basis, path, and result, with no faults to eliminate and no positive qualities to establish. In support, he cites the following famous passage from the *Sublime Continuum:*

> There is nothing to eliminate here,
> Nothing at all to establish.
> Reality is to be viewed as reality.
> Having seen [it], one is liberated.[36]

He interprets the passage as saying that as a result of that which exists on the level of the basis having been purified on the level of the path, the final way of being (*gnas lugs mthar thug*) is manifested and liberation thereby achieved.

In brief, he writes, all happiness and goodness (*bde legs*) of saṃsāra and nirvāṇa, including all happiness and joy in the three realms together with the positive qualities of āryas—all these ray-like qualities of mahāmudrā emerge from within the sun-like mahāmudrā. These qualities are different only in their clarity and extent, in inverse proportion to the levels of density of the cloud-like obscurations. In support, again linking mahāmudrā and the perfection of wisdom, Dorjé Sherap cites the *Abbreviated Perfection of Wisdom Sūtra:* "Whatever compounded happiness and uncompounded happiness they are—/ All those types of happiness are to be known as emerging from this."[37] Also,

> As many as there are phenomena of happiness and joy of buddhas with sons,
> Śrāvakas, pratyekabuddhas, gods, and all migrators—
> All of them have emerged from the supreme perfection of wisdom.[38]

Dorjé Sherap's position moves between presenting mahāmudrā as the source of all positive qualities and presenting it as actually possessing all positive qualities. The two are not the same; in contrast to the latter, the former can be understood as something with the potential to issue or manifest positive qualities without actually possessing them. His position also allows for the overlap between the ultimate reality—especially under the name "perfection of wisdom"—with what realizes it. While on the level of the path that is not problematic, on the level of the basis it might, depending on interpretation, entail unwanted consequences.

Another place to consider is where Dorjé Sherap comments on the *Single Intent*'s line "If emptiness is realized, emptiness emerges as causes and results."[39] He presents Jikten Gönpo's position as follows: All phenomena of saṃsāra and nirvāṇa are mind. Mind is not established as any entity at all. Although it primordially pervades all phenomena, the interdependence of causes and results (*rgyu 'bras kyi rten 'brel*) emerges from it incessantly and nondeceptively. Thus, emptiness emerges as causes and results. In support of this interpretation of the noncontradictory relationship of interdependent origination and emptiness, Dorjé Sherap cites well-known passages from Madhyamaka works, such as Nāgārjuna's *Wisdom:*

> There are not dharmas
> Other than interdependent origination.
> Therefore, there are not any dharmas
> That are not emptiness.[40]

Similar to this passage, Dorjé Sherap's claim of interpenetration of the empty mind as the nature of phenomena on the one hand and such conventional phenomena as karmas and results on the other is open to many discordant interpretations. That said, it too can be taken as contributing to the overlap between ultimate reality and virtue, as well as to the interpretation of the ultimate as a functional phenomenon that can be dedicated.

Dorjé Sherap's sources and interpretations demonstrate that his position is informed primarily by ideas related to the last dharmacakra. He does appeal to such second dharmacakra texts as the *Perfection of Wisdom* sūtras, as well as Nāgārjuna's works based on them, but his main emphasis is clearly on the third. Another feature of his approach is that of the two main argumentative tools used by Tibetan thinkers—textual statements (*lung*) and reasoning (*rigs pa*)—he relies primarily on the former, and he has little interest in purely logical arguments. Both of these elements of Dorjé Sherap's approach make it vulnerable to criticism and polemical attacks, especially by those thinkers whose views are grounded mainly in the second dharmacakra (although, as we will see, they appeal to the last dharmacakra texts too) and who put more emphasis on logical reasoning.

4 | The Ultimate Is Not a Virtue Unless You Do Not Mean It

Sakya Pandita's Objections

The discussion in this chapter is based on Sakya Pandita's *Thorough Differentiation of the Three Types of Vows,* one of the earliest Tibetan polemical treatises.[1] The text was written around 1232.[2] Looking at the religious and social milieu of Sakya Pandita's time, we learn, among other things, about sectarian and political rivalry between his Sakya and certain Kagyü traditions. But the text itself deals primarily with philosophical, ritual, and contemplative issues, including those related to the ultimate virtue.[3] While it is impossible for us to know details of Sakya Pandita's motivation, there is no reason to doubt that he genuinely wished to benefit Buddhism and its followers. The text leaves no doubt that Sakya Pandita saw himself as a righteous defender of the virtuous teachings of the Buddha, ready to fight to the virtual end to keep them pure and unadulterated. This text has been taken as authoritative by Sakya followers, but it has provoked responses from followers of other traditions, who have defended their own ways of interpreting and practicing Buddhism.[4]

In chapter 1 of the *Thorough Differentiation,* which deals with the vows of individual liberation (*so sor thar pa'i sdom pa*), Sakya Pandita criticizes those Tibetan thinkers who uphold the possibility of dedicating ultimate reality, interpret the tenth Vajradhvaja dedication—"As many virtues of migrators as there exist," and so on—as referring to the self-arisen existent virtue, and treat that virtue as the sugata-essence. According to Sakya Pandita, they thereby wrongly assert the existence of a result within a cause, which must be refuted.[5]

Sakya Pandita does not specify who those Tibetan thinkers are; however, commentators on his text, such as Gorampa, identify them as followers of several Kagyü lineages. In particular, he could not have been refuting Dorjé Sherap, because the latter's *Illuminating Lamp* was written in 1267, more than thirty years after Sakya Pandita composed the *Thorough Differentiation.* Yet it is obvious that Sakya Pandita's polemics directly target key ideas attributed to Jikten Gönpo outlined and elaborated upon in the *Illuminating Lamp.*[6] In his elaborate refutation of those ideas, Sakya Pandita focuses on three interrelated claims—that there is a primordially existent virtue, that the sugata-essence is a virtue, and that the sugata-essence can be dedicated—all of which, as we have seen, were accepted by Dorjé Sherap as valid. While Sakya Pandita does not refute the claim of the unchangeability of the dharma-sphere (because he accepts it), he does show its incompatibility with the claim that the dharma-sphere can be dedicated. As we will see below, his polemics extend to many related issues as well.

The verses of the *Thorough Differentiation* that specifically target the claim that reality is a dedicatable virtue are preceded by the verses focusing on karmas, starting with verses 42–43:

> The Victor taught in sūtras that among karmas
> There are virtuous, evil, and unspecified.
> Virtue is what is well performed,
> Producing happiness as its fruition.
>
> Evil is what is faultily performed,
> Producing suffering as its fruition.
> Because equanimity [*btang snyoms*][7] is neither of the two,
> Its fruition too is neither of the two.[8]

Verses 44–45 address well-known divisions of karmas and explicitly state that reality, or the dharma-sphere, is uncompounded and thus beyond virtue and evil. The verses also show that Sakya Pandita argues against reality's being a virtue on the grounds of its not being a karma:

> Because these are produced karmas,
> They are to be known as compounded.
> Because the dharma-sphere is uncompounded,
> It is not a karma. Thus, it is neither a virtue nor an evil.
>
> Among karmas, there are two types taught by the Sage:
> Intention and intended.
> Intentions are the mental karmas,
> Intended are the physical and verbal ones.
> The dharma-sphere is neither of the two.
> Therefore, it is free from virtuous and evil karmas.[9]

The passage should not be incorrectly read as implying that according to Sakya Pandita, virtues and evils necessarily have to be karmas. Rather, for him the uncompoundedness of the dharma-sphere is the reason why it is not a karma and also the reason why it is neither a virtue nor an evil.

The next twelve verses discuss different types and divisions of karmas. Verses 46–49 analyze one such division that addresses four types of karmas:

> Also, four types of karmas were taught:
> White karmas with white fruitions,
> Black karmas with black fruitions,
> White karmas with black fruitions,
> Black karmas with white fruitions.
>
> Because acts of generosity and the like, associated with pure intentions,
> Are white in both respects, wise ones should perform them.
>
> Because killing for the sake of food and the like
> Are black in both respects, wise ones should abandon them.
>
> If killing one for the sake of protecting many and the like
> Are black karmas with white fruitions, they are to be performed.
> Acts of generosity for the sake of killing and the like
> Are white karmas with black fruitions and should be abandoned.[10]

Another division, outlined in verses 50–51, addresses four possible combinations of two types of karmas:

> Also, two types of karmas were taught:
> Projecting karmas and completing karmas.
> If divided, there are four alternatives.
>
> [Results can be] projected by projecting virtues
> With completing [karmas] also being virtues.
>
> [They can be] projected by projecting evils
> With completing [karmas] also being evils.
> [Other options are] projecting virtues with completing evils
> And projecting evils with completing virtues.[11]

In verses 53–55, providing examples of the four, Sakya Pandita explains that rebirth in any of the three high states is projected by virtuous karmas and that happiness there is created by completing virtues. Rebirth in any of the three bad transmigrations is projected by evils, and different types of suffering there are created by completing evils. Although high states are projected by virtues, sufferings there are created by completing evils. While bad transmigrations are projected by evils, happiness there is created by completing virtues.

Yet another division, addressed in verses 56–57, is into three types of karmas:

> Also, the Sage taught three types of karmas:
> Solely white, solely black,
> And mixed.
>
> Solely white ones produce happiness.
> Solely black ones produce suffering.
> Mixed karmas produce mixed
> Happiness and suffering, he taught.[12]

The actual refutation of the claims about the dedicatable ultimate virtue begins with verses 59–62. Sakya Pandita writes:

> Sāṃkhya heretics, saying that virtue and evil
> Exist within the primal nature [*gshis*],
> Assert that results are present in causes.
> Some Tibetans also follow that [approach].
>
> Explaining the intent of
> The *Vajradhvaja's Dedication*'s
> "As many virtues of migrators as there exist,
> Created, to be created, and being created,"
>
> Some, similar to the Sāṃkhya tradition,
> Assert that the "existent virtue" [*yod pa'i dge ba*]
> Is established as self-arisen [*rang byung*],
> And treat it as the sugata-essence.
>
> Because this Sāṃkhya[-like] system is infeasible,
> It is to be refuted with scripture and reasoning.
> What is called "sugata-essence"
> Is the the unchangeable dharma-sphere [*chos dbyings 'gyur med*].[13]

Sakya Pandita's assertion that the sugata-essence is none other than the unchangeable dharma-sphere is a position that Dorjé Sherap would happily agree with. Nevertheless, the conclusion he draws is in direct contradiction with that of Dorjé Sherap. Referring in verses 63–66 to the *Sublime Continuum,* which describes mind as luminous and changeless, like space; Nāgārjuna's *Wisdom,* which describes the natures of buddhas and sentient beings as the same and then states that neither of them has nature; the sūtras' statement that the tathāgata-essence is changeless; and in particular the *Perfection of Wisdom*'s description of the dharma-sphere as transcending the three times and the three spheres, as well as virtues and nonvirtues, Sakya Pandita states: "Therefore, the Victor explained that / There is no dedication for the dharma-sphere."[14]

In verses 67–71, he cites the teaching of the *Union Tantra*[15] that both evils and positive qualities are concepts (*rnam par rtog pa*) and are abandoned by the wise, arguing that all tantras teach likewise. He also refers to Nāgārjuna's *Precious Garland of Advice for the King*,[16] which teaches that reality is beyond evil and positive qualities, and so forth. In doing so, Sakya Pandita essentially equates the dharma-sphere with the ultimate reality taught in the *Perfection of Wisdom* literature and Nāgārjuna's texts and uses those scriptural sources to demonstrate that the dharma-sphere cannot be dedicated, because it is changeless and transcends virtue and evil.

It might be objected that Sakya Pandita's interpretation of the sugata-essence as transcending virtue and evil is incorrect because the dharma-sphere has more to it than just emptiness and transcendence of dualistic concepts. Objecting to this interpretation, in verse 72 he writes:

> Some assert the term *sugata-essence*
> As emptiness with the essence of compassion [*stong nyid snying rje'i snying po* [*can*]].
> [No.] This is what purifies the element of the sugata-essence [*bde gshegs snying po'i khams sbyong byed*].
> It is not the actual element [*khams*].[17]

Sakya Pandita further claims, in verses 73–74, that his interpretation agrees with Dharmakīrti's *Commentary on Valid Cognition*,[18] Śāntideva's *Compendium of Training*,[19] and all sūtras and tantras in general. He demonstrates, in verses 84–85, that such virtuous states of mind as compassion do not belong to ultimate reality.[20] Sakya Pandita is no doubt aware that many sūtras and Indian commentarial works (some of which we have already referred to) appear to teach that the dharma-sphere is a virtue either by listing it among many categories that include the word *virtue* or by explicitly describing it as a virtue. Nevertheless, he persistently treats such passages as referring to either virtues or the ultimate, and never to something that is both a virtue and the ultimate. For example, he points out that virtues in terms of entity taught in the *Summary of Abhidharma* refer to the eleven virtues of śrāvakas, such as faith, and so on,[21] a claim supported in the writings of Asaṅga. He thereby shows that one should not be misled by the word *entity,* which can also be applied to the ultimate, because here it refers not to the dharma-sphere, the ultimate reality of virtues, or the ultimate as a virtue but rather to that which makes faith, and so on, a virtue with respect to its conventional nature or entity.

Regarding the ultimate virtue taught in the *Summary of Abhidharma,* Sakya Pandita reiterates Asaṅga's statement that it refers to suchness. While this interpretation agrees with what Asaṅga's text explicitly says, the conclusion drawn by Sakya Pandita is not explicitly stated there. While Asaṅga's position is open to different interpretations, Sakya Pandita states unequivocally that precisely because the ultimate virtue refers to ultimate reality, it cannot refer to an actual virtue. In other words, contending that the word *ultimate* (*don dam*) here refers to the ultimate itself, he gives this as a reason why the ultimate virtue cannot be an actual virtue.

To demonstrate that the *Summary of Abhidharma* does not treat the ultimate virtue as a real virtue, Sakya Pandita refers to the passages we encountered in the introduction and points out that the same text also describes the evil in terms of the ultimate / the ultimate evil (*don dam sdig pa,* i.e., nonvirtue in terms of the ultimate) as the whole saṃsāra, and the unspecified phenomena in terms of the ultimate / ultimate unspecified phenomena (*don dam lung ma bstan*) as the uncompounded space and the nonanalytical cessation. As he puts it in verse 76,

> What is explained as the ultimate virtue
> Was taught to be suchness,
> The ultimate evil—the whole saṃsāra,
> And the two, space and the nonanalytical cessation,
> Were explained as the ultimate unspecified.[22]

He thereby argues that were one to treat the ultimate virtue as an actual virtue, there should be no reason why the ultimate evil, and so on, could not be treated as an actual evil, and so on. This, of course, would entail such contradictions as, for example, virtues within saṃsāra turning out to be actual evils.

But if suchness, or the dharma-sphere, is not an actual, real virtue, what is the reason for calling it "virtue" in the first place? According to Sakya Pandita, the dharma-sphere is called "virtue" simply because of the absence of evil (*sdig pa med pa tsam*), not because it involves any additional virtuous qualities. This is similar, he says, to the reason for calling the freedom from illness "physical happiness" and the absence of sorrow "mental happiness." Although neither of these involves any additional elements other than the lack of suffering, that very lack of suffering itself is called "happiness." As he puts it in verses 77–79,

> The intent in explaining
> Suchness as "virtue" is as follows.

For example, the world calls
The freedom from illness "physical happiness"
And the absence of sorrow "mental happiness."

Although these do not have happiness
Other than the absence of suffering,
The mere absence of suffering
Is known to all as "happiness."

Likewise, although the dharma-sphere too
Does not have virtue in addition to
The mere absence of evil,
It ended up being imputed as "virtue."[23]

This line of argumentation makes it clear that according to Sakya Pandita, unless something functions as a productive cause of happiness and therefore is impermanent, compounded, and thereby falls outside the scope of ultimate reality, it cannot be an actual virtue—only an imputed one. In verse 81, this logic applies to the dharma-sphere in particular:

Likewise, although the dharma-sphere too
Was said to be a virtue,
It is not an actual virtue [*dge ba dngos*]
That produces happiness as its result.[24]

This shows that he limits the scope of what can be called "virtue" to functional phenomena producing happiness.

In verses 82–83, Sakya Pandita further argues that

If the dharma-sphere were a virtue itself,
The following absurd consequence would be entailed:

Because there are no other dharmas
Apart from the dharma-sphere, evils and
Unspecified [phenomena] too would become virtues.
If that were the case, it would be impossible
For any sentient being to go to bad transmigrations.[25]

In other words, taking for granted that the opponent agrees that nothing exists apart from the dharma-sphere (as stated in Maitreya's *Ornament of Mahāyāna Sūtras*[26] and *Differentiation of the Middle and Extremes*), Sakya Pandita argues that were the dharma-sphere an actual virtue, then in the light of the basic Buddhist teachings that good rebirths are caused by virtuous karmas and bad by nonvirtuous ones, no rebirth in the low transmigrations would be possible, because nonvirtues, not existing apart from the dharma-sphere, would turn out to be virtues.

Turning to the *Vajradhvaja's Dedication* passage that starts with "As many virtues of migrators as there exist," in verse 86 Sakya Pandita explains that it refers not to the innate primordially existent virtue but simply to virtues created by all beings. If this passage were referring to the dharma-sphere, neither the words *as many* (*ji snyed*) nor *exist* (*yod*) would be applicable. This is because *as many* indicates multiplicity, while the dharma-sphere, being free from proliferations (*spros bral*), is beyond multiplicity and scarcity. Not only that but the dharma-sphere transcends the category of existence itself. As he puts it in verse 89,

> The dharma-sphere is not even existent;
> Dharmakīrti taught well that
> Mere existence [*yod tsam*] is pervaded by impermanence.[27]

As we already know, the characteristic of impermanence, in Sakya Pandita's opinion, does not apply to the dharma-sphere.

In verse 90, Sakya Pandita also quotes Nāgārjuna's *Wisdom:*

> If nirvāṇa were a thing,
> Nirvāṇa would be compounded.
> No thing exists anywhere
> That is not compounded.[28]

After quoting a few more passages from Nāgārjuna that in his opinion demonstrate that the dharma-sphere is neither existent nor nonexistent, in verses 91–95 he admonishes his readers that if they respect the Buddha's teachings, they should not treat the dharma-sphere as either of the two.

In verse 96 Sakya Pandita further argues:

> It is also established by reasoning,
> Because the mere existence is a phenomenon able to function [*don byed nus pa*].
> The dharma-sphere is devoid of performing function
> Because it is freedom from proliferations.[29]

Providing additional arguments, in verse 97 Sakya Pandita writes:

> Also, if the existent virtue
> Were the dharma-sphere, then,
> Needless to mention "virtues,"

> Why not dedicate the reality [*chos nyid*] of
> Inanimate matter, nonthings, and āryas as well?[30]

In other words, the dharma-sphere, or reality, of inanimate matter, and so on, should be suitable for dedication because, there being no difference in the reality of sentient beings on the one hand and inanimate matter, and so on, on the other, there should be no difference between dedicating the former and dedicating the latter.

Regarding the meaning of the *Vajradhvaja's Dedication* passage, in verses 98–102 Sakya Pandita provides three interpretations, all of which he deems acceptable. According to one, the first line, "As many virtues of migrators as there exist," provides a general description, and the second, "Created, to be created, and likewise being created," addresses specific details. Alternatively, the first line can be understood as referring to virtues of others, and the second to Vajradhvaja's own virtues. Yet another possibility is that the first line is a brief statement, and the second a more extensive explanation. Whichever interpretation is chosen, what the passage addresses is similar to confessing, in buddhas' presence, as many evils as there exist—created, to be created, and likewise being created. There exist no evils outside the three times. Likewise, there exist no virtues outside the three times, he writes.

In verse 103 he adds: "The *Vajradhvaja['s Dedication]* itself also explains / 'Existent' in terms of accomplishment [*bsgrub pa*]."[31]The implication is that were the dharma-sphere existent, it would have to be treated as accomplished and, by extension, produced and impermanent, which contradicts its being described as uncreated.

Another reason why Sakya Pandita objects to the interpretation of the dharma-sphere as a virtue suitable for dedication is that, as he points out in verses 104–5, dedication would render it a functional thing because it would have to transform it. Otherwise, dedication that does not involve transformation or change is useless. Furthermore, accepting that the dharma-sphere can undergo transformation or change would contradict the Buddha's teaching that the dharma-sphere is unchangeable:

> If transformed through dedication, it will be compounded.
> Dedication without transformation is meaningless.
>
> The Victor taught in sūtras that
> The dharma-sphere is unchangeable.[32]

In other words, he points out the following contradiction: were it possible to dedicate the dharma-sphere, it would be suitable for change and therefore not the actual dharma-sphere; were it not suitable for change through dedication, that dedication would not act as a transformative force and thus would not be an actual dedication.

For support of his position that the dharma-sphere, the nature of phenomena, is unchangeable and thus cannot be a virtue, in verses 106–8 Sakya Pandita again turns to Nāgārjuna's *Wisdom:*

> It is not reasonable for nature
> To emerge from causes and conditions.
> Nature that emerges from causes and conditions
> Will turn out to be produced.
>
> How is it suitable for nature
> To be called "produced"?
> Natures are not fabricated
> And do not depend on something else.[33]

and

> If something exists by nature
> It will not transform into being nonexistent.
> It is never feasible
> For nature to transform into something else.[34]

In verse 110, Sakya Pandita addresses the following objection:

> One might think that although reality, suchness,
> Is not a virtue liable to dedication,
> There is no fault in its dedication
> Within a bodhisattva's mind training [*blo sbyong*].[35]

In other words, one can arguably reap the benefits of imagining the dedication of the dharma-sphere even though its actual dedication is not possible. In verse 111, Sakya Pandita refutes this position too:

> No. There is a fault in it. Because of involving
> Discrimination of objects of observation [*dmigs pa'i 'du shes*],
> Such dedication will be poisonous.[36]

Not only that, he adds in verses 112–13, but such dedication will thereby spoil all other dedications. The reason is that the actual bodhisattva's mind training consists in dedicating virtues from within the state of the dharma-sphere free from proliferations. Consequently, he writes in verse 114, "If reality is used as a dedicatable cause, / It is not suitable even as mind training."[37] The reason, he explains, is that if one treats the dharma-sphere free from proliferations as a virtue, it will render it an object of observation (*dmigs pa*). But it was taught that if dedication involves discrimination that has objects of observation, such dedication is poisonous, similar to eating good food mixed with poison. In verses 114–17, citing Maitreya's *Ornament of Clear Realizations*—"Special complete dedication— / Its function is supreme, / It has an aspect of nonobservation, / [And] non-erroneous characteristics"[38]—Sakya Pandita writes that all sūtras and tantras agree on that point.

These arguments demonstrate that the dharma-sphere should be treated differently from other phenomena involved in mind training because it is the ultimate reality, while the other phenomena belong to the conventional reality. We can say that although taking upon oneself sufferings of others and giving them one's own happiness, for example, is impossible in actuality, imagining doing it as a part of mind training can indeed bring benefit. That benefit derives from the virtuous intentions behind such acts of imagination, and that practice does not contradict the proper understanding of conventional reality. The same does not apply to ultimate reality: although imagining its dedication is based on a virtuous motivation, this imaginative process itself conflicts with the proper understanding of that very reality and therefore is counterproductive. Not only that but it contradicts the very factor that enhances mind training: engaging in that training from within the realization of reality understood as the state of nonobservation.

In verses 118–20, Sakya Pandita adds that making even the nonobservable dharma-sphere observable by calling it "existing virtue" will make other subjects observable. Furthermore, it is contradictory to treat reality, suchness, as an object of dedication and also claim that reality is the unchangeable bliss (*chos nyid mi 'gyur bde ba*).

Another approach Sakya Pandita criticizes is summarized by him in verse 121 as follows:

> Without saying that the term *sugata-essence*
> Refers to the dharma-sphere, some assert that
> [It refers] to the element of sentient beings only [*sems can kho na'i khams*].[39]

In verses 122–25, he rejects this position too:

> That element is either a thing, a nonthing, or,
> Not being either of the two, freedom from proliferations [*spros bral*];
> Apart from these three options, others are impossible.

If it were a thing, it would be determined
As either matter or cognition.
Asserting matter as the element of sentient beings
Is a system of some heretics;
Buddhists do not have it.

If it were cognition, it would not go beyond
Just the eight collections of consciousness.

Since all eight collections of consciousness are compounded,
They are not feasible as the sugata-essence,
Because it is taught in sūtras
That the sugata-essence is uncompounded.[40]

In this context, Sakya Pandita also disagrees with treating as the virtuous sugata-essence the stainless mental continuum (*zag med sems rgyud*) taught in some texts. He argues that what is intended by this term is the clarity aspect (*gsal cha*) of the universal basis consciousness. Because that clarity aspect is an unobscured unspecified (*ma bsgribs lung ma bstan*) phenomenon, it cannot be a virtue. Not subsuming the stainless mental continuum under the eight types of consciousness is not an option either, because it would entail that there are nine collections of consciousness—a position unacceptable to him. As he puts it in verses 126–27,

The teachings on the "stainless mental continuum"
Given in some [texts] intended
The clarity aspect of the universal basis consciousness.
Because it is an unobscured unspecified [phenomenon]
No convention of "virtue" [is applicable to it].

And if there were the "stainless mental continuum"
Apart from the eight collections of consciousness,
In that case there would be nine collections.
Therefore, the stainless mental continuum
Apart from the eight collections is not feasible.[41]

In verse 128 he points out that if the element of sentient beings were a non-thing, then owing to its being excluded from the category of functional things it could be neither a virtue nor a nonvirtue:

If it is a nonthing, then it does not function.
Virtues and evils are not feasible for it.[42]

This argument also demonstrates that Sakya Pandita treats virtue in the narrow sense of something capable of producing positive results.

In verse 129 he argues that were one to side with the third option—that the element of sentient beings is freedom from proliferations, which is neither a thing nor a nonthing—one would have to agree that it is none other than the previously discussed dharma-sphere (both *freedom from proliferations* and *dharma-sphere* indicating for him the same ultimate reality):

> If the element of sentient beings,
> Being neither a thing nor a nonthing,
> Is freedom from proliferations, then it will not transcend
> The previously explained dharma-sphere.
> In that case, as has already been explained,
> The dharma-sphere is beyond virtue and evil.[43]

Yet another opinion that Sakya Pandita argues against is that although the dharma-sphere of inanimate matter is not the sugata-essence, the dharma-sphere of sentient beings is. He rejects this opinion on the grounds that the dharma-sphere has no divisions—a point that he says was made by the Buddha and is also established by reasoning. As he puts it in verses 130–31,

> One may wonder, "Although the dharma-sphere of inanimate matter
> Is not the sugata-essence,
> The dharma-sphere of sentient beings
> Is the sugata-essence."
>
> No. The Victor taught that
> The dharma-sphere does not have divisions.
> Reasoning also proves this.[44]

It should be noted that although Sakya Pandita treats the tathāgata-essence as freedom from proliferations transcending the notions of virtue and evil, he does not understand it as unrelated to them either. On the contrary, in verse 132 he argues:

> Thus, because the tathāgata-essence
> Is freedom from proliferations,
> It is feasible for both buddhahood and saṃsāra
> To emerge from sentient beings.[45]

That said, he clearly treats the tathāgata-essence as emptiness, because in support of this line of reasoning, in verse 133 he quotes Nāgārjuna's *Wisdom:*

> For whom emptiness is suitable,
> To that one everything is suitable.
> For whom emptiness is unsuitable,
> To that one nothing is suitable.[46]

In verse 134, he also writes that the same was intended by the *Sublime Continuum,* which provides the following proof of the sugata-element (*bde gshegs khams*):

> If the sugata-element did not exist,
> No weariness of sufferings would arise, and
> No desire for, interest in, and
> Aspiration toward nirvāṇa would arise either.[47]

In verse 135, he explains why the latter passage teaches that proof:

> Because the appropriated aggregates
> Are suffering
> And nirvāṇa is happiness,
> Mind pursuits its own abode.[48]

As an example, in verse 136 he uses fire and heat: "[This is] suitable as a proof of the sugata-element / Similar to heat being a proof of fire."[49]

Consequently, when addressing some sūtras' and the *Sublime Continuum*'s teachings of the existence of the buddha-essence within sentient beings, similar to a precious image wrapped in rags, in verses 138–40 Sakya Pandita argues that they should not be taken literally:

> Nevertheless, the teachings in some sūtras
> And the *Sublime Continuum of Mahāyāna*
> That the buddha-essence exists
> In sentient beings,
> Like a precious image in rags,
>
> Are to be known as [having a special] intent.
> It is taught that their basis of intent is emptiness,
> And the purpose is the elimination of the five faults.[50]
>
> The valid cognition [realizing] the damage to the explicit [meaning exists]
> Because if such buddha-element existed,
> It would be equivalent to the self [taught by] non-Buddhists,
> And would turn out to be a true thing [*bden pa'i dngos po*].
> This is also because it would entirely contradict
> The sūtras of definitive meaning.[51]

To support this position, Sakya Pandita refers in verse 142 to, among other sources, Candrakīrti's *Engaging in Madhyamaka,*[52] which treats the sugata-essence teachings as having an interpretive meaning.

In verse 144, Sakya Pandita addresses two types of dedication, realistic (*gnas kyi bsngo ba*) and unrealistic (*gnas min gyi bsngo ba*):

> In brief, there are two types of dedication,
> Realistic and unrealistic.
> The realistic dedication is taught to be accomplishable.
> The unrealistic one, even if performed, will not be accomplished.[53]

In verses 145–48, he refers to what he sees as their scriptural sources:

> Both of them were taught in sūtras.
> It is the realistic one that was intended
> In the passage from the *Mañjuśrī's Buddha-Field:*
>
> "All dharmas accord with conditions,
> Thoroughly relying on desire-to-act as the root.
> Whatever aspirational resolve one has made,
> A corresponding result will be obtained."[54]
>
> It is the unrealistic dedication
> That was intended in the passage from the *Sūtra Requested by Vimaladattā:*
> "The reality of dharmas is not transformed
> Through dedication. Were it transformable, then
>
> Why has the dedication by even the first buddha alone
> Not been accomplished [until] these days?"[55]

In verse 149, Sakya Pandita also argues against dedication of virtues that have not been produced:

> Thus, the dedicatable virtues,
> As well as the confessable evils,
> Are the created virtues and evils.
> There is no virtue or evil in the uncreated.[56]

This argument further contributes to his exclusion of such uncompounded phenomena as the dharma-sphere from the category of virtue.

Overall, Sakya Pandita's position, which is supported not only by textual references but also by multiple logical arguments, looks much stronger than that of Dorjé Sherap, who appeals primarily to scriptural authority. Nevertheless, on the surface at least it is one-sided in the sense of siding with only one interpretation of the ultimate virtue and rejecting others as invalid or at best having an interpretive meaning. This position, based mainly on the teachings of the second dharmacakra and related commentarial literature, can be and has been understood as a straightforward endorsement of the idea of the dharma-sphere as freedom from proliferations, which is beyond virtue, nonvirtue, and even existence as such. That being said, later thinkers did feel the need to critically approach, further articulate, and reinterpret this position. One of those thinkers was Shakya Chokden, whose critical questions are listed in the next chapter.

5 | Admiring Your Virtues, I Have Questions to Ask

Shakya Chokden's Inquiry

This chapter lists Shakya Chokden's questions regarding Sakya Pandita's position on the ultimate virtue, which are taken from the *Good Questions about the "Thorough Differentiation of the Three Types of Vows."*[1] The text, composed in 1475 and sent to scholars of Ü (*dbus*), Tsang (*gtsang*), and Kham (*khams*),[2] poses more than one hundred critical questions about Sakya Pandita's *Thorough Differentiation.* Shakya Chokden's stated intention was to clarify the *Thorough Differentiation,* not to criticize it. At the end of the *Good Questions,* he also explicitly expressed his devotion to the *Thorough Differentiation* and stated that if people who lacked a solid understanding of the points of inquiry and refutation said that these questions were intended to refute Sakya Pandita's text, it was their problem, not his. But the questions did provoke considerable controversy among Sakya scholars, and a few of them attempted to provide answers.[3] One of these was Gorampa, who during the next year (1476) wrote the *Elimination of Mistakes about the Three Types of Vows: Answers to the Polemics and Questions Regarding the "[Thorough Differentiation of the] Three Types of Vows" Treatise.*[4] In 1481 Shakya Chokden answered his own questions in the *Golden Lancet: Resolved Abundant Discourse on the "Thorough Differentiation of the Three Types of Vows" Treatise.*[5] We will explore both of these texts in the three chapters following this one.

The twenty-four questions translated below[6] can be divided into three parts. Questions 1–7 refer to the nature and functioning of virtues and their results. They are not directly related to the question of the ultimate virtue, but they point to problems involved in interpreting virtues and related topics. Hence their inclusion here. Likewise, questions 22–24, while not addressing the issue of the ultimate virtue per se, deal predominantly with the tathāgata-essence and in the process further contribute to clarification of the nature of the ultimate virtue. These two sets of questions, targeting the conventional realm of karmic relationships and the ultimate realm of innate awakening, flank questions 8–21, which lie at the very heart of the topic of the ultimate virtue, focusing on its nature, its dedicatability, and related issues.

1. (9/13a)
If everything that is a virtue
Produces happiness as its fruition,
Then what are the fruitions of the stainless virtues [*zag med dge ba*]?[7]

2. (10/13b)
If equanimity [*btang snyoms*] is neither of the two,
Then what are the fruitions of the stained virtues [*zag bcas dge ba*]
Of the fourth absorption and above?
If what is called "equanimity" is an unspecified [phenomenon],
Then what about the emergence of fruitions
From the seeds of the universal basis [*kun gzhi'i sa bon*]?[8]

3. (11a/14)
If "white karmas" are explained as virtues,
Then how [can they have] black fruitions?
If "black karmas" are said to refer to evils,
Then how [can they have] white fruitions?[9]

4. (11b/15)
Was it not explained in the lower Abhidharma
That if the causal motivation [*rgyu yi kun slong*] is evil,
Even though the concurrent motivation [*dus kyi kun slong*] is virtuous,
That karma will not become white?[10]

5. (11c/16)
Did [the teaching] not emerge in the higher Abhidharma
That virtues concordant with
Nonvirtuous concurrent motivations
Are similar to sons of a barren woman?[11]

6. (11d/17)
Did the higher and lower [Abhidharmas] not teach in agreement
That because causal motivations are the main
Among projectors [*'phen byed*], they are projecting causes [*'phen byed rgyu*],
And because concurrent motivations are the main
Among accomplishers [*'grub byed*], they are accomplishing causes [*'grub byed rgyu*]?[12]

7. (11e/18)
Similar to white and black karmas
Deposited as a blend on the desire [realm's] basis,
Are the fruitions blended as well?
In such a case, will there not have to be accepted
The possibility of fruitions of bad transmigrations and high states
In one [and the same] mental continuum?[13]

8. (12a/19)
If the dharma-sphere is not a virtue,
Then what about its being taught [as such]
In the *Ornament of Clear Realizations,* the *Sublime Continuum,*
The *Summary of Mahāyāna,* and
The *Differentiation of the Middle and Extremes?*[14]

9. (12b/20)
If the mere absence of evil was intended [when calling the dharma-sphere "virtue"],
Then what about all unobscured unspecified [phenomena]?[15]

10. (13/21)
Dharmakīrti taught that actual existence [*yod pa nyid*]
Is pervaded by impermanence [i.e., necessarily impermanent].
[But] what textual systems of reasoning teach
That mere existence [*yod tsam*] is pervaded by that?[16]

11. (14/22)
Was it not taught in Nāgārjuna's *[Wisdom: Root Stanzas on] Madhyamaka*
That nonthings [*dngos med*] too
Are pervaded by [being] compounded?
Thus, does it not follow that
The dharma-sphere is compounded?[17]

12. (16a/24)
If emptiness with the essence of compassion [*stong nyid snying rje'i snying po can*]
Is not the sugata-essence,
Then what about the developmental lineage [*rgyas 'gyur rigs*]
Being taught as the sugata-essence?[18]

13. (17/25)
If the dharma-sphere cannot become
A cause of the perfect awakening, then what about the dharma-sphere's
Being posited as the causal lineage [*rgyu yi rigs*]?

And what about passages in valid scriptures
Stating that "because of being a cause of ārya dharmas
The dharma-sphere is posited as the lineage [*rigs*]"?[19]

14. (12c/26)
Are the "dharma-sphere,"
"Holy dharma" [*dam pa'i chos*], and "holy" [*dam pa*]
Not taught in valid scriptures as virtues?
Is the entity of the dharma-sphere, Nairātmyā—
The illusory body of great bliss—
Also asserted to not be a virtue?
In that case, is she not called
In her praise "Lady Virtue" either?[20]

15. (18a/27)
If the dharma-sphere were an unspecified phenomenon,
Then would the following doubt not arise:
Since there are no dharmas apart from the dharma-sphere,
Virtues and evils too
Will turn out to be unspecified phenomena?[21]

16. (18b/28)
If the dharma-sphere is unsuitable as [any of] the three,
Then why do no corresponding doubts arise [here] as well?[22]

17. (18c/29)
If the dharma-sphere is not asserted as existent,
Then, since there are no things
Apart from the dharma-sphere,
Why is it not [the case that] all things too are not asserted as existent?[23]

18. (19/30)
How does the explanation of existent as a positive phenomenon [*sgrub pa*]
Invalidate the dharma-sphere's being a virtue?[24]

19. (20/31)
If a dedication without transformation is meaningless,
Then what about that making of aspirational resolve
By the merchant chief Maitrakanyaka?[25]

20. (21/32)
If using reality as a dedicatable cause
Is not suitable even as mind training,
Then what about the teachings on the unrealistic dedication?[26]

21. (22/33)
If there are no uncreated virtues [*ma byas pa yi dge ba*],
Then what about the *Summary of Mahāyāna*'s explaining as virtues
The stainless seeds
On the universal basis,
Uncreated since beginningless time?
If such [seeds] do not exist, then what is that
Which is explained as the antidote of the universal basis?[27]

22. (16b/34)
If whatever was taught as the sugata-essence
Were uncompounded,
Then what about the nine essences
Taught in the *Sublime Continuum of Mahāyāna*?[28]

23. (23/35)
If the dharma-sphere of not only sentient beings
But matter too were the essence,
Then what about the explanation of sentient beings alone
As possessors of the buddha-essence?
If apart from [the dharma-sphere of] sentient beings,
The dharma-sphere of matter were not the essence,
Then what about tantras'
And the *Three Bodhisattva Commentaries*'s[29] teaching
That the buddha-essence exists in everything inanimate and animate?[30]

24. (24/36)
If what is demonstrated by the example
Of a precious image in rags had a [special] intent,
Would it not turn out that sentient beings
Do not have the naturally abiding lineage [*rang bzhin gyi gnas rigs*]?[31]

Despite Shakya Chokden's claim that in raising questions about the *Thorough Differentiation* he intended to clarify—not criticize—Sakya Pandita's text, these twenty-four (as well as other) questions in the *Good Questions* seem to express doubts regarding Sakya Pandita's position. Indeed, they can be viewed as a straightforward challenge to some of the key points. In particular, these twenty-four questions can be read as challenging the three key components of Sakya Pandita's position: that there is no such a thing as a primordially existent virtue, that the sugata-essence is not a virtue, and that the sugata-essence cannot be dedicated.

In the next three chapters we will explore the answers to these questions provided by Shakya Chokden and Gorampa. Addressing the latter thinker's position is particularly important because it came to be accepted within Sakya as correctly expressing the view of Sakya Pandita himself. Gorampa's answers also serve as a foil to Shakya Chokden's approach. Chapter 6 addresses the two thinkers' take on the workings of karma, facilitating understanding of their interpretation of the ultimate virtue, a topic of chapter 7. That chapter is followed by additional details of their interpretations of the buddha-essence in connection with the ultimate virtue in chapter 8.

6 | What Colors Are Virtues?

Gorampa vs. Shakya Chokden on Karmic Causes and Results

Chapters 6 through 8 provide detailed summaries of Gorampa's and Shakya Chokden's replies to each of the twenty-four questions in chapter 5, skipping over less important details and clarifying difficult points pertinent to the main topic of this book. In many cases, the question is followed first by Gorampa's and then by Shakya Chokden's reply. Because these replies are spread across three chapters, and because some of Shakya Chokden's replies respond to several questions at the same time, certain replies are relegated to the later chapters, and not each of Gorampa's replies is immediately followed by a reply from Shakya Chokden.[1]

While overall Gorampa's reasoning is incisive, demonstrating his virtuosity as a scholar and polemicist, he focuses primarily on refuting Shakya Chokden by showing logical inconsistencies in his questions rather than elucidating the deeper meaning of Sakya Pandita's position.[2] For example, when responding to Shakya Chokden's question whether the dharma-sphere was taught as a virtue in such and such an Indian text, he dismisses it as "pointless questioning" because Sakya Pandita has already explained that all such instances of presenting the dharma-sphere as a virtue refer to an imputed, not real, virtue. While this works well as a polemical tool, it still leaves us searching for deeper reasons why ultimate reality was treated as a virtue in so many Indian texts, as well as what persuaded Sakya Pandita (on surface at least) that all those passages deal only with an imputed virtue.

Shakya Chokden's answers to his own questions are much more detailed and nuanced. When responding to the questions in the *Golden Lancet,* he first considers the question, then offers an actual response. In considering the question, he explains why the question needed to be asked and points out faults or problems with not asking it. The actual response to the question has several subdivisions and sometimes is followed by a discussion of auxiliary topics. In his interpretive approach, rather than siding with just one position, Shakya Chokden addresses and elaborates on alternative, often conflicting perspectives, pointing out which ones were adopted in the *Thorough Differentiation.*

Let us now look at the two thinkers' answers to the twenty-four questions raised by Shakya Chokden. This chapter explores their responses to questions 1 through 7. While they do not address the issue of the ultimate virtue per se, they do clarify their positions on virtue more generally, addressing, among other things, relationships between fruitions and their causes and different types of motivations and actions.

*

1. If everything that is a virtue
   Produces happiness as its fruition,
   Then what are the fruitions of the stainless virtues?

Questions 1 and 2 target verses 42 and 43 of the *Thorough Differentiation.* In particular, question 1 targets the last two lines of verse 42: "Virtue is what is well performed, / Producing happiness as its fruition."

Gorampa replies that despite the statements to the contrary in the higher and lower Abhidharmas, fruitions of stainless seeds are accepted in the *Ornament of Clear Realizations.* He also implies that the *Ornament of Clear Realizations*'s approach supersedes that of the Abhidharmas. Shakya Chokden, by contrast, sides with—and reads into Sakya Pandita's verses—the widespread position that it is specifically stained virtues that produce happiness as their result.

Gorampa's Reply to Question 1

Gorampa writes that in fact there is a scriptural source that demonstrates that there are fruitions (*rnam smin*) of stainless virtues. The *Ornament of Clear Realizations* presents the dharma-body of a buddha as a fruition of the momentary training (*skad cig ma'i sbyor ba*) in the following passage: "The final conclusion of that and its fruition."[3] Gorampa thereby demonstrates that stainless virtues—in this case the last moment on the Mahāyāna path preceding buddhahood—are taught to bring about their fruition by none other than Maitreya himself. He also adds that if one were to object that this is refuted by the position of the higher Abhidharma (*mngon pa gong ma*, the *Summary of Abhidharma*) and the lower Abhidharma (*mngon pa 'og ma*, the *Treasury of Abhidharma*) that fruitional causes (*rnam smin gyi rgyu*) are limited to nonvirtues and stained virtues (*dge ba zag bcas*), one should recollect Haribhadra's words in the *Clear Meaning* about different ways of practicing the path by Mahāyāna and non-Mahāyāna practitioners: "This is exclusively a different presentation. Therefore, no refutations should be made anywhere based on other vehicles."[4] In other words, one cannot refute the *Ornament of Clear Realizations*'s position on the grounds of its contradicting that of other systems, such as Abhidharma.

Shakya Chokden's Reply to Question 1

Shakya Chokden writes that the reason for asking question 1 is that such commentators as Pökhangpa Rinchen Gyeltshen (*spos khang pa rin chen rgyal mtshan*, 1348–1430) did not go into sufficient detail in their discussion of virtues. If the question were not asked, there would still remain unsolved problems pertaining to apparent contradictions of Sakya Pandita's position (v. 42) and the explanation that fruitional causes necessarily have to be either nonvirtues or stained virtues. In the actual answer, Shakya Chokden argues that Sakya Pandita used *virtue* to refer specifically to stained virtues, which are of two types: those of partial concordance with merits (*bsod nams cha mthun*) and those of partial concordance with liberation (*thar pa cha mthun*). The first type issues four of the five results—excluding the separative result (*bral 'bras*). Its fruitional result is happiness of the three high states within saṃsāra. The second type brings about the separative result and the other four. What separation refers to is happiness of liberation (*thar pa'i bde ba*). In this context, it has to be explained as the ultimate virtue. The fruitional happiness (*rnam smin gyi bde ba*), by contrast, has to be explained as the ultimate nonvirtue because all varieties of saṃsāra that are fruitions of karmas and afflictions have to be explained as such.[5]

*

2. If equanimity is neither of the two,
   Then what are the fruitions of the stained virtues
   Of the fourth absorption and above?
   If what is called "equanimity" is an unspecified
      [phenomenon],

Then what about the emergence of fruitions
From the seeds of the universal basis?

Question 2 targets the last two lines of verse 43 of the *Thorough Differentiation*: "Because equanimity is neither of the two, / Its fruition too is neither of the two."

In this question, as well as in its answers provided by Shakya Chokden and Gorampa, the term *universal basis* stands for the *universal basis consciousness* and the two are treated as synonymous. The same applies to other questions and answers by Shakya Chokden and Gorampa in which the universal basis is mentioned.[6]

Elaborating on several context-dependent applications of *equanimity*, Gorampa defends Sakya Pandita's usage of the term to refer to unspecified phenomena. He also clarifies how the universal basis's seeds, which according to him are necessarily unspecified phenomena, can nonetheless produce karmic results of happiness and suffering.

In contrast to Gorampa, Shakya Chokden argues for the narrow usage of the term *equanimity*, limiting it to one of the three karmic results and the feeling of equanimity that can accompany karmas (including the virtuous ones), their results, and the universal basis. He also points out the problem with treating equanimity as referring to unspecified phenomena and treating them as necessarily *not* producers of fruitions. He stresses the importance of distinguishing between causes of fruitions and producers of fruitions, in particular where the universal basis is accepted. That distinction allows him to claim that the seeds of the universal basis do not necessarily have to be neutral; in his answers to questions 13 and 21 he will explicitly argue that they can also be virtues or nonvirtues.

Gorampa's Reply to Question 2

Regarding the first three lines of question 2, Gorampa suggests that Shakya Chokden was attempting to refute Sakya Pandita by referring to the feeling of equanimity (*tshor ba btang snyoms*). Nevertheless, he argues, *equanimity* does not always refer to that; it can also refer to the compositional factor of equanimity (*'du byed btang snyoms*). However, *equanimity* in verse 43 refers to neither of these two. Rather, to make "equanimous" the line containing that word,[7] Sakya Pandita referred to unspecified phenomena as *equanimity*. Thus one should know, he writes, that depending on context, one and the same word *equanimity* can refer to multiple phenomena: to unspecified phenomena in the trio of virtue, evil, and equanimity; to the feeling of equanimity in the trio of happiness, suffering, and equanimity; to the compositional factor of equanimity in the trio of equanimity, shame, and decorum; and so forth.

Addressing the issue raised in the last three lines of Shakya Chokden's question, Gorampa specifies that the idea of planting seeds on the universal basis belongs to the Cittamātra system, not to the lower Abhidharma. According to Cittamātra, as soon as virtuous or nonvirtuous karmas have been performed, their seeds are planted on the universal basis, and from their nourishment by "external" conditions fruitions eventually emerge. In that process, the fruitions are those of virtuous and nonvirtuous karmas that planted the seeds, not of the seeds per se. That allows, without contradiction, for the seeds themselves to be unspecified phenomena and for fruitions of virtuous and nonvirtuous karmas to arise from them. Gorampa thereby clarifies the problematic issue of the universal basis's seeds being neutral or unspecified phenomena and at the same time producing happiness and suffering, which are results of virtuous and nonvirtuous karmas.[8]

To further clarify his position, Gorampa provides an interesting example: In spring, one invests three coins for profit and signs a contract testifying to that. In fall, he shows that same document and receives four coins. The additional coin is the interest made on the previously invested three coins, not on the signed contract. (The three coins in this example stand for karmas, the contract for seeds, and the interest for fruitions.)

Gorampa also shows unwanted consequences of the claim that fruitions in future lives are fruitions of the seeds because they emerge or originate from those seeds. Mocking that claim's logic, he writes that it will then follow that the head of a statue is the head of the statue maker because that head originates from (i.e., issued, was created by) the statue maker; the eye of a needle is the eye of the smith because it originates from the smith; the nose of a shoe (i.e., the toe box) is the nose of the shoemaker because it originates from him; and so forth.[9]

Shakya Chokden's Reply to Question 2

Shakya Chokden subdivides question 2 into two parts: the context-related question (the first three lines) and the auxiliary question (the remaining lines). He explains the need for asking the first one: The term *equanimity* (*btang snyoms*) is used when addressing the division into happiness and suffering as results. The term *unspecified* (*lung du ma bstan pa*) is used when addressing the division into virtues and nonvirtues as causes; the Buddha's teachings addressed no equanimity in that context. Using the term *equanimity* is confusing also because equanimity itself can be virtuous or nonvirtuous. The problem with not asking this question is that according to the literal reading of the passage mentioning equanimity (vv. 42–43), equanimity is the cause producing fruitions that are neither happiness nor suffering. However, numerous writers on the *Thorough Differentiation,* including Pökhangpa, argued that equanimity does not have fruitions.

In the actual response, Shakya Chokden writes that the six lines in verses 42 and 43 that discuss virtues, nonvirtues, and equanimity apparently explain the meaning of the *Treasury of Abhidharma* passage:

> Fruitions of virtuous karmas
> Devoid of applied thought [*rnam par rtog pa*]
> Are asserted as exclusively mental feelings.
> Those of nonvirtuous, as bodily ones.[10]

Elaborating on those lines, he suggests the following reading:

> Fruitions of nonvirtuous karmas
> Are the bodily feelings of suffering.
> Virtuous karmas include both the ones
> With and devoid of applied thought.
> Fruitions of virtues with applied thought
> Are ascertained as bodily feelings of happiness.
> Virtues devoid of applied thought include
> Those with happiness and with only equanimity.
> Fruitions of both are mental feelings.
> Fruitions of the ones with happiness
> Are the mental feelings of happiness.
> Fruitions of the ones with only equanimity
> Are the mental feelings of equanimity.[11]

He adds that this interpretation is also informed by an additional verse from the *Treasury of Abhidharma:*

> Virtues through the third absorption [have]
> Experiences of manifest happiness. Above that
> [They have] experiences of neither suffering nor happiness.[12]

The above discussion revolves around various mental states that are present or absent on different planes of existence. Applied thought is present among mental states of the desire realm and the first of the four absorptions that correspond or lead to rebirth on the four levels of the form realm. The feeling of happiness is present among mental states of the desire realm and the first three of the four absorptions. The feeling of equanimity devoid of suffering and happiness is present starting from the fourth absorption. In contrast to the mental states of the desire realm and the first absorption, where both bodily and purely mental feelings of happiness occur, only mental feelings of happiness are present in the second and third absorptions, and only mental feelings of equanimity are present in the fourth absorption. These feelings of happiness and equanimity are also experienced in respective states within the form realm, where one can take birth as a karmic fruition of respective absorptions. Two things should be noted in this scenario. First, all mental states in the four absorptions—including the feeling of equanimity in the fourth absorption—are virtues, albeit stained owing to their not serving as the causes of nirvāṇa. Second, all four absorptions can serve as fruitional causes leading to rebirth in the form realm, which is a fortunate state of existence.

Moving to the auxiliary question, Shakya Chokden writes that the reason for asking it is that all commentators on the *Thorough Differentiation* interpreted *equanimity* as referring to unspecified phenomena and explained that they are not producers of fruitions (*rnam smin skyed byed*). The problem with not asking the question is that there is a very big difference between fruitional causes / causes of fruitions (*rnam smin gyi rgyu*) and producers of fruitions. If that distinction is not maintained, it will follow that it is impossible for any unspecified afflictions (*nyong mongs pa lung ma bstan,* i.e., afflictions that are not nonvirtues) to be producers of fruitions. Such is unacceptable, he argues, because they do produce fruitions through becoming motivations of virtuous karmas. Also, in a context in which the universal basis is accepted, such as Asaṅga's *Summary of Mahāyāna,* it will follow that seeds on the universal basis (*kun gzhi'i steng gi sa bon*) are fruitional causes because they are producers of fruitions. That would go against Asaṅga's system, which differentiates between two types of causes: projecting causes (*'phen byed kyi rgyu*) and producing causes (*skyed byed kyi rgyu*). The former are karmas depositing predispositions (*bag chags 'jog byed kyi las*), the latter predispositions deposited by them (*des gzhag pa'i bag chags*). According to Asaṅga, nonvirtues and stained virtues are projecting causes of fruitions. Their predispositions are producing causes of fruitions.[13]

Shakya Chokden's actual response to the auxiliary question is that in general *equanimity* refers to the feeling of equanimity, and in particular it refers to the equanimity of the fourth absorption and above (i.e., the formless realm). According to him, the meaning of the *Thorough Differentiation* lines mentioning equanimity is this: "Because equanimity is neither of the two—neither happiness nor suffering—/ Its fruition is equanimity, which is neither of the two."[14]

*

3. If "white karmas" are explained as virtues,
   Then how [can they have] black fruitions?
   If "black karmas" are said to refer to evils,
   Then how [can they have] white fruitions?

4. Was it not explained in the lower Abhidharma
   That if the causal motivation is evil,
   Even though the concurrent motivation is virtuous,
   That karma will not become white?

5. Did [the teaching] not emerge in the higher Abhidharma
   That virtues concordant with
   Nonvirtuous concurrent motivations
   Are similar to sons of a barren woman?

6. Did the higher and lower [Abhidharmas] not teach in agreement
   That because causal motivations are the main
   Among projectors, they are projecting causes,
   And because concurrent motivations are the main
   Among accomplishers, they are accomplishing causes?

7. Similar to white and black karmas
   Deposited as a blend on the desire [realm's] basis,
   Are the fruitions blended as well?
   In such a case, will there not have to be accepted
   The possibility of fruitions of bad transmigrations and high states
   In one [and the same] mental continuum?

Questions 3 through 7 target verses 46–57 of the *Thorough Differentiation,* in particular verse 46:

> Also, four types of karmas were taught:
> White karmas with white fruitions,
> Black karmas with black fruitions,

> White karmas with black fruitions,
> Black karmas with white fruitions.

verses 50–51:

> Also, two types of karmas were taught:
> Projecting karmas and completing karmas.
> If divided, there are four alternatives.
>
> [Results can be] projected by projecting virtues
> With completing [karmas] also being virtues.
> [They can be] projected by projecting evils
> With completing [karmas] also being evils.
> [Other options are] projecting virtues with completing evils
> And projecting evils with completing virtues.

and verses 56–57:

> Also, the Sage taught three types of karmas:
> Solely white, solely black,
> And mixed.
>
> Solely white ones produce happiness.
> Solely black ones produce suffering.
> Mixed karmas produce mixed
> Happiness and suffering, he taught.

While Shakya Chokden answers these questions together (hence I have listed them together here), Gorampa replies to them one by one.

Gorampa's reply to question 3 demonstrates that he cannot take literally Sakya Pandita's statements about karmas' producing fruitions whose "colors" are different from their own. As a result, he resorts to the common tactics of claiming that Sakya Pandita did not literally mean what he said. In particular, he argues that when writing that there are white karmas with black fruitions and black karmas with white fruitions, Sakya Pandita called them "virtues," and so on, only because they appear as such.

In his reply to question 4, he explains that karmas with negative causal motivations cannot be positive, and their being called so should not be taken literally. Not only that but such karmas' concurrent motivations cannot be virtuous either.

Responding to question 5, he reiterates the points that he has already made. Other than that, he does not see the question itself as relevant to the discussion of the *Thorough Differentiation*.

Answering question 6, Gorampa explores technicalities of karmic causality, addressing nuanced differences between accomplishing and concordant causes, as well as between three types of "projectors": those paired with "completors," those paired with "accomplishers," and those paired with "concordant engagers." He does that in part because in his opinion, Shakya Chokden misunderstood the meaning of relevant textual passages. He also demonstrates differences between the two Abhidharmas' approaches to the topic.

In his reply to question 7, Gorampa addresses three distinct ways of dividing positive and negative karmas and points out which of these approaches was followed in the *Thorough Differentiation.* He also specifies that the mixed fruitions addressed in that text are the ones integrated in the same mental continuum, which does not entail blending of their entities.

In his reply to questions 3 through 7, Shakya Chokden focuses on several issues related to blended white-black karmas. Like Gorampa, he does not accept literally the *Thorough Differentiation*'s claim that white karmas can issue black fruitions, and vice versa. Explaining that the term *blended white-black karmas* is found only in the lower Abhidharma, he argues that that system accepts neither the possibility of white karmas' issuing black fruitions nor the possibility of distinguishing between white and black karmas based on both causal and concurrent motivations. According to the higher Abhidharma, it is exclusively the concurrent motivation that makes a karma virtuous or nonvirtuous. That system also does not accept white karmas' issuing black fruitions, and vice versa.

Going into details of karmic causality, Shakya Chokden addresses "accomplishers," "projectors," and different types of results. He specifies differences between approaches of the higher and lower Abhidharmas, arguing that the *Thorough Differentiation*'s presentation agrees with the higher Abhidharma's presentation of white-black karmas' having white-black fruitions. This, nonetheless, does not entail the acceptance of the possibility of one and the same karma's issuing both white and black fruitions. Rather, it is that within the two parts, preparatory and actual, of one and the same path of karma, one part issues white fruitions, and the other black. Regarding the lower Abhidharma, Shakya Chokden argues that it accepts the blending of karmic causes but rejects the possibility of their fruitions' simultaneously emerging in the same mental continuum.

Gorampa's Reply to Question 3

Gorampa replies to question 3 that although genuine white karmas are in general virtues, in this context (i.e., verses 46–49 of the *Thorough Differentiation,* where it is stated that there are white karmas with black fruitions and black karmas with white fruitions), such physical and verbal applications (*sbyor ba*) of black karmas as acts of generosity, and so on, are called "virtues" only because they appear as such. In fact, because both their causal motivations and their concurrent motivations are black, those karmas are black too. Likewise, such physical and verbal applications of white karmas as killing, and so on, are called black only because they appear as such. In fact, they should be understood as white. Otherwise, if it were incorrect to call white karmas "black" and black karmas "white," then it would be contradictory to call one and the same stainless karma (*zag med kyi las*) "nonwhite" in the lower Abhidharma and "white" in the higher Abhidharma, because the same logic should be applicable in that context too.[15]

Gorampa's Reply to Question 4

In his reply to question 4, Gorampa interrogates the original inquiry with a counterquestion: "What are you asking about"? Presuming that the only possibility is that Shakya Chokden was asking about the acts of generosity for the sake of killing, and so on, as an illustration of white karmas with black fruitions, Gorampa writes that he has just explained that they are not genuine white karmas. He also points out that it is incorrect to claim that such karmas' concurrent motivation is virtuous. Otherwise, it would follow that they are blended white-black karmas.[16]

Gorampa's Reply to Question 5

It is true, writes Gorampa in reply to question 5, that in the higher Abhidharma virtues concordant with nonvirtues are analogized to "sons of a barren woman." But how does that invalidate the words or the meaning of Sakya Pandita's treatise? In the *Thorough Differentiation,* Sakya Pandita intended to say that if both the causal and concurrent motivations are black, the karmas motivated by them are solely black. If both are white, the motivated karmas are exclusively white. If they are blended, the karmas will also be blended. As for the physical and verbal applications that appear as white or black, they are merely the bases for imputing the names of white and black karmas, which does not turn them into actual white or black karmas.[17]

Gorampa's Reply to Question 6

Gorampa replies to question 6 that Sakya Pandita's text provides no basis for asking this question, the question's wording does not derive from the higher or the lower Abhidharma, and the question's meaning is undermined by reasoning. Regarding the former, Gorampa writes that if the question refers to white karmas with black fruitions and black karmas with white fruitions, then it can be answered as he has just done. If it refers to the four possibilities between projectors and completors (*'phen rdzogs*, i.e., projecting and completing karmas), then within the twofold division into projectors and completors it is entirely incorrect to identify projectors as causal motivations and completors as concurrent motivations. This is because in that context, projectors are different from projectors within the twofold division into projectors and accomplishers (*'phen 'grub gnyis*), and completors are also different from accomplishers within that division.

Regarding the second issue, Gorampa writes that the higher and lower Abhidharmas' approaches to the issue are not in agreement. In contrast to the higher Abhidharma, the *Treasury of Abhidharma* and Vasubandhu's autocommentary do not discuss projectors and accomplishers when dealing with the twelve links of dependent origination (*rten 'brel yan lag bcu gnyis*). But they do discuss the causal and concurrent motivations, addressing causal motivations as projectors, which according to Gorampa is likely what misled Shakya Chokden. The root text says:

> There are two types of motivations, called
> "Causal" and "concurrent" motivations;
> The first of the two thoroughly engages,
> The second subsequently engages.[18]

The autocommentary explains: "Because the causal motivation projects [*'phen par byed pa*], it thoroughly engages [*rab tu 'jug par byed pa*]. Because the concurrent motivation concordantly engages [*mthun par 'jug pa*] during the activity [*bya ba*], it subsequently engages [*rjes su 'jug par byed pa*]. Now what potential [*nus pa*] of that [former motivation] does that activity have? Even though projected [by the causal motivation], if that [concurrent motivation] is not present, as if someone dropping dead [prior to reaching a desired destination] that [karma] will not occur."[19]

Gorampa explains that in that context, the causal motivation is not the same as the projector within the twofold division into projectors and accomplishers. "Projectors" in that twofold division project entities of fruitions (*rnam smin gyi ngo bo*), while "projectors" in this context project entities of karmas (*las kyi ngo bo*). Regarding the concurrent motivation, these texts do not explain it as an "accomplisher." Were one to accept it as such, it would follow that there are not karmas projected by projectors but not yet nourished by accomplishers, because it is clearly stated in those texts that no karma occurs without a concurrent motivation even if there is a causal motivation.[20]

Gorampa thereby refers to quotations from Vasubandhu's writings demonstrating that according to the lower Abhidharma, causal motivations, also termed *projectors*, together with concurrent motivations, project karmas, not their fruitions. Furthermore, a concurrent motivation is required for a karma to be performed. Otherwise, despite the existence of a causal motivation, no actual karma will be formed, which is similar to someone's expiring prior to reaching a destination despite a previous intention to reach it. The twofold division into projectors and accomplishers deals specifically with how karmas produce their fruitions, not with how karmas themselves are produced through motivations. If one mistakenly matches this division with that into the two motivations, it will follow that no projecting karma can exist without the presence of the accomplishing karma, which, as we will see below, is incorrect.

Gorampa argues that matching these two divisions is incorrect in the context of the higher Abhidharma as well, in particular when addressing the twelve links of dependent origination. Were one to do so, the trio of ignorance, compositional factors, and consciousness (*ma rig pa 'du byed rnam shes*), being projectors, would have to be counted as causal motivations, and the trio of craving, clinging, and existence (*sred len srid pa gsum*), being accomplishers, would have to be counted as concurrent motivations, which is simply laughable.[21]

Regarding the third issue, Gorampa posits an unwanted consequence: that according to the system of the higher Abhidharma, when the causal motivation of such karmas as killing has been generated and before the concurrent motivation has been produced, the karma of killing is completed. This is because when projectors of such karmas as killing have been completed, such karmas as killing are completed. If this is accepted, it will follow that the concurrent motivation occurs after the karma has been completed. If such is not established, it will follow that even when the compositional factors (*'du byed*)—the second within the twelve links—have been completed, those karmas are not completed.

An additional unwanted consequence is that if concurrent motivations are accomplishers, it will follow that if something is a karma it necessarily has to be an accomplishing karma. This is because if something is a karma it has to have a concurrent motivation. If such is accepted, it will wrongly follow that compositional factors within the twelve links are accomplishing karmas because they are karmas.

Further, Gorampa continues, it is entirely wrong to claim that if something is an accomplishing cause it must be a concordant cause: because accomplishing causes have to be identified as craving, clinging, and existence, it will follow that all concordant results (*rgyu mthun gyi 'bras bu*) are results concordant with afflicted causes (*nyon mongs can gyi rgyu mthun gyi 'bras bu*).

Thus, Gorampa concludes, one should not confuse three types of projectors: projectors within the twofold division into projectors and completors, projectors within the twofold division into projectors and accomplishers, and projectors within the twofold division into projectors and concordant engagers (*mthun par 'jug par byed pa*) when activity takes place. The first refers to both projectors and accomplishers as fruitional causes only. The second refers to the first three among the twelve links of dependent origination. The third refers to the causal motivations.[22]

Gorampa's Reply to Question 7

Gorampa divides his answer to question 7 into three parts: individual explanation of the four alternatives between white and black karmas, the way of explaining blended fruitions in the lower Abhidharma, and the way blended fruitions are *not* discussed in the higher Abhidharma.

In the first part he explains that there appear to be three different approaches to dividing white and black karmas. The first is that of Vasubandhu's *Explanation of the "Treasury of Abhidharma."* Presenting there the Vaibhāṣika position, Vasubandhu explains that black karmas producing black fruitions are nonvirtues, because their entity is afflicted and their fruitions are unpleasant. White karmas producing white fruitions are virtues of the form realm, because they are not blended with nonvirtues and their fruitions are pleasant. Virtues of the formless realm are not included in the category of white karmas with white fruitions because that category should include, with respect to those karmas' fruitions, both the intermediate existence (*srid pa bar ma*) and the rebirth existence (*skye ba'i srid pa*), and with respect to those karmas' entities, all three types of karmas: those of the body, speech, and mind.[23]

Articulating his own position, Vasubandhu adds that white-black karmas producing white-black fruitions are virtues of the desire realm because they are blended with nonvirtues in one and the same mental continuum (*rgyud*) and because their fruitions are also blended. Nonwhite-nonblack karmas extinguishing karmas and lacking fruitions (*mi dkar mi gnag cing rnam par smin pa med pa la las zad par byed pa'i las*) are stainless karmas (*zag pa med pa'i las*). Having no white fruitions, they are called "nonwhite" and "lacking fruitions" (*rnam smin med pa*). Because their entities (*ngo bo*) are not afflicted, they are nonblack. Because they extinguish all three types of karmas (white, black, and white-black), they are called "extinguishing karmas." Gorampa points out (as he has done in his answer to question 3) that Vasubandhu interprets teachings on nonwhite karmas as intentional (i.e., nonliteral).[24]

The second approach is that of the higher Abhidharma, in which these four types of karmas are explained as, respectively, nonvirtues, virtues of all three realms, blended karmas thoroughly possessing desires (*'dod pa dang rab tu ldan pa'i 'dren ma*), and stainless karmas that are the preparation and unobstructed paths (*sbyor ba dang / bar chad med pa'i lam*). The meaning of the third type of karmas is explained by Asaṅga in terms of intentions (*bsam pa*) and applications (*sbyor ba*) being respectively black and white, and vice versa. The essential point, according to Gorampa, is that intentions and applications here refer to the causal and concurrent motivations. The fourth type is described by Asaṅga as nonblack white karmas with no fruitions being issued and with karmas being extinguished (*mi gnag cing / dkar la rnam par smin par mi 'byung zhing / las zad par 'gyur ba'i las*).[25] According to Gorampa, with the *Treasury of Abhidharma*'s explaining that the nonwhite karmas were called so in a nonliteral sense, their interpretation there and that of the fourth type of karmas outlined here appear to have the same meaning.[26]

The third approach is followed in, among other texts, those sūtras that provide a threefold division of karmas into solely white, solely black, and blended, a division that is also used in the *Thorough Differentiation*. While the meaning of *blended* is explained differently in the higher and lower Abhidharmas, the *Thorough Differentiation*'s explanation is clearly in accordance with that of the higher Abhidharma because it accepts that if both the causal and concordant motivations are white, fruitions will also be exclusively white. In the lower Abhidharma, Vasubandhu specifies that the phrase *blended white-black karmas of the desire realm* refers to their being blended in one and the same mental continuum (*rgyud 'dres pa*), not to their having blended entities (*ngo bo 'dres pa*). This is because if a karma's entity is virtuous, it is contradictory for it to be blended with nonvirtues. The description of fruitions as *blended* likewise pertains to their being integrated in one and the same mental continuum, not to their entities being blended. Regarding the question whether nonvirtues of the desire realm are mixed white-black karmas owing to their being blended with virtues, Vasubandhu specifies that because in the desire realm nonvirtues are powerful, they do not blend with virtues. On the other hand, virtues there are weaker and thus do blend with nonvirtues.[27]

Now directly answering Shakya Chokden's question, Gorampa writes that in brief, according to this approach, there are blended fruitions in one and the same mental continuum because one and the same mental continuum can possess both pleasant and unpleasant fruitions. Nevertheless, this does not make it possible for the happy transmigrations (*bde 'gro*) and bad transmigrations (*ngan 'gro*) to be blended in one and the same mental continuum. This is because if something is a fruition of a virtue, it necessarily ripens on the basis of happy transmigrations (*bde 'gro'i rten*), and if something is a fruition of a nonvirtue, it necessarily ripens on the basis of bad transmigrations (*ngan 'gro'i rten*).[28] Gorampa thereby argues that in the context of multiple lifetimes, one and the same continuum can have pleasant fruitions of being reborn in happy transmigrations and unpleasant fruitions of being reborn in bad transmigrations. But such fruitions cannot co-occur on one and the same basis, because fruitional causes' main function is to produce mental and physical aggregates within different realms of rebirth.

Turning to the higher Abhidharma, Gorampa writes that he has already explained the meaning of blended white and black karmas. As for the phrase *blended fruitions,* it refers to the results concordant with causes (*rgyu mthun*) and dominant results (*bdag po'i 'bras bu*), which were simply given the name *fruitions.* It is impossible for genuine fruitional results to blend on one and the same basis. This is because the main type of fruition is the feeling of equanimity within the surroundings (*'khor*) of the universal basis, through whose power the universal basis itself, together with its surroundings, also becomes a genuine fruition. Regarding feelings of happiness and suffering being explained as fruitions, Gorampa explains that because they are termed *fruitions,* their blending within one and the same mental continuum too is posited as *blended fruitions.* It is impossible, argues Gorampa, for the universal bases of happy and bad transmigrations to simultaneously emerge in one and the same mental continuum, because in this system, when the universal basis of a particular transmigration is established, it is treated as taking rebirth in that particular transmigration.[29]

Shakya Chokden's Reply to Questions 3 through 7

Shakya Chokden divides questions 3–7 into two sections: the context-related questions (3–6) and the auxiliary question (7). Regarding the former, explaining the reason for asking them, he writes that they target specifically blended white-black karmas. While the *Thorough Differentiation* explained that white karmas can issue black fruitions, and black karmas[30] white fruitions, not only is it incorrect to accept that explanation literally but the Abhidharma did not provide such an explanation. The problem with not asking is that none of the commentators on the *Thorough Differentiation* provided explanations that did more than simply add details to the words of the text. Because they have accepted that nonvirtues can cause fruitions of happiness, and virtues can cause fruitions of suffering, a common locus (*gzhi mthun*) between white and black karmas would be possible, which is absurd.

Regarding the reason for asking the auxiliary question, he writes that it might be objected that the category of blended white-black karmas refers to karmas whose causal motivations are nonvirtues and whose concurrent motivations are virtues and that such karmas also issue fruitions of both happiness and suffering. He explains that the term *blended white-black karmas* is found only in the lower Abhidharma. He makes two points regarding the lower Abhidharma: that white karmas' issuing black fruitions is not accepted in that system and that the possibility of distinguishing between white and black karmas on the basis of both causal and concurrent motivations is not accepted in it either. Addressing the first, he quotes from the *Explanation of the "Treasury of Abhidharma"*: "Virtues belonging to the desire realm are white-black because of being blended with nonvirtues. Because their fruitions are blended, those fruitions are also white-black. This is presented in terms of the mental continuum—not in terms of the entity. There does not exist one [and the same] karma or fruition that is white and also black. This is because they are mutually contradictory."[31]

Citing the passage immediately following that quote, he explains that the *Treasury of Abhidharma* also does not accept the possibility of nonvirtues' issuing white fruitions interpreted in terms of blended white-black karmas: "It might be asked: in such a case will nonvirtues [of the desire realm] too, as a result of being blended with virtues, not turn into white-black? [The answer is that] as for the desire realm, nonvirtues there do not doubtlessly blend with virtues. That is because they are powerful. Virtues [by contrast] blend, because they are weaker."[32] According to Shakya Chokden, the meaning of that passage is that at the time when virtuous karmas within the desire realm are present in one's mental continuum, nonvirtuous karmas in that same mental continuum can issue black fruitions. But as long as nonvirtuous karmas are present in that mental continuum, virtues cannot issue white fruitions. In particular, when the correct view (*yang dag pa'i lta ba*) within the desire realm is present in one's mental continuum, the wrong view (*log lta*) can still issue black fruitions. But as long as the wrong view is present, the correct view cannot issue fruitions. This is because within the desire realm the root of the correct view can be severed by the wrong view, but not vice versa.[33]

Moving to the second point, Shakya Chokden explains that it is incorrect to claim that according to the lower Abhidharma an example of black karmas with white fruitions is a karma created by a nonvirtuous concurrent motivation and a virtuous causal motivation that issues a white fruition and that an example of white karmas with black fruitions is a karma created by a virtuous concurrent motivation and a nonvirtuous causal motivation that issues a black fruition. This is because what makes bodily and verbal karmas virtuous and nonvirtuous according to this system is the causal motivation, not the concurrent one. Explaining that is the fact that according to the lower Abhidharma the causal motivation brings about exclusively the nonrevelatory materiality (*rnam par rig byed ma yin pa*) that is the actual part of the path of karma (*las lam gyi dngos gzhi*). The concurrent motivation, by contrast, brings about subsequent activity with the entity of the revelatory materiality (*rnam par rig byed*). In support of this interpretation, he cites the *Treasury of Abhidharma:*

> There are two types of motivations, called
> "Causal" and "concurrent" motivations;
> The first of the two thoroughly engages,
> The second subsequently engages.[34]

One might object, he writes, that according to the higher Abhidharma system too karmas are posited as based on their causal motivations. He replies that this is also incorrect, because in that system, no matter what the causal motivation is, what makes a karma virtuous or nonvirtuous is exclusively the concurrent motivation. That also explains why according to that system it is impossible for white karmas to issue black fruitions, and vice versa.

Some might also object that karmas with nonvirtuous causal motivations and virtuous concurrent motivations are exclusively white but issue black fruitions because their fruitional causes are nonvirtuous. Shakya Chokden's answer is that such white karmas are accomplishers of distinctive features (*khyad par 'grub byed*) of black fruitions but not projectors of entities (*ngo bo 'phen byed*) of those fruitions. This is because they are not their fruitional causes and also because black fruitions are results concordant with causes (*rgyu mthun gyi 'bras bu*) based on those karmas, not their fruitional results (*rnam smin gyi 'bras bu*).

Shakya Chokden also explains that the presentation of the two karmas motivated by the causal and concurrent motivations as predominantly projecting and accomplishing causes is exclusively in terms of actions within the desire realm, because that is the context of dealing with the issue of blended white-black karmas. For the same reason, it specifically pertains to the karmas that are objects of abandonment by the path of meditation. As stated in the *Treasury of Abhidharma,* "As for others, the objects of abandonment by [the path of] seeing are black; / Others, produced from within the desire [realm], are white-black."[35] He also writes that some claim that although karmas with white fruitions are called black, in fact they are genuine white karmas, and that they also claim that the same applies to calling karmas with black fruitions white, although they are genuine black. According to him, that is wrong too because in that case karmas would be divided into just two types: white and black karmas issuing, respectively, white and black fruitions.[36]

The actual answer is divided into two parts: giving answer in accordance with the higher Abhidharma and separately raising and resolving doubts with respect to the lower Abhidharma. In the first part he explains that the *Thorough Differentiation*'s presentation of white-black karmas is not in agreement with the lower Abhidharma. This is because that Abhidharma system explains only three types of karmas, while the *Thorough Differentiation* explains four. Furthermore, in the lower Abhidharma, black karmas with white fruitions are taken as the opponent's position and refuted. In contrast to that, Sakya Pandita's explanation agrees with the higher Abhidharma's presentation of white-black karmas' having white-black fruitions. That said, the meaning of such a presentation is not that one and the same karma can issue both white and black fruitions. Rather, it is that within the two parts of one and the same path of karma, preparatory and actual (*las lam gcig gi sbyor dngos gnyis*), one part issues white fruitions and the other issues black. Regarding a karma with a black causal motivation and a white concurrent motivation, although its entity is white, since its causal motivation issues a black fruition, that karma itself is posited as a producer of a black fruition. For example, when, with hatred as a causal motivation, one donates lots of wealth in order to kill, even though it is just one path of karma, that causal motivation of hatred is the projector of a black fruition, while the concurrent motivation, which is the root of the virtue of nonattachment, is the accomplishing cause of that black fruition. The same logic applies to karmas with white causal and black concurrent motivations.

Providing a verse summary, Shakya Chokden writes:

There are four types of karmas: white, black, blended,
And extinguishing them. Owing to the divisions into black karmas'
Being accomplishers of white fruitions and white karmas' also
Being accomplishers of black fruitions,
[White and black karmas are] explained as twofold.

The distinctions responsible for there being no repetitiveness between
These [karmas] and mixed karmas explained below
Pertain to the systems of the higher and the lower Abhidharma: [According to the lower one,]
Actions [can also] be material [*gzugs can*]; [according to the higher, they can] not.[37]

In the second section addressing question 7, Shakya Chokden explains his thoughts underlying the question and then moves to the actual answer. In the former part he returns to the *Explanation of the "Treasury of Abhidharma"* passage that reads, "Virtues belonging to the desire realm are white-black because of being blended with nonvirtues. Because their fruitions are blended, those fruitions are also white-black. This is presented in terms of the mental continuum—not in terms of the entity." According to him, the passage indicates that although it is impossible for the entities of the causal virtues and nonvirtues to be blended, it is not contradictory for them to simultaneously emerge, and this is why they are explained as blended. One might then mistakenly presume that in that case the meaning of blended fruitions too should be explained as their simultaneous emergence in the same mental continuum. But were such the case, it would follow that high states and bad transmigrations can simultaneously emerge in the same mental continuum because fruitional results of virtuous and nonvirtuous karmas are none other than aggregates (*phung po*) of the good and bad transmigrations.

Shakya Chokden's actual answer is that if it could be accepted that similar to the blending of causes, there are fruitions that simultaneously emerge in one and the same mental continuum, that fault would indeed apply. But such is not acceptable. This is because the meaning of *blended* (*rnam par 'dres pa*) is "mixture" (*'dren ma*), and the meaning of *mixture* is explained as "intertwining" (*spel ma*). For example, when a powerful hatred is produced in the mental continuum of someone who upholds the vows of individual liberation (*so thar sdom ldan*), that hatred and the vows with the nature of materiality (*sdom pa gzugs can*) that were motivated by hatred-lacking virtues emerge simultaneously. At that time, they cannot mutually destroy each other's potentials, which is what "blending of the two via the mental continuum" (*gnyis po rgyud kyi sgo nas 'dres pa*) refers to. Their fruitions ripen first in higher states and then in bad transmigrations. This is what is referred to as "mixture."

One might object that in that case it will be possible for a nonvirtuous karma on the basis of the desire realm to be a mixed karma for the same reason. Shakya Chokden's answer is that such is indeed possible. The reason why such a possibility was not explicitly addressed in the lower Abhidharma is that virtues of the desire realm necessarily can *not* annihilate fruitions of their opposite nonvirtues, while some nonvirtues, such as the wrong view deprecating causes and results (*rgyu 'bras la skur 'debs kyi log lta*), can indeed annihilate fruitions of their opposite virtues.

To conclude, he writes, if something is a virtue of the desire realm, it is necessarily suitable for blending with nonvirtues, because it cannot eliminate nonvirtues—its opposite. That does not apply to nonvirtues, because it is possible that some of them have the potential to eliminate their opposite—virtues.[38]

In their interpretations of karmic processes, Gorampa and Shakya Chokden agree that certain statements in the *Thorough Differentiation*, such as the notion of mixed black-white karmas, cannot be taken literally, while some statements that can be taken literally are limited to specific scriptural sources. Important differences between the two thinkers' positions include, but are far from limited to, how to interpret certain terms used by Sakya Pandita, how to interpret different elements involved in the process of karmic causality, and how to interpret the nature of seeds on the universal basis. Most importantly, the two thinkers understand very differently what can be included in the category of virtue. This results in their contradictory approaches to understanding numerous textual passages that treat ultimate reality as a virtue—the topic to which we now turn.

7 | Is the Ultimate an Actual Virtue?

Gorampa vs. Shakya Chokden on the Dharma-Sphere

The two thinkers' responses in this chapter start with replying to questions 8, 9, and 14 (addressed by Shakya Chokden together), which deal specifically with interpreting ultimate reality, the dharma-sphere, as a virtue. Questions 10 and 11 raise the issues of the dharma-sphere's existence and its momentariness. Question 13 prompts further discussion of the momentary—and thus active, functional, and causal—nature of the dharma-sphere. Questions 15 through 18 prompt analysis of the existence of the virtuous dharma-sphere, particularly in the context of its encompassing all phenomena. Questions 19 and 20 target the dedicatability of the ultimate virtue. Question 21 leads to the discussion of the primordially existent stainless seeds.

*

8. If the dharma-sphere is not a virtue,
Then what about its being taught [as such]
In the *Ornament of Clear Realizations*, the *Sublime Continuum*,
The *Summary of Mahāyāna*, and
The *Differentiation of the Middle and Extremes?*

9. If the mere absence of evil was intended [when calling the dharma-sphere "virtue"],
Then what about all unobscured unspecified [phenomena]?

14. Are the "dharma-sphere,"
 "Holy dharma," and "holy"
 Not taught in valid scriptures as virtues?
 Is the entity of the dharma-sphere, Nairātmyā—
 The illusory body of great bliss—
 Also asserted to not be a virtue?

These questions target verses 76 through 79 of the *Thorough Differentiation:*

> What is explained as the ultimate virtue
> Was taught to be suchness,
> The ultimate evil—the whole saṃsāra,
> And the two, space and the non-analytical cessation,
> Were explained as the ultimate unspecified.
>
> The intent in explaining
> Suchness as "virtue" is as follows.
> For example, the world calls
> The freedom from illness "physical happiness"
> And the absence of sorrow "mental happiness."
>
> Although these do not have happiness
> Other than the absence of suffering,
> The mere absence of suffering
> Is known to all as "happiness."
>
> Likewise, although the dharma-sphere too
> Does not have virtue in addition to
> The mere absence of evil,
> It ended up being imputed as "virtue."

References to texts presenting the dharma-sphere as a virtue are crucial for reinforcing Shakya Chokden's claim that it is indeed the case. But in his reply to question 8, Gorampa is satisfied with reiterating that Sakya Pandita has already explained that all such interpretations of the dharma-sphere as a virtue refer only to an imputed virtue and concluding that therefore Shakya Chokden's question amounts to pointless questioning. He also points out that Shakya Chokden misinterpreted several texts he was referring to. In his replies to questions 9 and 14 too, without providing much detail, Gorampa largely dismisses Shakya Chokden's inquiries as pointless questioning.

In his extensive reply to questions 8, 9, and 14, Shakya Chokden is clearly concerned that if taken literally, as was done by other commentators, the

Thorough Differentiation argues that the dharma-sphere cannot be a virtue. To demonstrate that it is indeed a virtue, he provides passages from influential texts related not only to the third but to the second dharmacakra as well. To reconcile their statements with Sakya Pandita's text, he differentiates between the other- and self-emptiness modes of identifying the dharma-sphere, and claims that when Sakya Pandita rejected the interpretation of suchness as a virtue he adopted the approach of self-emptiness, which he did to refute the *Single Intent*'s self-emptiness interpretation of the dharma-sphere. In Shakya Chokden's opinion, that move by Sakya Pandita does not undermine the validity of the other-emptiness approach, according to which ultimate reality—the nondual primordial mind—is a virtue.

Gorampa's Reply to Question 8

Gorampa replies that in the *Ornament of Clear Realizations* the dharma-sphere was not explained as a virtue at all. Regarding the eight latter objects of observation of accomplishing Mahāyāna (*theg chen bsgrub pa'i dmigs pa*),[1] he argues that it is logically absurd to treat them as actual virtues. He does agree that both the *Sublime Continuum* and the *Differentiation of the Middle and Extremes* refer to the dharma-sphere as a "virtue."[2] Nevertheless, he again points out that Sakya Pandita has explained that all such interpretations of the dharma-sphere as a virtue refer only to an imputed virtue (*dge ba btags pa ba*).[3] Consequently, asking questions about such texts as the *Sublime Continuum* teaching the dharma-sphere as a virtue after Sakya Pandita has already determined such a "virtue" to be imputed amounts to pointless questioning (*thug med kyi dri ba*).[4]

Gorampa clearly thinks that Sakya Pandita's explanation of the ultimate as merely an imputed virtue is sufficient and exhaustive in itself. As a result, he brushes aside Shakya Chokden's question. Needless to say, Shakya Chokden expected a more detailed explanation of why those Indian texts call the dharma-sphere "virtue" in the first place and how their interpretation by Sakya Pandita as referring to a merely imputed virtue is justified. Yet it is also true that Shakya Chokden's question as it stands does not explicitly ask for such details and might sound like asking why again and again after the reason has already been provided. Be that as it may, Gorampa himself does not go into those details here.

Gorampa's Reply to Question 9

In his reply to question 9 too Gorampa largely dismisses Shakya Chokden's question without going into much detail. He writes that while Sakya Pandita explained that the mere absence of evil had been intended as the reason—literally, "causative condition" (*rgyu mtshan*)—for calling the dharma-sphere a virtue, Shakya Chokden's question implies the following absurd consequence: that the unobscured unspecified phenomena are virtues because of being the mere absence of evil. He mocks this argument. In his opinion the argument is similar to someone saying that the intended reason for giving the *Perfection of Wisdom* texts their name is that they teach the perfection of wisdom as their topic. That someone's opponent replies that it follows that the excellent words of the Buddha that teach a pot as their topic are a pot because they teach a pot as their topic. If, continues Gorampa, the meaning of the question lies in the fact that causative conditions for naming the unobscured unspecified phenomena *virtue* are indeed complete, then he accepts it. But in his opinion, that in itself is not enough: even when causative conditions for giving a name to something are complete, it is an approach of those with inquisitive minds not to provide a name if there is no purpose (*dgos pa*) in doing so.[5]

In other words, Gorampa argues that similar to calling the *Perfection of Wisdom* sūtras "perfection of wisdom," there is a specific purpose in calling the dharma-sphere "virtue." But similar to there being no purpose in calling "pot" the Buddha's teachings whose topic is a pot, there is no purpose in calling unobscured unspecified phenomena "virtues." This is despite the fact that in both cases there are causative conditions for giving the name of the topic to what expresses that topic.

Gorampa's Reply to Question 14

Gorampa reads the last five lines of the question differently from those in the *Good Questions*:

> If the entity of the dharma-sphere is not a virtue,
> Then is the illusory body of great bliss
> Also asserted to not be a virtue?
> In that case, is it not called
> In its praise "virtue" either?[6]

But this does not affect the main point of Gorampa's answer: similar to his reply to question 8, here too Gorampa basically dismisses Shakya Chokden's question as pointless questioning. Mocking the reasoning underlying the question, Gorampa writes that it is similar to arguing the following: "If a bramin boy named Siṃha [Lion] is not the king of beasts, then was he not named Siṃha? And does the word *siṃha* not apply to the king of beasts?"

Gorampa is also unclear about what the illusory body of great bliss in Shakya Chokden's question refers to. He writes that if it refers to the dharma-sphere, then it is subsumed under the categories addressed above. If not, what is the connection? In other words, in the former case the same logic that applies to the dharma-sphere (such as its being freedom from proliferations, transcending compoundedness, etc.) will apply to the illusory body of great bliss; consequently, referring to the illusory body of great bliss here will add nothing new. In the latter case, referring to it will be irrelevant.[7]

Shakya Chokden's Reply to Questions 8, 9, and 14

Shakya Chokden writes that according to the explicit teachings (*dngos bstan*) of Sakya Pandita's *Thorough Differentiation,* if something is the dharma-sphere it cannot be a virtue. He further claims that all earlier and later commentators on the text, without going into any detail, took that explanation literally and interpreted it accordingly. What makes this literal reading faulty is that it contradicts both textual statements and reasoning.

Contradiction with Textual Statements

The first authoritative textual passage Shakya Chokden refers to is the *Ornament of Clear Realizations*'s two-verse explanation of the objects of observation (*dmigs pa*), which groups all dharmas into virtuous, nonvirtuous, and unspecified:

> The objects of observation are all dharmas.
> They are furthermore virtues and so forth,
> Worldly realizations and
> Those which are asserted as world-transcending,
>
> Stained and stainless dharmas,
> Those that are compounded and uncompounded,
> Dharmas common with those of disciples and
> Those that are the Sage's uncommon ones.[8]

Shakya Chokden argues that according to Haribhadra's *Clear Meaning*[9] commentary on the text, the remaining objects of observation listed in the lines starting with "Worldly realizations and" should be subsumed under "virtues and so forth," referred to in the first two lines. Included in that list is "uncompounded" (*'dus ma byas*), which the *Clear Meaning* describes as "suchness that does not rely on causes" (*rgyu la mi ltos pa'i de bzhin nyid*). According to Shakya Chokden, because it cannot be interpreted as a nonvirtue or an unspecified phenomenon, it has to be interpreted as a virtue.[10] Thus, taking Haribhadra's interpretation of the two verses as authoritative, he argues that the *Ornament of Clear Realizations* treats reality as one of the three types of phenomena (rather than transcending them all) and then advances his own understanding of it as a virtue by excluding it from the two remaining categories.

Next, Shakya Chokden turns to the *Sublime Continuum,* writing that the text explains suchness as the sugata-essence, which also should be interpreted as a virtue. This is because, he argues, sūtras interpreted by it taught the essence as "virtuous tathāgata-essence" (*de bzhin gshegs pa'i snying po dge*), and the *Sublime Continuum* itself states that "because of [being] a virtue and purity" when addressing it.[11] Furthermore, the *Sublime Continuum* teaches that it has to be accepted as purity, bliss, permanence, and self (*gtsang bde rtag bdag*), as well as permanence, stability, peace, and eternity (*rtag brtan zhi ba g.yung drung*).

The implication here is that the tathāgata-essence is presented in such texts as the *Sublime Continuum* as an existent phenomenon rather than transcending all proliferations of existence, nonexistence, and so forth. Based on these passages and referring to Sakya Pandita's admonition not to apprehend the dharma-sphere as either existent or nonexistent if one respects the Buddha's teachings, Shakya Chokden points out the discordance in the explanations provided in the above texts and in the *Thorough Differentiation,* which presents the dharma-sphere as unsuited to be even merely existent (*yod pa tsam*).[12]

Turning to further textual sources, and treating the dharma-sphere as the perfect (*yongs su grub pa*), Shakya Chokden proceeds to quote the *Summary of Mahāyāna,* which describes the perfect as the best type of virtue: "Why is it called 'perfect'? It is perfect because of not changing into another; because of being a pure object of observation and the supreme of all virtuous dharmas [*dge ba'i chos thams cad kyi mchog*], owing to [having] the supreme meaning, it is perfect."[13] He also points out that the *Differentiation of the Middle and Extremes* explains the uncompounded virtue (*'dus ma byas kyi dge ba*) as obtainable (*thob bya*) when it says "In order to obtain the two virtues."[14] The implication is that because the ultimate reality—in this case nirvāṇa,[15] the uncompounded virtue—is obtainable, it is not beyond existence and nonexistence.

Next, Shakya Chokden quotes from Vasubandhu's *Praise to the Three Buddha-Bodies:*

> I respectfully prostrate to
> The pure dharma-sphere,
> The eight ārya paths of accomplishment,
> The Teacher's holy Dharma.[16]

He argues that texts common to both Mahāyāna and non-Mahāyāna Buddhist systems explain nirvāṇa as the Jewel of Dharma, while the uncommon Mahāyāna texts, such as the *Sublime Continuum,* explain the three ultimate Jewels in terms of the dharma-sphere. The Jewel of Dharma is necessarily a virtue because sūtras teach that "the holy Dharma is a virtue at the beginning, a virtue at the end, and a virtue in the middle."[17] Thus, once again he points out that because the dharma-sphere and nirvāṇa are the Jewel of Dharma, and because the Jewel of Dharma is necessarily a virtue, they too have to be virtues.

Shakya Chokden also shows how the term *virtue* (*dge ba*) is combined with what can be translated as "ultimate" (*dam pa*) in Vasubandhu's *Explanation of the "Treasury of Abhidharma."* Referring to the term *dam pa,* which, depending on the context, can mean "holy" or "excellent" but also "ultimate" (as in *don dam pa,* "ultimate meaning," usually translated as simply "ultimate"), he cites the *Treasury of Abhidharma*—"Engaging and not engaging in what is holy/ultimate and not holy/ultimate [*dam min*]"[18]—and then the *Explanation of the "Treasury of Abhidharma,"* which states: "[One is] called 'holy/ultimate being' [*skyes bu dam pa*] because of engaging exclusively in what is holy/ultimate—virtue—and not engaging in what is not holy/ultimate—nonvirtue." Shakya Chokden is apparently paraphrasing the latter text in a way that suggests that *dam pa* can include the ultimate as such even if defined in a non-Mahāyāna Abhidharma way.[19]

Shakya Chokden likewise writes that if the dharma-sphere, which is also called "natural perfection of wisdom" (*rang bzhin shes phyin*), is not interpreted as a virtue, it will contradict, among other texts, the *Hundred and Eight Names of the Perfection of Wisdom,* which says:

> Whoever the past, future, and present Victors are,
> The mother of them all

> Is you, Lady Virtue;
> You are a goddess, Victors' Daughter!
>
> I express virtuous names of the one
> With the nature of naturelessness,
> The Mother of Buddhas.[20]

Interestingly, the above quotations derive not only from the teachings on the buddha-essence that are usually linked with the third dharmacakra but also from those that (like the last one) are linked with the second dharmacakra, and even those that (like the *Treasury of Abhidharma*) are not unique to Mahāyāna at all. Referring to these diverse sources helps Shakya Chokden prepare the ground for arguing that one cannot conclude that all of them treat the ultimate as a virtue merely in terms of the absence of evil—a point to which he now turns.

Shakya Chokden admits that one might object that what is intended in all such statements is the mere absence of evil (*sdig pa med tsam*), similar to the mere absence of suffering being universally known as happiness, and so on—the position articulated in the *Thorough Differentiation* (vv. 77–79). As we also know, this very position was reiterated by Gorampa. In contrast to Gorampa, who unquestionably accepted Sakya Pandita's position, Shakya Chokden prefers to reinterpret it, arguing that Sakya Pandita provided his explanation of suchness as "virtue" in such texts as the *Summary of Abhidharma,* when *he himself accepted the approach of self-emptiness.* Nevertheless, he thereby *did not* demonstrate the reason for explaining suchness as an imputed virtue according to the Abhidharma's own system (*chos mngon pa'i rang lugs*) itself.[21] Thus, Shakya Chokden disagrees with the literal reading of the *Thorough Differentiation,* claiming that in that text Sakya Pandita adopted a special point of view and therefore his interpretation itself is provisional.

Resisting the literal take on Sakya Pandita's position, Shakya Chokden argues that the unobscured unspecified phenomena addressed in the Abhidharma system could also be imputed as the ultimate virtue for the same reason of being qualified by the absence of evil. Yet this is unacceptable, he objects, because that system specifically treats the analytical cessations (*so sor brtags 'gog*) as the ultimate virtues and the nonanalytical cessations (*so sor brtags min gyi 'gog pa*) as the ultimate unspecified phenomena (*don dam pa'i lung ma bstan*).[22]

He also refers to the passage from what he calls the *Treatise on Engaging in Primordial Mind,*[23] quoted in the *Explanation of the "Treasury of*

Abhidharma"—"What are the white dharmas? The virtuous dharmas and the unobscured unspecified ones"[24]—and argues that the virtue in terms of the mere absence of evil is related to the unobscured unspecified phenomena. Consequently, he writes that while the three factors (*chos gsum*) involved in imputing the name *virtue*[25] are complete when that term is applied to the nonanalytical cessation, such is not applicable to the analytical cessation.[26] In other words, in the context of the Abhidharma system, while such unobscured unspecified phenomena as the nonanalytical cessation can be imputed as virtues even though they are not actual virtues, such ultimate virtues as the analytical cessation—the most prominent of which is nirvāṇa—cannot be just imputed virtues, because they are real virtues.

Shakya Chokden also addresses the issue raised in the *Thorough Differentiation* (v. 76): If according to the Abhidharma literature the ultimate virtue fills the role of a virtue, then it follows that the ultimate nonvirtue fills the role of a nonvirtue. In that case, it will follow that the contaminated virtues (*zag bcas kyi dge ba*) produce sufferings as their fruitional results. In other words, because contaminated virtues are a part of saṃsāra, which is treated as the ultimate nonvirtue in the *Summary of Abhidharma,* if one treats the ultimate nonvirtue as an actual nonvirtue, the contaminated virtues will also be nonvirtues, which by definition produce sufferings, in particular sufferings of pain (one of the three types of sufferings).[27]

He responds that the ultimate virtue and the ultimate nonvirtue are not concordant as actual virtues and nonvirtues. He thereby indicates that while ultimate virtues are necessarily virtues, ultimate nonvirtues are not necessarily nonvirtues. As an analogy, he refers to his opponents' unanimous agreement that while the subsequently connected unspecified phenomena (*rjes su 'brel pa'i lung ma bstan*) fill the role of unspecified phenomena, the subsequently connected virtues and nonvirtues (*rjes su 'brel pa'i dge mi dge*) do not fill the role of virtues and nonvirtues.[28] What he is referring to is the *Summary of Abhidharma*'s treatment of predispositions or propensities (*bag chags*) formed by unspecified (neutral) minds and mental states as the subsequently connected unspecified phenomena,[29] propensities of the eleven virtuous mental states and states concordant with them as the subsequently connected virtues,[30] and propensities of the states concordant with primary and secondary afflictions as the subsequently connected nonvirtues.[31] Because predispositions of virtues, nonvirtues, and unspecified phenomena are usually treated as unspecified phenomena, Shakya Chokden points out that others will find no problem with treating those predispositions as actual unspecified phenomena and will indeed see problems in treating predispositions of virtues and nonvirtues as actual virtues or nonvirtues. He refers to this discrepancy to support his claim that the ultimate virtue and the ultimate nonvirtue also should be treated in different ways.

Shakya Chokden further argues that according to the lower Abhidharma, while separative results (*bral ba'i 'bras bu*) can fill the role of virtues, fruitional results (*rnam smin gyi 'bras bu*) cannot fill the role of nonvirtues. Also, according to the higher Abhidharma, the ultimate happiness (*don dam pa'i bde ba*) fills the role of happiness, but the ultimate suffering (*don dam pa'i sdug bsngal*) does not fill the role of suffering.[32] He thereby shows what he sees as further differences in the ways the two Abhidharmas treat virtues, nonvirtues, and their results. Separative results, such as nirvāṇa, can be treated as virtues. Fruitional results, such as suffering, cannot be treated as nonvirtues. The ultimate happiness, nirvāṇa, is happiness, while the ultimate suffering, the five aggregates, is not (at least if we limit the meaning of *suffering* to the suffering of pain).[33] This line of reasoning provides additional support for the claim that the ultimate virtue and the ultimate nonvirtue should be approached differently. It also shows diversity of approaches in the Abhidharma writings to results, virtue, and other categories, whose meanings change depending on context and additional categories they are combined with.

Contradiction with Reasoning

Advancing reasons against the literal acceptance of Sakya Pandita's statement that the dharma-sphere is not an actual virtue, Shakya Chokden connects interpretation of the ultimate as a virtue with the Buddhist contemplative practice. In particular, he refers to the tantric views and contemplative techniques. He writes that the line "Is the entity of the dharma-sphere, Nairātmyā" in his question was just an example intended to illustrate the absurd consequence that according to Mantrayāna the primordial mind of the dharma-sphere (*chos kyi dbyings kyi ye shes*) is not the dharma-sphere or not a virtue. But this is problematic because when accumulating the two collections through the tantric practice, one accumulates the collection of primordial mind (*ye shes kyi tshogs*) by purifying into emptiness all dharmas subsumed under the categories of the apprehended and the apprehender (*gzung 'dzin*) through the *svabhāva* mantra.[34] Then, having generated divine pride (*[lha'i] nga rgyal*) by identifying oneself as the vajra of primordial mind of emptiness (*stong pa nyid kyi ye shes kyi rdo rje*) through the *śūnyatā* mantra,[35] one proceeds to accumulate the collection of merits (*bsod nams kyi tshogs*), which are the positive qualities of the support and supported [maṇḍalas] (*rten dang brten par bcas pa'i yon tan gyi tshogs*) established by that primordial mind of emptiness (*stong pa nyid kyi ye shes*). Consequently, it will follow that both of those collections are exclusively *not* virtues because they have the entity of the dharma-sphere![36] Clearly, such a position is unacceptable for Shakya Chokden, who views the above process as the standard way of accumulating the collection of merits in tantric practice. For him, the whole process boils down to and has the nature of primordial mind, which is none other than the dharma-sphere.[37] Were the dharma-sphere not a virtue, none of the elements of the process would be virtues either. Put in positive terms, the above absurd consequence demonstrates that precisely because tantric practitioners *do* accumulate the two collections in the above manner, the dharma-sphere *has* to be a virtue.

Next Shakya Chokden turns to the nontantric Mahāyāna teachings based on the explanatory system of the *Perfection of Wisdom* sūtras' "Chapter Requested by Maitreya,"[38] certain Maitreya's treatises, and certain writings of those who follow or comment on those treatises—these texts divide all phenomena into the "imaginary" (*kun btags pa*), the "imputational" (*rnam par brtags pa*), and the "reality" (*chos nyid*).[39] Positing yet another absurd consequence, he writes that the reality-powers (*chos nyid kyi stobs*) and other positive qualities will turn out not to fill the role of powers and other positive qualities because the reality-virtue (*chos nyid kyi dge ba*) does not fill the role of virtue. If this consequence is accepted, it will follow that the imaginary and imputational powers, and so on, fill the role of powers, and so on. But this is unacceptable because the imaginary is explained as not being established by valid cognition (*tshad mas ma grub pa*), while the imputational is explained as the unreal ideation (*yang dag pa ma yin pa'i kun tu rtog pa*). Furthermore, although imputational dharmas are emphasized when positing conventional reality, it is reality (*chos nyid*) itself that has to be emphasized when positing pure dharmas (*rnam byang gi chos*).[40] In other words, in the context of this threefold division, if one does not accept the reality-virtues as actual virtues, one will have no other choice but to posit buddha-powers and other pure dharmas as the unreal ideation with its projections. That position will entail such contradictions as pure dharmas' being posited by or existing as impure consciousness, the unreal ideation's participating in the virtuous qualities of buddhahood, and so forth.

Thus far, Shakya Chokden has not even started to provide the actual answer—only the reasons for asking the questions, and so on. Now the actual answer starts.

Actual Answer

The actual answer involves a general explanation and connecting the explanation with textual sources.

General Explanation

According to Shakya Chokden, there are two dissimilar modes of identifying the dharma-sphere, deriving from the systems of the advocates of other-emptiness (*gzhan stong du smra ba*) and the advocates of self-emptiness (*rang stong du smra ba*). According to the former mode, the dharma-sphere is the primordial mind free from the duality of the apprehended and the apprehender (*gzung 'dzin gnyis med kyi ye shes*), which persists throughout all the levels of the basis, the path, and the result. According to the latter mode, the nonimplicative negation qua the mere negation of the entire mass of proliferations (*spros pa'i tshogs mtha' dag bkag tsam gyi med par dgag pa*) is given the name *dharma-sphere* when applying conventions during the subsequent attainment (*rjes thob*) following the meditative equipoise (*mnyam gzhag*). In other words, while the advocates of other-emptiness identify ultimate reality as the nondual primordial mind, the advocates of self-emptiness do not identify it as anything at all and merely impute the name *dharma-sphere* after one has emerged from the state of meditative equipoise in which no proliferations are present.

Shakya Chokden acknowledges that according to the self-emptiness system, not only can the dharma-sphere not be dedicated but it is not a virtue either since being any extreme of proliferations (*spros pa'i mtha'*)—virtue, nonvirtue, or anything else—contradicts being the dharma-sphere. According to the other-emptiness system, the entity of the dharma-sphere is a knowing (*shes pa*) and a functional thing (*dngos po*). It is also permanent (*rtag pa*)[41] because it does not change into something else. Furthermore, it is uncompounded (*'dus ma byas pa*) because it is neither a continuity of a similar class (*rigs 'dra'i rgyun*) that did not exist previously and emerges anew nor compounded by karmas and afflictions.[42] However, it *is* a virtue—an interpretation supported by the textual passages and reasons, provided in the previous section, that issue from the explanatory approach of other-emptiness. Nevertheless, it is *not* a virtue that can be dedicated, because according to that system its entity cannot be changed into anything else.

Having distinguished between the two interpretations of the dharma-sphere, Shakya Chokden turns to the question of Sakya Pandita's own position in his *Thorough Differentiation*. Shakya Chokden writes that the text identified the dharma-sphere in accordance with the approach of self-emptiness, and although it quoted some passages articulating the mode of other-emptiness, that was done in order to demonstrate not that the dharma-sphere is not a virtue but that it cannot be changed through dedication into something else. As a side note, he points out that in general if something is a virtue, it does not necessarily have to be dedicatable. As an illustration, he cites the positive qualities of the buddha-ground (*sangs rgyas kyi sa'i yon tan*).[43]

Shakya Chokden argues that when Sakya Pandita stated that such texts as the *Summary of Abhidharma* called ultimate reality a "virtue" to mean the mere absence of evil, Sakya Pandita himself accepted the self-emptiness approach—not the approach of those texts per se—and this interpretation should not be understood as a denial of the other-emptiness position outlined there. Furthermore, although Sakya Pandita quoted some passages from those other-emptiness texts in order to refute what he deemed the wrong interpretation of the dharma-sphere, he did so in order to refute what is extrinsic to those texts—the claim that the dharma-sphere can be dedicated—and not what is intrinsic to them—the view of the dharma-sphere as a virtue. Shakya Chokden clearly disagrees with the literal reading of Sakya Pandita's text, but instead of saying that Sakya Pandita was wrong, he argues that in the *Thorough Differentiation* Sakya Pandita himself adopted a special point of view and therefore his interpretation itself is liable to reinterpretation. This approach allows Shakya Chokden to advance his own position, which on the surface is very different from that of Sakya Pandita but in Shakya Chokden's opinion is implicitly endorsed by him: ultimate reality is the nondual primordial mind and a virtue.

Connecting the Explanation with Textual Sources

Connecting the explanation with textual sources includes presenting the position of Sakya Pandita's opponent and explaining the way it was refuted in the *Thorough Differentiation.*

Identifying the opponent's position as that of the *Single Intent,*[44] Shakya Chokden provides its summary, outlines points already familiar to us from chapter 3, and adds some additional information. He writes that according to the *Single Intent* the tathāgata-essence is the naturally pure element, which has the same meaning as mahāmudrā. It is ornamented with the major and minor marks of a buddha, all positive qualities of powers, and so on, and pervades all sentient beings. It is the root of virtues of partial concordance with liberation (*thar pa cha mthun gyi dge ba'i rtsa ba*), is called "existent virtue" (*yod pa'i dge ba*), and should be dedicated to awakening.

Next he lists scriptural sources and reasonings provided by the *Writings*[45] in support of this position. In addition to the passages we dealt with in chapter 3, he also quotes Sherap Jungné's *Refined Gold* more extensively:

> The ocean-like virtuous element
> Ornamented with the great weaves of the created-accumulated [virtues]—
> I dedicate such virtue
> To the unsurpassed awakening![46]

Turning to the reasonings, Shakya Chokden refers to the aforementioned argument that the ultimate reality is changeless but because sentient beings do not realize it as such, there is no contradiction in positing it as the cause-effect qua the change of state (*gnas gyur gyi rgyu 'bras*) resulting from the purification of erroneous defilements. He also adds that referring to the *Sublime Continuum*'s "There is nothing to eliminate here," and so on, the *Single Intent* argues that mahāmudrā abides as the nature of all positive qualities throughout the basis, the path, and the result, with no faults to eliminate or positive qualities to establish.[47]

Explaining the way this position was refuted in the *Thorough Differentiation,* Shakya Chokden highlights three points made in Sakya Pandita's refutation. One point, dealt with in verses 59–62 and 138–40, is the refutation of a result present within a cause. This refers to Sakya Pandita's statement that the teachings of some sūtras and the *Sublime Continuum* on the existence of the buddha-essence within sentient beings, like a precious image wrapped in rags, have a special intent and should not be taken literally. Another point, dealt with starting in verse 62, is Sakya Pandita's argument that because the tathāgata-essence is unchangeable, it is unsuitable for dedication. The third point consists in Sakya Pandita's quoting from Madhyamaka (i.e., Niḥsvabhāvavāda)[48] writings in order to demonstrate that because his opponent, treating mahāmudrā and the tathāgata-essence as the same, treats both as self-emptiness, they are unsuitable even as a mere virtue.[49]

Note that regarding the third point, Shakya Chokden is not just saying that having assumed the standpoint of self-emptiness, Sakya Pandita refuted the *Single Intent*'s interpretation of the tathāgata-essence as a virtue. Rather, he points out *why* Sakya Pandita did that: because the *Single Intent* itself interpreted mahāmudrā and the tathāgata-essence from what Shakya Chokden sees as the standpoint of self-emptiness. This justifies, in part at least, Shakya Chokden's claim that Sakya Pandita only provisionally assumed the position of self-emptiness.

In anticipation of the discussion that will unfold in his reply to question 10,

Shakya Chokden addresses the following issue: since in Dharmakīrti's textual system the dharma-sphere is posited in terms of other-emptiness and as truly established, does it not follow that it is impermanent? His answer, which reflects his own unique position on the nature of reality, is yes.[50] Nevertheless, he continues, this does not contradict the dharma-sphere's being taught as permanent, because according to the textual system of other-emptiness there is no contradiction in being posited as permanent with regard to the permanence of continuity (*rgyun gyi rtag pa*) and as impermanent with regard to the momentary impermanence (*skad cig gi mi rtag pa*). As an example, he refers to the presentation of the three bodies of a buddha as permanent in the *Sublime Continuum*.[51] In other words, he argues that according to the other-emptiness system, the dharma-sphere is momentary in that its continuity is made up of discrete moments, but that continuity itself never ceases. Depending on which of these two features is emphasized, the dharma-sphere can be described as either permanent or impermanent.

Turning to the *Thorough Differentiation*'s verse 89, which states that the "the dharma-sphere is not even existent," Shakya Chokden explains that this statement was made from the standpoint of self-emptiness, in the context of refuting the interpretation of the dharma-sphere and mahāmudrā as synonymous and as an "existent virtue." (As we have just seen, he claims that the opponent's own position there was that of self-emptiness.) Otherwise, he argues, the following question would arise: is the primordial mind of the dharma-sphere nonexistent or permanent? Whichever is accepted, it would not be primordial mind. And if it is accepted as existent, it will follow that it is impermanent. In other words, Shakya Chokden argues that if the claim that "the dharma-sphere is not even existent" were made from the standpoint of the Dharmakīrtian system of other-emptiness, which presents the dharma-sphere as primordial mind, it would be contradictory, because according to that system, being a mind, it has to be impermanent, and being ultimate reality, it has to be existent.

Completing the answer, he writes that some thinkers claim that the primordial mind of the dharma-sphere is not taught in the Vehicle of Characteristics (*mtshan nyid theg pa*, i.e., the nontantric Mahāyāna). He objects to that claim, arguing that it contradicts Asaṅga's teachings on the buddha-ground (*sangs rgyas sa*)[52] and Drakpa Gyeltsen's writings.[53] He also adds that as long as the primordial mind of the dharma-sphere is asserted as ultimate reality, there is no contradiction in accepting it as existent and impermanent. With respect to Sakya Paṇḍita's statement that the dharma-sphere is not existent, he claims that it was made in terms of eventually dispelling all conceptual proliferations.[54] This last point appears to provide yet another reason why, according to Shakya Chokden, Sakya Pandita wrote that "the dharma-sphere is not even existent."

*

10. Dharmakīrti taught that actual existence
    Is pervaded by impermanence [i.e., necessarily
        impermanent].
    [But] what textual systems of reasoning teach
    That mere existence is pervaded by that?

This question targets verse 89 of the *Thorough Differentiation:*

> The dharma-sphere is not even existent;
> Dharmakīrti taught well that
> Mere existence is pervaded by impermanence.

In his response, Gorampa provides several Dharmakīrtian passages that in his opinion demonstrate that Dharmakīrti did in fact indicate that mere existence is necessarily impermanent.

Shakya Chokden's answer goes into detail about the phrases "mere existence" and "actual existence." Importantly, it displays several key elements of his interpretation of ultimate reality that contribute to its interpretation as a virtue. The most unique is his claim that the dharma-sphere qua primordial mind, being existent, is a momentary phenomenon.

Gorampa's Reply to Question 10

Gorampa cites passages that include the following three from Dharmakīrti's *Commentary on Valid Cognition:* "Also [used as a reason is] an entity that has connection / [With a probandum] through the mere existence of [its] nature";[55] "Precisely because the destruction is connected with / Mere existence, sound is only impermanent";[56] and "The destruction, because of being connected with / A mere thing, is not permanent."[57] According to Gorampa, when asking this question, Shakya Chokden apparently thought that the only passage in the *Commentary on Valid Cognition* stating that if something is existent, it has to be impermanent, was "The result and actual existence [are used as reasons] for [proving] destruction."[58] Regarding that, he explains that depending on the context, the same Sanskrit term *bhava* is translated into

Tibetan as *yod pa* ("existence") and *dngos po* ("thing"). Both were used when proving sound as impermanent. This passage, which discusses different types of reasoning, also addresses both the result, which refers to product (*byas pa*), and existence, which refers to thing (*dngos po*). Gorampa points to Sakya Pandita's explanation in the *Treasure of the Science of Valid Cognition*[59] of why such division was made: because some non-Buddhist opponents do not accept self, Lord, vedic sounds, and so on, as products, in order to prove them as impermanent one first uses existence as the reason and then, when the opponent realizes that it is impossible for something existent not to be produced by causes and conditions, uses product as the reason.[60]

Shakya Chokden's Reply to Question 10

Explaining the reason for asking this question, Shakya Chokden writes that while mere existence and actual existence should be differentiated, none of those who commented on Sakya Pandita's treatise made that distinction. If the question is not raised, this will result in two problems: the lack of differentiation between mere existence and actual existence, and the wrong assumption that no identification of the dharma-sphere was provided in Dharmakīrti's system.

Starting with the first problem, he explains that in general there is a big difference between mere existence (*yod pa tsam*) and actual existence (*yod pa nyid*). The word *nyid* can be used for emphasis (*nges bzung gi don*) or for referring to phenomenal conditions (*dngos po'i rkyen*);[61] which of the two is meant should be clear from the context. Regarding *nyid*'s meaning as phenomenal conditions, according to a general approach of textual systems that accept the existence of truly established things or phenomena (*bden grub kyi dngos po*), it signifies exclusively what is established as a thing (*dngos por grub pa*). Examples include suchness (*de bzhin nyid*), entityness (*ngo bo nyid,* also translated as "entity"), dharmaness (*chos nyid,* also translated as "reality"), emptiness (*stong pa nyid*), and "own characteristic-ness" (*rang gi mtshan nyid,* translated as "own characteristics").

An interesting question arises as to whether this applies to the general characteristics ("general characteristic-ness," *spyi'i mtshan nyid*). Shakya Chokden explains that there are two types of general characteristics: those relating to things (*dngos po*) and those relating to elimination of other isolates (*ldog pa gzhan sel*). The former refers to, for example, impermanence that is posited as the general characteristics of what is compounded (*'dus byas*), and pervades it. The latter refers to knowables (*shes bya*), comprehendables (*gzhal *bya*), and so on, that appear as existent in the face of conceptuality. Although they are things in the face of elimination (*sel ngo*), they are not things in general and therefore are not suitable as genuine phenomenal conditions.[62]

Thus, he continues, the term *existence* can refer to either mere existence or actual existence. The former exists in the face of elimination, the latter in the face of appearance (*snang ngo*). According to Dharmakīrti, if something exists in the face of appearance, it must be impermanent, while such categories as the universal principle, for example, are only merely existent. In his *Treasure of the Science of Valid Cognition,* Sakya Pandita also accepted that if something exists, it has to be impermanent.[63] Explaining the reason why *actual* (*nyid*) is added to *existence,* Shakya Chokden writes that it is done in order to differentiate existence from mere existence. Resorting to quotations from Dharmakīrti's *Ascertainment of Valid Cognition,*[64] he argues that the same logic applies to such terms as *mere thing* (*dngos po tsam*) and *actual thing* ("thing-ness," *dngos po nyid*). *Mere thing, mere pot,* and so on, should be understood merely as other-eliminations (*gzhan sel*) that pervade all their instances (*gsal ba*).

In other words, he argues that the term *existence* refers to functional, impermanent things that actually exist and appear to mind without being conceptually constructed. The suffix *nyid* is added in order to emphasize that and to distinguish what actually exists from what is merely conceptually constructed, such as the category of the universal principle (*gtso bo, prakṛti*), whose existence, accepted by Sāṃkhya, is denied by Buddhists.[65] That conceptual process, in turn, is understood as other-elimination, wherein a concept (whether of an existent or a nonexistent thing) is constructed through the conceptual elimination or exclusion of what the conceived thing is not.

Referring to two passages from Dharmakīrti's *Commentary on Valid Cognition* (also quoted in Gorampa's answer)—"Also [used as a reason is] an entity that has connection / [With a probandum] through the mere existence of [its] nature" and "Precisely because the destruction is connected with / Mere existence, sound is only impermanent"—he rejects the claim that they demonstrate that the mere existence is pervaded by impermanence. In his opinion, this position is based on "getting backwards" (*go zlog pa*) the object connected to (*'brel yul*) with what is connected to it (*'brel po*).[66] In other words, instead of treating the mere existence, and so on, as what is conceptually connected to the actual existent objects via elimination of what they are not, one mistakenly takes the mere existence as the actual thing or object that impermanent things, such as sounds, and so on, are connected to.

Moving to the second problem, Shakya Chokden writes that one might suspect that according to Dharmakīrti's own system, owing to existence being pervaded by impermanence, the dharma-sphere does not exist. He argues that if such is accepted, then no dharma-sphere taught in Dharmakīrti's writings and the four subsequent *Dharmas of Maitreya*[67] will be identifiable, because those texts explain the entity of the dharma-sphere exclusively as the primordial mind free from the duality of the apprehended and the apprehender (*gzung 'dzin gnyis med kyi ye shes*).

While this argument in and of itself does not sound unusual, in what follows next Shakya Chokden displays one of the most characteristic and uncommon features of his position: he argues that therefore the dharma-sphere itself *has* to be accepted as impermanent (*mi rtag pa*). This is because, he writes, if something is a thing (*dngos po*), it has to be accepted as momentarily disintegrating (*skad cig gis 'jig pa*). Yet, he continues, this does not contradict the dharma-sphere's being explained as permanent (*rtag pa*) on other occasions, because it was explained as such with the permanence of continuity (*rgyun gyi rtag pa*) in mind. For support he cites Maitreya's *Ornament of Clear Realizations*: "Because that very [buddhahood] is inexhaustible, / It is described as 'permanent' as well."[68]

Now Shakya Chokden has to address the following challenge: If the dharma-sphere is accepted as a thing, it will follow that it is compounded (*'dus byas*), and in that case one will have to accept those same claims that have been refuted by the *Thorough Differentiation*. In response, he explains that in general, Buddhist teachings provide three ways of presenting something as compounded or uncompounded. Something can be treated as compounded (*'dus byas pa*) in the sense that it (*a*) undergoes production, disintegration, and abiding (*skye 'jig gnas gsum*); (*b*) is produced by karmas and afflictions, by the ground of predispositions of ignorance (*ma rig bag chags kyi sa*), and so on; or (*c*) has its own entity (*rang gi ngo bo*) being newly fabricated by causes and conditions (*rgyu rkyen gyis gsar du bcos pa*). He accepts that the dharma-sphere is compounded in the first sense but argues that it is uncompounded in the latter two. In other words, he argues that being primordial mind, the dharma-sphere is impermanent in the sense of undergoing momentary change and therefore is the first of the three types of compounded phenomena.

For support of this interpretation, he refers to Asaṅga's *Summary of Abhidharma*, which approaches phenomena "that are not the appropriated aggregates" (*nye bar len pa'i phung po ma yin pa rnams*) as follows: "Because of being actually uncompounded by karmas and afflictions, they are not compounded,"[69] and "because of being actual things, they are not uncompounded either."[70] He also writes that when in sūtras it is said that all compounded phenomena are deceiving (*slu ba'i chos can*), that refers to the latter two of the three types of compoundedness. Otherwise, were it not limited to those, the ultimate dharma-body (*don dam pa'i chos kyi sku*) would also be deceiving. He thereby points out that the dharma-body is primordial mind and thus compounded in the first of the three senses. He further adds that this view is not limited to that of Vastusatpadārthavāda[71] but is accepted in the tantric teachings as well, because in agreement with the *Dharmas of Maitreya* they identify reality, the dharma-sphere—under such names as "emptiness with the supreme of all aspects" (*rnam kun mchog ldan gyi stong pa nyid*), "vajra of bodhicitta" (*byang chub kyi sems kyi rdo rje*), and so on—as primordial mind, not as a nonimplicative negation.

As a result of the above deliberations, when finally moving to the actual answer to his question Shakya Chokden argues that the words of Sakya Pandita's text have to be read as follows:

> The dharma-sphere is not even existent;
> Dharmakīrti taught well that
> Existence [*yod*] is pervaded by impermanence.[72]

That way, he suggests that *mere* (*tsam*) has to be removed. Having pointed out several other passages in Sakya Pandita's text whose words, in his opinion, have to be altered in order to avoid confusion, Shakya Chokden completes this section by raising and answering an auxiliary question regarding the existence of the dharma-sphere: "If the dharma-sphere did not exist, / Then how would the primordial mind of the dharma-sphere exist?"[73] He thereby asks how primordial mind can exist if the dharma-sphere, which constitutes its very nature, "component," or "object," is denied existence.[74] His answer is that the primordial mind of the dharma-sphere is accepted according to the provisional (*gnas skabs*) position of other-emptiness; by contrast, the dharma-sphere is explained in accordance with the final (*mthar thug pa*) position of the self-emptiness system in Sakya Pandita's text.[75] In other words, according to Shakya Chokden, while both the existence of the dharma-sphere and the primordial mind of the dharma-sphere are accepted in the system of other-emptiness whose view the *Thorough Differentiation* relegates only to the provisional level, neither is accepted in the self-emptiness system whose view in that text is adopted as the final position of Sakya Pandita.

*

11. Was it not taught in Nāgārjuna's [*Wisdom: Root Stanzas on*] *Madhyamaka*
    That nonthings too
    Are pervaded by [being] compounded?
    Thus, does it not follow that
    The dharma-sphere is compounded?

This question targets the *Thorough Differentiation*'s verse 90, which quotes from Nāgārjuna's *Wisdom:*

> If nirvāṇa were a thing,
> Nirvāṇa would be compounded.
> No thing exists anywhere
> That is not compounded.

In his reply, Gorampa wonders what specific consequence Shakya Chokden intended in his question and to whom it applies. According to Gorampa, whichever way it is put it does not work. He also reiterates that Sakya Pandita asserted that the dharma-sphere was the freedom from proliferations transcending both things and nonthings. Regarding Nāgārjuna's passage, Gorampa explains that it was written as a refutation of the Vaibhāṣika position on nirvāṇa.

Shakya Chokden's inquiry and its answer go into additional details on the compoundedness of the dharma-sphere, further contributing to the discussion of whether the dharma-sphere can be treated as a virtue. He also explains Sakya Pandita's position in connection with Nāgārjuna's passage and like Gorampa writes that the passage criticizes the Vastusatpadārthavāda interpretation of nirvāṇa. He also explains why Nāgārjuna's passage works outside that context as well.

Gorampa's Reply to Question 11

As Gorampa understands him, Shakya Chokden puts forward the following consequence: "It follows that the subject, the dharma-sphere, is compounded because of being a nonthing. The pervasion applies to Nāgārjuna." Wondering whether such reasoning is accepted by Shakya Chokden himself or applies to Sakya Pandita's treatise, he writes that the former option entails that Shakya Chokden accepts the explicit contradiction. The latter does not work either, because Sakya Pandita himself asserted that the dharma-sphere was the freedom from proliferations transcending both things and nonthings (v. 129). Gorampa also adds that if, according to Shakya Chokden, Nāgārjuna simply meant to say that if something is a nonthing it necessarily has to be compounded, then why not raise criticisms by using as a subject of the consequence not the dharma-sphere but rabbit horns?

Providing his own understanding of Nāgārjuna's statement quoted in verse 90 of the *Thorough Differentiation,* Gorampa explains the context in which it was made: the refutation of the Vaibhāṣika position that nirvāṇa, as an analytical cessation (*so sor brtags 'gog*), is both a substantially existent thing (*rdzas su yod pa'i dngos po*) with respect to its entity and also a nonthing with respect to the nonexistence of an object of abandonment (*spang bya'i dngos med*) because nirvāṇa emerges from the destruction by antidotes of the previously existent objects of abandonment. Nāgārjuna's response, according to Gorampa, is that this is incorrect because both such a thing and a nonthing must be accepted as being compounded through causes and conditions, while nirvāṇa is uncompounded.[76] "Do not belittle Nāgārjuna by attributing to him the claim that a nonthing is necessarily compounded!" Gorampa warns.[77]

Shakya Chokden's Reply to Question 11

Shakya Chokden provides two reasons for asking the question. One is that in the context of discussing the dharma-sphere in verse 90, Sakya Pandita quoted the passage from the *Wisdom* as the means of negating the claim that the natural nirvāṇa (*rang bzhin gyi myang 'das*), which is synonymous with the dharma-sphere, is a thing, while that passage itself negates the Vastusatpadārthavāda assertion that nirvāṇa wherein saṃsāra is abandoned (*'khor ba spangs pa'i mya ngan las das pa*) is a true thing (*bden ngos*). The other reason is the claim, made by later Tibetan thinkers, that proponents of all the four Buddhist tenets reason in common that if something is not a thing (*dngos po*), it has to be a nonthing (*dngos med*).[78]

One problem with not asking that question is the probability of the following unwanted consequence: that the subject, nirvāṇa, is compounded because of being a nonthing. The pervasion is established by such passages as the *Wisdom*'s "Things and nonthings are compounded."[79] Another problem is that none of the commentaries on the *Thorough Differentiation* provided explanations that could dispel the objection that even if the argument that it will follow that nirvāṇa is a thing is indeed an unwanted consequence for those who accept nirvāṇa as existent, it is unreasonable to give being a thing as a reason and argue that it will follow that it is compounded, because nirvāṇa being a thing is not accepted by the opponent criticized in the *Thorough Differentiation.*[80]

Proceeding to the actual answer, Shakya Chokden explains Sakya Pandita's position as follows: When determining the meaning of the dharma-sphere, the system of Nāgārjuna has to be accepted as valid. According to that system, the dharma-sphere has the same meaning as the natural nirvāṇa, which transcends abandonment, achievement, permanence, annihilation, cessation, and production. In that context, the following consequence is used against the opponent: it follows that the dharma-sphere/nirvāṇa is either a thing or a nonthing because it exists. The reason (*rtags*) of this consequence is accepted by the opponent, and the pervasion (*khyab pa*) is established by the valid cognition known to others (*gzhan la grags pa'i tshad ma*). If this consequence is accepted by the opponent, then the next consequence is posited: it will follow that the dharma-sphere is compounded because of being either a thing or a nonthing. The reason and the predicate of this consequence (*thal chos*) are accepted by the opponent, and the pervasion is established by what is known to others (*gzhan grags*) because no uncompounded things (*'dus byas ma yin pa'i dngos po*) are known in the world. And it is what is known in the world (*'jig rten gyi grags pa*), not what is posited by tenets, that is counted as valid cognition when positing conventional reality (*tha snyad kyi bden pa*). Shakya Chokden thereby points out that having accepted the consequence that the dharma-sphere/nirvāṇa is either a thing or a nonthing because it exists, and having also accepted the existence of compounded phenomena, the opponent is now one step away from "connecting the dots" between the two points and accepting, on the basis of "common sense" or "what is known in the world," that the dharma-sphere therefore should be compounded.

Furthermore, although Nāgārjuna's passage quoted by Sakya Pandita criticizes nirvāṇa as posited by Vastusatpadārthavāda, that passage can indeed serve to support the above line of reasoning. This is because with nirvāṇa interpreted by others having been refuted as either a thing or a nonthing, and nirvāṇa in one's own system being established as the freedom from extremes of proliferations (*spros pa'i mtha' bral*), the dharma-sphere is established as free from all extremes of existence, nonexistence, and so forth.[81]

*

13. If the dharma-sphere cannot become
    A cause of the perfect awakening, then what about the
        dharma-sphere's
    Being posited as the causal lineage?
    And what about passages in valid scriptures

> Stating that "because of being a cause of ārya dharmas
> The dharma-sphere is posited as the lineage"?

This question targets, among other verses, the *Thorough Differentiation's* verse 96:

> It is also established by reasoning,
> Because the mere existence is a phenomenon able to function.
> The dharma-sphere is devoid of performing function
> Because it is freedom from proliferations.

At stake here is the dharma-sphere's compoundedness and thus its ability to function as a productive cause.

In his reply, Gorampa defends Sakya Pandita's position, arguing that the dharma-sphere is posited as the causal lineage and the cause of ārya dharmas because it is the nature-cause that is not liable to transformation. Were it the productive cause of ārya dharmas, it would have to be compounded—a possibility he rejects, in contrast to Shakya Chokden.

Shakya Chokden's reply highlights key points of his interpretation of the ultimate as a virtue: the dharma-sphere does undergo momentary production and disintegration; it is an actual cause of ārya dharmas; and it is a virtue, but not a dedicatable one. According to him, the interpretation of reality as primordial mind, which is a functional phenomenon, is shared by the *Dharmas of Maitreya* and related texts. His answer also provides a nuanced discussion of different types of causes and predispositions and elaborates on the stainless predispositions' meaning, their synonyms, and their relationship with the universal basis consciousness.

Gorampa's Reply to Question 13

Gorampa replies that in general there are two types of causes: productive causes (*skyed byed kyi rgyu*) and nature-causes (*rang bzhin gyi rgyu*). While the former do have to undergo change or transformation (*'gyur ba*), the latter do not. Were such not the case, nature-causes would also be productive causes. The dharma-sphere is posited as the causal lineage with regard to its being the nature-cause because apart from its being or not being separated from adventitious defilements (*blo bur gyi dri ma*), no changes to its own entity (*ngo bo*) occur. The same also applies to its being called the "cause of ārya dharmas." Were it the productive cause of ārya dharmas, it would follow that it is compounded.[82]

This answer further explains Gorampa's insistence on ultimate reality's being called "virtue" only in terms of the absence of evil. For him, because ultimate reality cannot function as a productive cause, treating it as a virtue capable of producing positive results is absurd. Were it capable of doing so, it would fall under the category of compounded—and thus not ultimate—phenomena.

Shakya Chokden's Reply to Question 13

Shakya Chokden's reply to question 13 lies at the heart of his interpretation of the ultimate as a virtue. He explains the reasons for asking this question as follows: There are many who claim that the dharma-sphere's being unchangeable (*'gyur med*) entails its being permanent and that permanence means not undergoing momentary production and disintegration (*skad cig gis skye 'jig mi byed pa*). Many also claim that when the *Dharmas of Maitreya* and texts of their followers explain that the dharma-sphere is a cause of ārya dharmas, they are not referring to the actual cause (*rgyu mtshan nyid pa*). Many others think that if the dharma-sphere is an actual cause of ārya dharmas, it can be treated as a dedicatable virtue. These three reasons point in the direction of three key features of Shakya Chokden's approach to the dharma-sphere that are clarified in his answer: the dharma-sphere is impermanent, it serves as a cause of ārya dharmas, and therefore it is a virtue—but not a virtue suitable for dedication.

Why is not raising this question problematic? Because both the final view (*mthar thug gi lta ba*) and the identification of the dharma-sphere in the *Thorough Differentiation* are posited in the self-emptiness mode, which also accords with Sakya Pandita's opponent's interpretation of mahāmudrā in the self-emptiness mode. Regarding the dharma-sphere as it is taught in the *Dharmas of Maitreya,* if it is explained in the way that is widespread among Shakya Chokden's contemporaries, its identification will fail. If these points are not understood, the approaches of both the *Dharmas of Maitreya* and the *Thorough Differentiation* will be misunderstood, he writes.[83] He thereby claims that the dharma-sphere is interpreted differently by Maitreya and Sakya Pandita, with the latter interpreting it in the self-emptiness mode to more efficiently refute his opponent.

The actual answer is divided into three parts, showing how the dharma-sphere is identified in the *Dharmas of Maitreya,* the way the dharma-sphere produces ārya dharmas, and the dharma-sphere's unsuitability as a dedicatable virtue. In the first part, Shakya Chokden provides quotations from several well-known texts, most importantly the *Differentiation of the Middle and Extremes,* where the dharma-sphere is explained as a thing (*dngos po*). When providing the definition of emptiness—also calling it "dharma-sphere," and so on—the text describes it as "the nonthing of the two and the nonthing's thing."[84] He also points out that other texts, such as Haribhadra's *Clear Meaning,* identify suchness as the nondual primordial mind.[85] These references are meant to further reiterate that reality in the *Dharmas of Maitreya* and texts that are related to them or share their approach is understood as primordial mind, which in his opinion is a functional phenomenon.

The second part is informative. Here, Shakya Chokden explains that in general there are two types of causes of the entirely afflicted and purified phenomena (*kun nas nyon mongs dang rnam byang gi chos*): projecting causes and producing causes. The former are the factors depositing individual predispositions, the latter the predispositions deposited by those factors.[86] The former are the dominant conditions (*bdag po'i rkyen*), the latter the causal conditions (*rgyu'i rkyen*).

There are two types of predispositions: stained and stainless. The former are commonly known as "seed factors of the universal basis consciousness" (*kun gzhi'i rnam shes kyi sa bon gyi cha*). The latter are the ones that exist on (*steng na*) the universal basis consciousness by virtue of coexisting with it in the same locality (*go sa tha mi dad pa*). Nevertheless, they are not posited as the universal basis consciousness itself because they are its antidote (*gnyen po*), stainless knowing (*zag pa med pa'i shes pa*), and also persist all the way into the buddha-ground (*sangs rgyas kyi sa*). The relationship between the universal basis consciousness and them is like that of the earth and gold present in it.[87]

Those stainless predispositions are also known as the naturally abiding lineage (*rang bzhin du gnas pa'i rigs*), stainless seeds (*zag pa med pa'i sa bon*), suitability of the abandonment of obscurations (*sgrib pa spang rung*), predispositions to listening (*thos pa'i bag chags*), distinctive features of the six sources (*skye mched drug gi khyad par*), and lineage serving as the basis of accomplishments (*sgrub pa'i rten du gyur pa'i rigs*). Their illustration (*mtshan gzhi*) is the nondual primordial mind, taught by such passages as the one from the *Commentary on Valid Cognition:* "Thus, that emptiness of duality / Is the thatness of that as well."[88] That primordial mind is also called "dharma-sphere" because of being a cause of all ārya dharmas.[89] Note that as this approach demonstrates, Shakya Chokden sees the ultimate reality and potentials or predispositions as overlapping, which is possible because of his interpretation of the dharma-sphere as a causally effective phenomenon.

Shakya Chokden also argues that in this context, *dharmas* should be interpreted as "ārya dharmas," and *sphere* as a cause, which is different from the self-emptiness approach, where *dharma* is explained as all knowables (*shes bya thams cad*) and *sphere* as their being empty of truth (*bden pas stong pa*). On the basis of this causal interpretation of the dharma-sphere, he explains that when āryas engage in contemplation observing the dharma-sphere in their mental continua and habituating with it in accordance with their modes of realization, their positive qualities are born from within the dharma-sphere. This process is similar to seeds in a field producing sprouts from themselves when nourished by water, manure, and so forth. For support of this interpretation, he cites the passage in Maitreya's *Ornament of Mahāyāna Sūtras* on subdivisions of the lineage:

> The naturally abiding and developmental—
> They should be understood as the support and the supported,
> Existent and nonexistent,
> And [having] the meaning of releasing positive qualities.[90]

He further points out that the meaning of "releasing" (*sgrol ba*) is explained as "giving birth" (*skyed pa*) in such texts as Āryavimuktisena's *Illumination of the "Twenty Thousand."*[91]

In the third part, Shakya Chokden explains that despite the points made above, the dharma-sphere is not a dedicatable virtue. This is because even without dedication the dharma-sphere of sentient beings abides from the very beginning as the buddha-lineage (*sangs rgyas kyi rigs*), and because its entity does not change into something else—just as when the cloudy sky clears up, the sky itself does not undergo change.

Although the dharma-sphere is not dedicatable, he continues, this does not mean that in general a dedication cannot "benefit" (*phan 'dogs*) the dharma-sphere. This is because the dedication of compounded roots of virtue (*'dus byas kyi dge rtsa*) to awakening nourishes the stainless seeds existing on that fertile soil-like dharma-sphere, and they give rise to sprouts of one of the three types of awakening.[92]

*

> 15. If the dharma-sphere were an unspecified phenomenon,
> Then would the following doubt not arise:
> Since there are no dharmas apart from the
> dharma-sphere,

Virtues and evils too
Will turn out to be unspecified phenomena?

16. If the dharma-sphere is unsuitable as [any of] the three,
Then why do no corresponding doubts arise [here] as well?

17. If the dharma-sphere is not asserted as existent,
Then, since there are no things
Apart from the dharma-sphere,
Why is it not [the case that] all things too are not asserted as existent?

These questions target the *Thorough Differentiation*'s verses 82–83:

> If the dharma-sphere were a virtue itself,
> The following absurd consequence would be entailed:
> Because there are no other dharmas
> Apart from the dharma-sphere, evils and
> Unspecified [phenomena] too would become virtues.
> If that were the case, it would be impossible
> For any sentient being to go to bad transmigrations.

Gorampa's reply to question 15 provides one among several possible interpretations of verse 83. That interpretation supports Sakya Pandita's argument and conclusion.

His reply to question 16 demonstrates why, according to him, Shakya Chokden's reasoning is wrong: Shakya Chokden mistakenly thought that a negative pervasion worked in the same way as a positive pervasion.

In his reply to question 17, Gorampa argues that as in the previous question, Shakya Chokden apparently presumed that the two types of pervasions functioned in the same way.

Shakya Chokden replies to questions 15 through 17 together. He explains that if taken literally, verses 82 and 83 of the *Thorough Differentiation* state that whatever exists—including evils and unspecified phenomena—has to be the dharma-sphere. In his opinion, this entails several problems, which he treats as absurd consequences. Going into detail about the meaning of there being no dharmas apart from the dharma-sphere, he highlights two different approaches: of self- and other-emptiness. His position is that according to either approach, no conventional phenomena exist, while in the other-emptiness case, what exists is only the dharma-sphere, which is the ultimate reality and a virtue. He further argues that in verses 82 and 83, on the basis of the self-emptiness system of Madhyamaka, Sakya Pandita provided a refutation of the Yogācāra position of other-emptiness.

Gorampa's Reply to Question 15

Gorampa provides the following explanation of the *Thorough Differentiation*'s verse 83: all evils and unspecified phenomena will turn out to have virtue because they all have the dharma-sphere. The pervasion is accepted by Sakya Pandita's opponent, according to whom the dharma-sphere is a virtue. The reason is established by the fact that there are no dharmas apart from the dharma-sphere. If such is accepted, then it will be impossible for anyone to be reborn in a low realm, because no matter whether one has performed virtuous, nonvirtuous, or unspecified deeds, in each case one would have created virtues.

We should note that the *Thorough Differentiation*'s verse is open to several interpretations. The straightforward reading of "there are no dharmas apart from the dharma-sphere"—a reading implied by Shakya Chokden's question (and elaborated upon in the *Golden Lancet*)—is that all phenomena *are* the dharma-sphere. But Gorampa interprets the passage as saying that all phenomena *have* the dharma-sphere or, to use an alternative translation, that the dharma-sphere exists or is present in all phenomena. After all, if the dharma-sphere is the ultimate nature of phenomena, phenomena do have it present in them as their nature. While that reading is less straightforward, it does align with Sakya Pandita's conclusion that no rebirth in bad transmigrations will be possible. That is, if all karmas necessarily have virtues present in them, those karmas have to be virtuous, in part at least.

To put it somewhat differently, we can say that if whatever karmas one performs necessarily have virtues attached to or accompanying them, those virtues will be only adding to other virtues, transforming unspecified karmas into virtues, and counterbalancing or neutralizing nonvirtuous karmas. If we substitute 1 for a virtue (however powerful), including the dharma-sphere, −1 for a nonvirtue (however powerful), and 0 for an unspecified phenomenon, this can be expressed in the following way: $(1 + 1) + (-1 + 1) + (0 + 1) = 3$.[93] Due to an overwhelming number of virtues accumulated by any of the three types of karmas, no rebirth in unfortunate states of existence will be possible.

Gorampa reads Shakya Chokden's question in a similar manner. According to him, Shakya Chokden puts forward the consequence that both virtues and nonvirtues have unspecified phenomena because they have the dharma-sphere. Not surprisingly, he asks why accepting this consequence is problematic. And he goes on to say that were Shakya Chokden to say that the same problem would arise here as in the case of the dharma-sphere's being a virtue, he would say no, because unspecified phenomena are not causes of either happy or bad transmigrations.[94]

To resort to arithmetic again, we can say that the fact that an unspecified phenomenon or quality is attached to virtuous and nonvirtuous karmas will not make them more (or less) virtuous or nonvirtuous. Neither 1 nor −1 nor 0 will change if we add 0 to it, and the end result will also be 0: $(1 + 0) + (-1 + 0) + (0 + 0) = 0$.

Gorampa's Reply to Question 16

Gorampa responds that because Sakya Pandita did *not* say that the dharma-sphere is none of the three, no rebuttal of faults attributed to such position is necessary. Nevertheless, he proceeds to demonstrate why Shakya Chokden's reasoning is faulty here as well: Sakya Pandita argued that if the dharma-sphere were a virtue, then nonvirtues and unspecified phenomena too would become virtues because there are no dharmas apart from the dharma-sphere. Shakya Chokden thinks he is using a similar reasoning when arguing that if the dharma-sphere were none of the three types of phenomena, it would follow that virtues are none of the three, nonvirtues are none of the three, and unspecified phenomena too are none of the three because there are no phenomena apart from the dharma-sphere.

According to Gorampa, this approach is similar to someone's claiming that a knowable (*shes bya*, i.e., an existent thing) is a pot and his opponent's then arguing that it would follow that a pillar too is a pot because it is a knowable. In response, the first person says since you, the opponent, assert that a knowable is not a pot, it follows that a golden pot too is not a pot because of being a knowable. The intended parallel here is with Sakya Pandita's opponent's claim that the dharma-sphere is a virtue, Sakya Pandita's responding that this position entails that nonvirtues, and so on, are virtues because of being the dharma-sphere, and then Shakya Chokden's arguing that if the dharma-sphere were not a virtue, it would follow that virtues, and so on—all of which are included within the dharma-sphere—are not virtues either.

In Gorampa's opinion, Shakya Chokden mistakenly thinks that a negative pervasion (*dgag khyab*) works in the same way as a positive pervasion (*bsgrub khyab*).[95] In other words, Gorampa points out that there is a difference between claiming that because A is B, all instances of A have to also be B, and claiming that because A is not B, all instances of A are not B. According to him, Shakya Chokden's question is based on misunderstanding this distinction.

Gorampa concludes his answer by writing that there is no need for Shakya Chokden to send such a question to all scholars of Ü, Tsang, and Kham: better to send it to students of Collected Topics (*bsdus ra ba*)![96]

Gorampa's Reply to Question 17

Gorampa replies that in question 17, as in the previous question, Shakya Chokden apparently treats the positive and negative pervasions as working in the same way. He therefore dismisses this question too as based on a mistaken presumption. He also adds that in general it is not befitting for an intelligent person to reply to the criticism of the claim that if something is a thing it necessarily has to be a pot by arguing that it will then likewise be wrong to claim that if something is not a thing it necessarily is not a pot.[97] He thus reads Shakya Chokden's question as implying that similar to the mistaken claim that if the dharma-sphere is existent it necessarily is a virtue, it is equally mistaken to claim that if the dharma-sphere is not existent it necessarily is not a virtue.

Shakya Chokden's Reply to Questions 15 through 17

The reason for asking these questions is that as long as existent phenomena are accepted, all of them have to be divided into virtuous, nonvirtuous, and unspecified. Yet according to the literal reading of Sakya Pandita's text (vv. 82–83), if something exists it has to be the dharma-sphere, and both evils and unspecified phenomena too appear to be explained as the dharma-sphere. That said, no commentators on the *Thorough Differentiation* have provided clear-cut explanations of this approach. Addressing the problem with not asking these questions, Shakya Chokden points out several issues. First, in the form of an absurd consequence, whose reason and pervasion in his opinion are established by valid cognition, he writes that it follows that the subject, the dharma-sphere, is any of the three because of being existent.[98] If this statement is accepted, then which of the three is it? Since it can not be other than an unspecified phenomenon,[99] it follows that virtues and evils are unspecified phenomena because of being the dharma-sphere. Paraphrasing a part of verse 83, he writes, furthermore:

> If such is the case, it will become impossible
> For sentient beings to go to the happy transmigrations.
> Nor will it be possible to go to the bad transmigrations.[100]

Proposing yet another absurd consequence, he writes that it follows that the subject, virtue, is the dharma-sphere because it exists. If this is asserted, then it indicates that one has accepted the common locus (*gzhi mthun*) between reality (*chos nyid*) and virtue.

If one claims that because the dharma-sphere is not accepted as existent, it is not accepted as any of the three either, then the following unwanted consequence issues: that the subject, each of the three (virtue, etc.), is individually not itself because of being the dharma-sphere. In other words, he argues that because the dharma-sphere does not exist, virtue, being the dharma-sphere, will not exist either and thus will not be virtue. The same applies to evil and unspecified phenomena.

If one were to argue that with respect to virtue there is no pervasion (i.e., that it is not necessarily the case that if something is the dharma-sphere it is not a virtue), that would entail a direct contradiction, because the contradiction between being a virtue and being the dharma-sphere is literally stated in the *Thorough Differentiation* and appears to be what Sakya Pandita himself asserts in that text. If, alternatively, one were to argue that there is no pervasion with respect to evil and unspecified phenomena, then one would have accepted the common locus between nonvirtues or unspecified phenomena on the one hand and the dharma-sphere on the other, thereby invalidating one's previous assertion that the dharma-sphere is none of the three because it is not accepted as existent.

Shakya Chokden writes that yet another issue can be raised: if the dharma-sphere is not existent (*yod pa ma yin*), then does one accept it as nonexistent (*med pa*) or as freedom from proliferations? If it is the former, then not only will it entail a direct contradiction but no phenomena called "existent" will be possible, because the dharma-sphere is nonexistent and there are no phenomena apart from it. If it is the latter, then the existent virtues described in the line "As many virtues of migrators as there exist" will turn out to be free from the extremes of existence and nonexistence (*yod med kyi mtha' dang bral*). This is because the dharma-sphere is freedom from extremes (*mtha' bral*) and there are no phenomena apart from the dharma-sphere. He writes that although the statement that "there are no dharmas apart from the dharma-sphere" is found in the pronouncements of the Buddha and many valid commentaries, commentators on not only the *Thorough Differentiation* but also the *Perfection of Wisdom* sūtras, the *Ornament of Mahāyāna Sūtras,* and the *Differentiation of the Middle and Extremes* have not gained confidence regarding its meaning.[101]

The actual answer is divided into an extensive explanation of the fact that there are no dharmas apart from the dharma-sphere and an explanation of the relevant passage from the *Thorough Differentiation.* The first explanation has two parts: an explanation of the intent behind teaching that there are no dharmas apart from the dharma-sphere in the *Perfection of Wisdom* sūtras and an explanation of the intent behind teaching this in the subsequent *Dharmas of Maitreya.*[102]

The intent behind the *Perfection of Wisdom* sūtras' teaching that there are no dharmas apart from the dharma-sphere is to show that all dharmas or phenomena are said to have two entities: the entity of the mode of appearance (*snang tshul gyi ngo bo*) and the entity of the mode of being (*gnas tshul gyi ngo bo*). Differences between the two are delineated in terms of the mode of appearance to unreal ideation (*yang dag min rtog la snang tshul*) versus the mode of seeing by the nonconceptual primordial mind (*mi rtog ye shes kyis gzigs tshul*). The mode of appearance to unreal ideation is the dualistic appearance as the apprehended and the apprehender (*gzung 'dzin gnyis su snang ba*) owing to the predispositions of ignorance to ordinary beings and in the subsequent attainment of the āryas on the path to awakening. The mode of seeing by the nonconceptual primordial mind is not appearing as anything at all (*cir yang mi snang*) through the power of manifestation of the nondual primordial mind in the meditative equipoise of āryas. The two "subjects" (*yul can*) in those respective contexts are described as consciousness and primordial mind. The two "objects" (*yul*) are described as reality-possessors/dharma-possessors (*chos can*) and reality/dharmaness (*chos nyid*), relativities (*kun rdzob*) and the ultimate (*don dam*), multiplicity (*ji snyed*) and the mode (*ji lta*). Of the two, the mode of being of all knowables is the dharma-sphere, or reality.[103] That mode of being is not reality-possessors. Were it otherwise, a buddha's primordial mind would see appearances as they arise to ordinary beings and in the subsequent attainment of the āryas prior to awakening, which is not the case. Consequently, dharma-possessors do not exist the way they appear because their modes of appearance and being are discordant, which is illustrated by the appearance of falling hair as a result of a cataract. The reason why there are no dharmas apart from the dharma-sphere is that the mode of being of all knowables is the dharma-sphere.[104]

Note that Shakya Chokden provides this interpretation by means of the self-emptiness approach, according to which, in his opinion, no phenomena, including reality, exist, because they do not exist in reality, and that lack of real existence is merely imputed as reality. He does *not* argue here, as he does in the contest of the other-emptiness approach, that of the two modes, the mode of appearance does not exist, the mode of being and the dharma-sphere are synonymous, and thus nothing exists apart from the dharma-sphere because only the dharma-sphere exists. Yet his position can be misinterpreted as arguing that. This is the issue he turns to next.

One might object, he writes, that if something does not exist, it is contradictory for its mode of being to exist. But that is not true, he says, because here the nonexistence of the mode of being is merely imputed as the mode of being. However, relative phenomena are not accepted as the dharma-sphere either, because otherwise it would follow that they are the ultimate reality. Finally, even the dharma-sphere itself is not accepted as the dharma-sphere, because otherwise it will follow that it is the ultimate reality, and thus not free from all extremes of proliferations. Thus, the meaning of there being no other dharmas apart from the dharma-sphere is *not* that all established bases (*gzhi grub*, i.e., existents) are the dharma-sphere. This is because if a dharma called "established" (*grub pa*) were accepted, it would be unsuitable as the dharma-sphere. And in general too, if something is accepted as any of the extremes of proliferations, it would contradict its being the dharma-sphere.

Clarifying the context, Shakya Chokden writes that the above explanation has been made with respect to severing proliferations by the view (*lta bas spros pa gcod pa*). By contrast, in the context of incorporation into experience through meditation (*sgom pas nyams su len pa*), one accepts and becomes familiar with just the object of experience of the individually self-cognizing primordial mind (*so sor rang gis rig pa'i ye shes kyi nyams su myong bya tsam*), which is called "yogic relativity" (*rnal 'byor pa'i kun rdzob*). In the context of training in the collection of merits through action (*spyod pas bsod nams kyi tshogs la slob pa*), one posits phenomena as they are known in the world, which is called "worldly relative reality serving as the method" (*'jig rten kun rdzob kyi bden pa thabs su gyur pa*).[105]

Moving to the subsequent *Dharmas of Maitreya,* Shakya Chokden writes that the meaning of such passages as the *Differentiation of the Middle and Extremes*'s "Thus, apart from the dharma-sphere / There are no dharmas"[106] and the *Ornament of Mahāyāna Sūtras*'s "Because there are no dharmas / Apart from the dharma-sphere"[107] is, once again, *not* that all afflicted and purified dharmas of saṃsāra and nirvāṇa are the dharma-sphere. Otherwise, it would follow that because of being the entity (*ngo bo nyid*) of the dharma-sphere,[108] both the imaginary (*kun btags*) and the dependent (*gzhan dbang*) are the perfect (*yongs grub*), the pure objects of observation (*rnam dag gi dmigs pa*), and the ultimate reality itself. What is the meaning of those passages then?

He explains that according to the final view of the three intermediate *Dharmas of Maitreya,* there are no dharmas apart from the dharma-sphere because only the dharma-sphere, and nothing else, exists. If something exists, it has to be the entity of the dharma-sphere because if something exists, it has to be the perfect. The apprehended (*gzung ba*) and the apprehender (*'dzin pa*) do not exist; what exists is exclusively the nondual primordial mind. This is attested in such passages as the *Ornament of Mahāyāna Sūtras*'s "Having cognized the nonexistence of both, the intelligent one / Dwells in the dharma-sphere devoid of them"[109] and the *Differentiation of the Middle and Extremes*'s

> Relying on observation,
> Nonobservation is thoroughly produced.
> Relying on nonobservation,
> Nonobservation is thoroughly produced.
>
> Therefore, observation is established
> As [having] the entity of nonobservation.
> Thus, observation and nonobservation
> Are to be known as equal.[110]

Importantly, he adds that according to this system, evils and unspecified phenomena are not accepted as even existent, let alone as the dharma-sphere, because they are subsumed under the apprehended and the apprehender.[111] This is a significant statement that demonstrates a special status assigned to virtue in this other-emptiness system, according to Shakya Chokden. In fact, it is safe to argue that according to its final view in his interpretation, only virtue—qua the dharma-sphere—exists because only the dharma-sphere exists and the dharma-sphere is a virtue!

Next, Shakya Chokden addresses the following question: is the conventional reality not accepted in this system? His answer is that what is known to the world (*'jig rten*) and to śrāvakas is not accepted as established by the valid cognition (*tshad ma*) known in Yogācāra's own tenets. Rather, the aspects of the apprehended (*gzung rnam*) as they appear to the knowing emerging from the firm and unfirm predispositions (*bag chags brtan pa dang mi brtan pa*) are termed, respectively, *correct conventionalities* (*yang dag pa'i kun rdzob*) and *wrong conventionalities* (*log pa'i kun rdzob*). Regarding their way of being (*gnas lugs*), those appearances exist as mind (*sems su gnas*), and that in turn is established by the direct self-cognition (*rang rig pa'i mngon sum*). Such is the way of positing the conventional reality in that system. Regarding the boundary of positing the ultimate reality, the aspect of mind appearing in the above way is itself also established as untrue (*mi bden pa*) and not existent (*yod pa ma yin pa*).[112] Note that when Shakya Chokden refers to the way of being, he means the conventional, not the ultimate, way of abiding of conventionalities.

Moving to the explanation of the *Thorough Differentiation* itself, Shakya Chokden explains that in verses 82 and 83, which articulate unwanted consequences of accepting the dharma-sphere as a virtue, Sakya Pandita, *on the basis of the system of Prāsaṅgika and Svātantrika Madhyamakas,* provided refutations of the Yogācāra position that if something exists it has to be the dharma-sphere and that only the dharma-sphere is the ultimate virtue. That position also includes the view that virtues projecting fruitions (*rnam smin 'phen byed kyi dge ba*) are relative virtues (*kun rdzob pa'i dge ba*), subsumed under the imaginary apprehended and apprehender (*gzung 'dzin kun btags*), and therefore do not exist. Challenging that position, Sakya Pandita argued that by claiming that there are no phenomena apart from the dharma-sphere and that only the dharma-sphere is real, it has misinterpreted both realities, because both the dharma-possessors and the dharma-sphere should be posited as equally existent conventionally and equally nonexistent ultimately. Because Yogācāras have no option other than to respond that neither reason is established, Sakya Pandita afterwards refuted the conventional and ultimate realities' not being equally existent conventionally and not being equally nonexistent ultimately.

According to this refutation, if the conventional and ultimate realities are not equally existent conventionally, it follows that evils and unspecified phenomena too are conventionally nonexistent because conventionally there are no phenomena apart from the dharma-sphere. If that were so, then no sentient being would be able to go to bad transmigrations. If the conventional and ultimate realities are not equally nonexistent ultimately, that is, if, in contrast to conventional reality, the dharma-sphere existed ultimately and were also a virtue, then the following unwanted consequence would apply: that the subject, the ultimate entity of evils and unspecified phenomena, is a virtue because of being the entity of the dharma-sphere. Yogācāras will have to accept that the ultimate entity of evils and unspecified phenomena is the entity of the dharma-sphere, because they assert that the ultimate entity of dharma-possessors or the dependent (*gzhan dbang*) is reality (*chos nyid*). Then it will turn out that the entity of both evils and unspecified phenomena is a virtue, because Yogācāras accept that the ultimate entity (*don dam pa'i ngo bo*) of them both is a virtue and that the relative entity (*kun rdzob kyi ngo bo*) does not exist even conventionally. In that case, the bad transmigrations will be impossible.

One might object that the first refutation applies to Niḥsvabhāvavāda as well because according to that system too there is nothing apart from the dharma-sphere. But then one can answer that there is no such fault because such reasoning is not established with respect to the conventional level (i.e., on the conventional level there *are* phenomena other than the dharma-sphere) and accepted with respect to the ultimate level (wherein nothing exists). Consequently, Shakya Chokden suggests paraphrasing verses 82 and 83 as follows:

> If the dharma-sphere were precisely a virtue itself,
> The following absurd consequence would be entailed:
> The entity of evils and unspecified [phenomena]
> Also would be a virtue, and
>
> Because there are no dharmas
> Apart from the dharma-sphere, evils and
> Unspecified [phenomena] too would become nonexistent.
> If that were the case, it would be impossible
> For any sentient being to go to bad transmigrations.[113]

*

> 18. How does the explanation of existent as a positive
> phenomenon
> Invalidate the dharma-sphere's being a virtue?

This question targets verse 103 of the *Thorough Differentiation:* "The *Vajradhvaja['s Dedication]* itself also explains / 'Existent' in terms of accomplishment." In his reply, Gorampa quotes a textual passage that in his opinion provides the answer. In his answer, Shakya Chokden explains that the existent virtue taught in the *Vajradhvaja's Dedication* is not the dharma-sphere, because it is taught as newly accomplished.

Gorampa's Reply to Question 18

Gorampa reads Shakya Chokden's question as follows: "How does the explanation of existent in terms of accomplishment [*bsgrub pa*] / Invalidate the dharma-sphere's being a virtue?"[114] In response, he quotes another passage from the *Vajradhvaja's Dedication:*

> Truly accomplishing those virtues
> That exist in the realms of the ten directions,

> With the thoughts of benefit and happiness for all migrators,
> I fully dedicate them to the mastery of primordial mind.[115]

He writes that it invalidates the interpretation of *exist* in "As many virtues of migrators as there exist" as referring to the dharma-sphere because in that context the existent virtue is described as being properly accomplished (*yang dag par bsgrub pa*) through efforts, while the dharma-sphere is not accomplished (*bsgrubs pa*) through efforts.[116]

Shakya Chokden's Reply to Question 18

While the explicit target of the question is the *Thorough Differentiation's* verse 103, the answer also addresses more generally different interpretations, provided in verses 98 through 102, of the passage from the *Vajradhvaja's Dedication:*

> As many virtues of migrators as there exist,
> Created, to be created, and likewise being created,
> In such grounds that accord with good,
> Let in all ways everything come in contact with good!

The reason for asking this question pertains to the spelling of the word in verse 103 that I translated as "accomplishment" (*bsgrub pa*). Shakya Chokden writes that all copies of the text available to him used "positive phenomenon" (*sgrub pa*). Read this way, Sakya Pandita's passage contradicts both scriptural statements and reasoning. In other words, Shakya Chokden reads *sgrub pa* as "positive phenomenon" or "affirmation"—one of the two types of phenomena, the other being "negative phenomenon" or "negation" (*dgag pa*)[117]—and sees it as problematic. The problem with not asking the question, according to him, is that the *Vajradhvaja's Dedication* does not explicitly treat the existent virtue in the sense of a positive phenomenon (*sgrub pa*). And if verse 103 were read to say that the virtue taught by the word *existent* in the *Vajradhvaja's Dedication* is not the dharma-sphere because of being a positive phenomenon, the pervasion in this consequence would not be ascertained, because such texts as the *Ornament of Mahāyāna Sūtras* and the *Differentiation of the Middle and Extremes* do teach the dharma-sphere as a positive phenomenon.

As the actual answer, Shakya Chokden quotes the *Vajradhvaja's Dedication* passage that presents the existent virtue as accomplished—the same one that was quoted by Gorampa in his answer but with the slightly altered first line in English (second in Tibetan):

Having properly accomplished [*bsgrubs pa*] those virtues
That exist in the realms of the ten directions,
With the thoughts of benefit and happiness for all migrators
I fully dedicate them to the mastery of primordial mind.[118]

He explains that the existent virtue taught in that sūtra is not the dharma-sphere because it is taught as newly accomplished (*gsar du bsgrubs pa*) in that scripture itself.[119]

*

19. If a dedication without transformation is meaningless,
Then what about that making of aspirational resolve
By the merchant chief Maitrakanyaka?

This question targets the passage from verses 104–5 of the *Thorough Differentiation:*

If transformed through dedication, it will be compounded.

Dedication without transformation is meaningless.
The Victor taught in sūtras that
The dharma-sphere is unchangeable.

Gorampa replies that the answer to this question lies in differentiating between two types of meaningless dedication and that Shakya Chokden failed to do so. In his reply, Shakya Chokden explores the dedicatability of the dharma-sphere, as well as the dharma-sphere's being a virtue and having causal efficiency. He argues that the dharma-sphere is not suitable for transformation or change through dedication. Differentiating between dedication and aspirational resolve, he writes that although the dharma-sphere is not a dedicatable cause, it can become a cause for aspirational resolve and such resolve can be realized.

Gorampa's Reply to Question 19

According to Gorampa, Shakya Chokden neglected to differentiate between two types of meaningless dedication: that pertaining to the roots of virtues being dedicated not being transformed (*bsngo rgyu'i dge rtsa mi 'gyur*) and that pertaining to the results of dedication not being accomplished (*bsngo ba'i 'bras bu 'grub par mi 'gyur*). The answer lies in differentiating between the two, he writes.[120] Gorampa implies that according to the story of Maitrakanyaka, the former type did not occur: the transformation of the roots of virtues did indeed happen. The latter, by contrast, did occur: the intended results of dedication were not accomplished.

This passage draws on the legend of Maitrakanyaka, who, as a karmic consequence of kicking his mother in the head, was tortured by a hot iron wheel spinning in his head. He was told that this torture would continue until another person who had accumulated a similar karma underwent a similar torture. Out of compassion, Maitrakanyaka aspired to continue undergoing the wheel torture forever so that nobody else would experience the suffering he experienced. As a result of this compassionate aspiration, the wheel disappeared and his suffering ended.[121] Thus, the intended result of such aspirational resolve, or "dedication,"[122] was not achieved, but compassion—the root of virtue in this case—did undergo transformation by bringing about positive results. Therefore, neither type of "dedication" was meaningless (in contrast to the dedication of the dharma-sphere, which, according to Sakya Pandita, is not only meaningless but also harmful).

Shakya Chokden's Reply to Question 19

Shakya Chokden writes that the reason for asking this question is that none of the commentators on the *Thorough Differentiation* correctly explained the difference between dedication (*bsngo ba*) and aspirational resolve (*smon lam*). The problem with not asking it is the possibility of a mistaken presumption that if it is impossible to dedicate what is not liable to change through dedication, then it is also unsuitable to make an aspirational resolve that cannot be accomplished.

In the actual answer, Shakya Chokden first delineates the well-known distinction between dedication and aspirational resolve: the former necessarily requires a substance to dedicate (*bsngo rgyu'i rdzas*); the latter, on the other hand, consists in striving for something desired (*'dod bya'i dngos po*), regardless of whether there is something to dedicate or not. The two also overlap: although there are numerous types of aspirational resolve that are not dedications, it is impossible for a dedication not to be an aspirational resolve.

Next, he explains that according to the *Vajradhvaja's Dedication*, what is dedicated is the created virtues (*byas pa'i dge ba*). They are of three types owing to the division into virtues accumulated in the three times. Furthermore, within the twofold division into virtues accumulated by oneself and by others, what one actually dedicates are virtues accumulated by oneself. With respect to the virtues accumulated by others, one dedicates not them but one's own virtues of rejoicing (*yi rang gi dge ba*) in them. Otherwise, as stated in the *Thorough Differentiation*, "Why has the dedication by even the first buddha alone / Not been accomplished [until] these days?" (v. 148).

What dedication is made toward is of two types: high state (*mngon mtho*, good rebirth in saṃsāra) and definite goodness (*nges legs*, nirvāṇa). If dedication is made only toward the former, the dedicated virtues will become just virtues of partial concordance with merits (*bsod nams cha mthun*) and will not serve as causes of attaining the actual separative result (*bral ba'i 'bras bu*, nirvāṇa). If dedication is made toward the latter, the dedicated virtues will become both virtues of partial concordance with merits and virtues of partial concordance with liberation (*thar pa cha mthun*). Furthermore, if such virtues are stained (*zag pa dang bcas pa*, i.e., connected with afflictions), they will serve as causes producing all five results.[123]

Now, the dharma-sphere is not suitable for transformation or change through dedication because dedication cannot transform it into a cause of any of those results. Although the separative result is indeed achieved when the dharma-sphere is purified of defilements, the actual cause of attaining that separative result is exclusively the truth of the path, not the dharma-sphere per se. One might object that when the dharma-sphere is accepted as cognition (*rig pa*), this allows for the subsequent continuity of a similar type (*rigs 'dra'i rgyun phyi ma*) to emerge, making the dharma-sphere a homogeneous cause (*skal mnyam gyi rgyu*). (In other words, the dharma-sphere as cognition can produce its result, which will also be the dharma-sphere as cognition when nirvāṇa is achieved.) Shakya Chokden agrees but also points out that no dedication is required for it to happen. He concludes that therefore, if reality (*chos nyid*) were suitable as a dedicatable cause (*bsngo rgyu*), it would have to be a cause of nirvāṇa of one of the three vehicles. But that is not the case because it is not any of the six causes with respect to nirvāṇa, nor is nirvāṇa any of the five results with respect to it.[124]

One might also object that nirvāṇa's own entity is cognition. Shakya Chokden agrees that there is a context when it is accepted as such. But that does not make his position faulty, he argues, because in that context nirvāṇa is posited as a result concordant with a cause (*rgyu mthun gyi 'bras bu*) with respect to its natural purity (*rang bzhin rnam dag*), not its purity from adventitious obscurations (*glo bur rnam dag*). In other words, he argues that when the entity of nirvāṇa is accepted as cognition (as in the system of other-emptiness), nirvāṇa can be treated as a result of preceding moments of the dharma-sphere, which is also a cognition. With respect to natural purity, that resultant nirvāṇa and that causal dharma-sphere are concordant. But they are not concordant with respect to the purity from adventitious obscurations, which is a quality of the former and not of the latter—as far as freedom from *all* adventitious obscurations is concerned.[125] Consequently, here too nirvāṇa and the dharma-sphere are not related to each other in terms of any of the abovementioned causes and results because the dedicatability of the dharma-sphere pertains to the dharma-sphere in its pre-nirvāṇic state, that is, the dharma-sphere that is not yet free from all adventitious defilements. And the main feature of the resultant nirvāṇa is not its natural purity—which, after all, is true of all existents—but its purity from all adventitious defilements.

Shakya Chokden also points out that the entity of the dharma-sphere was treated as cognition by Sakya Pandita himself when he provisionally accepted the Yogācāra position. He specifically refers to verse 418 in chapter 2 of the *Thorough Differentiation,* which deals with bodhisattva vows:

> Intending the conformity with the world in mind,
> Phenomena were taught as external objects.
> Intending the reasoning analyzing conventionalities,
> Phenomena were taught as mind.[126]

When the dharma-sphere is treated that way, he writes, it is indeed accepted as producing its own result, but it still is not a dedicatable cause. This is because dedication is made for the purpose of nonexhaustion (*mi zad pa*) and nonwastage (*chud mi za ba*), while it is impossible for the entity of the dharma-sphere and cognition (*dbyings rig gi ngo bo*) to become exhausted or wasted even if not dedicated.[127]

Returning to the distinction between dedication and aspirational resolve, Shakya Chokden writes that although the dharma-sphere is not a dedicatable cause, it can become a cause for aspirational resolve with respect to two factors: that to which and that toward which one aspires (*gang zhig gang du smon pa*). This is because when one aspires to attain awakening, with respect to that person's ultimate entity (*don dam pa'i ngo bo*) both factors have the entity of suchness. Also, it is not an unaccomplishable aspirational resolve (*mi 'grub pa'i smon lam*). In other words, he argues that both of the abovementioned factors have the nature of the dharma-sphere: the dharma-sphere that is not pure of all adventitious defilements prior to buddhahood and the dharma-sphere that is pure of them all when buddhahood is achieved. The former is that to which one aspires when one aspires to achieve buddhahood, because it is what one wants to purify to achieve it. The latter is that toward which one aspires when one aspires to achieve buddhahood. And such an aspirational resolve can be realized.

To clarify this point, Shakya Chokden draws parallel with tantric practice, where, on the basis of familiarization with viewing oneself as an awakened being, one aspires to reality as a buddha and accomplishes it as such (*chos nyid sangs rgyas su smon nas der grub pa nyid*), a process commonly described as follows: "if engaged with adherence, what is nondeceptive emerges through connection" (*zhen pas zhugs na / 'brel pas mi slu ba zhig byung*). In other words, imagining oneself as a buddha eventually results in becoming one owing to the connection between the pre-awakening dharma-sphere, which is only imagined as fully awakened, and the post-awakening dharma-sphere, which is accomplished as such.

Consequently, Shakya Chokden argues against those who, claiming that their approach is based on sūtras, divide dedication into that which involves transformation and that which does not and treat as the latter the dedication that takes the dharma-sphere as a dedicatable cause, calling it an "unrealistic dedication" (*gnas min bsngo ba*). This is because, he argues, that latter type is meaningless and was not taught in sūtras among different types of dedication. Nevertheless, he accepts two types of aspirational resolve: that which will be accomplished if made (*btab na 'grub pa'i smon lam*) and that which needs to be made even though it will not be accomplished (*mi 'grub kyang 'debs dgos pa'i smon lam*). An example of the latter is the shepherd-like bodhicitta that is needed for a bodhisattva's mind training.[128]

*

> 20. If using reality as a dedicatable cause
> Is not suitable even as mind training,
> Then what about the teachings on the unrealistic
> dedication?

This question targets the *Thorough Differentiation*'s verses 111 through 117, in particular two lines of verse 114: "If reality is used as a dedicatable cause, / It is not suitable even as mind training."

Reading the question as referring to the dedication of reality addressed in verses 147 and 148 of the *Thorough Differentiation,* Gorampa replies that those verses address the textual passage in which reality refers not to freedom from proliferations but to dependent origination. He explains that what cannot be transformed or accomplished in that context is the result of dedication, while the cause being dedicated can in fact be transformed.

Shakya Chokden replies that the question was motivated by the apparent contradiction between the *Thorough Differentiation*'s verses 105 and 144–48. He also indicates that although unrealistic dedication cannot be accomplished or fulfilled, it is not meaningless and can serve as mind training. As for the twofold division into realistic and unrealistic made in the *Thorough Differentiation,* he claims that it pertains not to dedication but to aspirational resolve.

Gorampa's Reply to Question 20

Gorampa reads the question regarding the unrealistic dedication as referring to the dedication of the reality itself. He reads the last line of the question as "Then what about [that dedication's] being taught as an unrealistic dedication?"[129] Consequently he asks where in the *Thorough Differentiation* the usage of reality as a dedicatable cause was taught as an unrealistic dedication. Gorampa presumes that Shakya Chokden had in mind verses 147 and 148:

> It is the unrealistic dedication
> That was intended in the passage from the *Sūtra Requested by Vimaladattā:*
> "The reality of dharmas is not transformed
> Through dedication. Were it transformable, then
> Why has the dedication by even the first buddha alone
> Not been accomplished [until] these days?"

He writes that they refer to the following passage from the *Jewel Heap Sūtra:*[130] "The girl said: 'Son of good family. The reality of dharmas cannot be transformed [*bsgyur*][131] by the power of aspirational resolve. If it could, then why have each tathāgata's intents[, "let all sentient beings achieve complete nirvāṇa,"] not been accomplished by the power of aspirational resolve? Thus, it is to be known that it cannot be transformed by the power of aspirational resolve.' "[132]

Gorampa explains that reality (*chos nyid*) in that context refers not to the reality qua freedom from proliferations (*spros bral gyi chos nyid*) but to the reality qua dependent origination (*rten 'brel gyi chos nyid*), such as the fact that saṃsāra has no limits. Implying the distinction between transformation of the roots of virtues and accomplishing the intended results of dedication mentioned in the previous answer, Gorampa writes that "cannot be transformed" here refers to the result of dedication (*bsngo ba'i 'bras bu*), which indeed cannot be accomplished. The cause being dedicated (*bsngo rgyu*) definitely can be transformed.[133] In other words, despite the buddhas' aspiration to free all sentient beings from sufferings, such aspiration cannot bring about that particular result (not yet at least). However, the virtue of their aspiration can indeed undergo transformation with respect to bringing about (other) positive results.

Shakya Chokden's Reply to Question 20

Shakya Chokden writes that the reason for asking this question is that on the one hand Sakya Pandita stated that the dharma-sphere cannot be changed through dedication and that dedication without transformation is meaningless (v. 105). On the other, when explaining the sūtras' division of dedication into realistic and unrealistic, he appears to have treated as an illustration of the latter taking the reality of dharmas as a cause of dedication and dedicating it (vv. 144–48). The problem with not asking this question is that were such the case, the twofold division of dedication would not be suitable because of the apparent contradiction: Sakya Pandita would have accepted that the unrealistic dedication is the one wherein what cannot be transformed through dedication is dedicated, and he would also have accepted that "dedication without transformation is meaningless."[134] The point Shakya Chokden is making is that even though unrealistic dedication cannot be accomplished or fulfilled, it is not meaningless or useless and in fact can serve as mind training.

With respect to the actual answer, Shakya Chokden writes that most of it was already provided in the preceding reply. Regarding the twofold division made in verse 144 of the *Thorough Differentiation,* he argues that Sakya Pandita actually had in mind aspirational resolve, not dedication proper, because the sūtra passages he quoted refer to the former. Shakya Chokden refers to the *Mañjuśrī's Buddha-Field* passage, quoted in verses 145 and 146, which explicitly mentions aspirational resolve rather than dedication. He also refers to the *Sūtra Requested by Vimaladattā,* which also discusses aspirational resolve but was paraphrased by Sakya Pandita as referring to dedication.[135]

Turning to the reasoning, Shakya Chokden refers to the preceding answer, also writing that there is no doubt that in general it is a correct aspirational resolve to aspire: "let the reality of mind [*sems kyi chos nyid*] of all sentient beings achieve complete nirvāṇa." Yet it is not a dedication, because such a reality is not suitable for dedication. Thus, of the two types of aspirational resolve, dedication is exclusively the realistic aspirational resolve (*gnas kyi smon lam*). This is because if it is a dedication taught by the Buddha, the substance being dedicated (*bsngo rgyu'i rdzas*) is necessarily suitable to be transformed into that which it is dedicated toward (*bsngos sa*). Consequently, he proposes to replace all references to dedication in verses 144–48 of Sakya Pandita's text with references to aspirational resolve. For example:

> In brief, there are two types of aspirational resolve:
> Realistic and unrealistic.
> The realistic aspirational resolve is taught to be accomplishable.
> The unrealistic one, even if performed, will not be accomplished.[136]

Clearly, then, while not explicitly refuting Sakya Pandita on the issue, Shakya Chokden thinks that what was presented in sūtras as two types of aspirational resolve was (mis)interpreted by Sakya Pandita as the two types of dedication and that that interpretation needs to be corrected.

*

> 21. If there are no uncreated virtues,
> Then what about the *Summary of Mahāyāna*'s explaining
> as virtues
> The stainless seeds
> On the universal basis,
> Uncreated since beginningless time?
> If such [seeds] do not exist, then what is that
> Which is explained as the antidote of the universal basis?

This question targets verse 149 of the *Thorough Differentiation:*

> Thus, the dedicatable virtues,
> As well as the confessable evils,
> Are the created virtues and evils.
> There is no virtue or evil in the uncreated.

Gorampa's response is that the question is both self-contradictory and in conflict with reasoning. Once again he stresses that not everything called "virtue" is an actual virtue. Regarding the stainless seeds, he argues that although they themselves cannot serve as antidotes of the universal basis, they turn into its antidotes when they become the truth of the path.

In his answer, Shakya Chokden argues against treating the dharmasphere as not momentary. He also rejects the interpretation of the clarity and cognition factor of experience on the universal basis as the universal basis. His position is that the stainless seeds on the universal basis are the universal basis's factor of experience and the antidotes of the universal basis. They are virtues (similar to some stained seeds also being virtues). Elaborating on two types of stainless seeds, he matches them with two lineages and presents them as momentary phenomena. He also argues that although the entity of the universal basis is neither virtue nor evil, not all predispositions on it are necessarily excluded from these two categories. As for the *Thorough Differentiation*'s statement that there is no virtue in the uncreated, he claims that it refers specifically to dedicatable virtues.

Gorampa's Reply to Question 21

Gorampa responds that the question itself is self-contradictory because he thinks that Shakya Chokden has previously accepted that the seeds existent on the universal basis (*kun gzhi'i steng gi sa bon*) are unspecified phenomena.[137] In Gorampa's opinion, this contradicts what is implied in the present question: that according to Shakya Chokden, stainless seeds on the universal basis are virtues. He argues that if there were both virtues and unspecified phenomena among the seeds of one and the same universal basis, it would follow that the seeds and the universal basis that possesses them have discordant entities (*ngo bo mi mtshungs pa*)—something he does not accept.

Gorampa also argues that this question contradicts reasoning: it entails that a person who from beginningless times possesses the uncreated seeds (*ma byas pa'i sa bon*) cannot have the roots of virtues severed through wrong views (*log lta*) because the stainless seeds (which are accepted by Shakya Chokden here as virtues) cannot be severed through wrong views. Furthermore, it would follow that such a universal basis is not an unspecified phenomenon because the stainless seeds on it are virtues and its entity is concordant (*ngo bo mtshungs pa*) with them.

Gorampa reiterates that it has already been explained that not everything called a virtue is necessarily a virtue. Regarding the meaning of the stainless seeds' being antidotes of the universal basis, he argues that the seeds do become such antidotes when, having been nourished by such conditions as learning, and so on, they become the truth of the path, which itself is stainless. The seeds themselves are not the antidotes. Otherwise, argues Gorampa, it should be explained why sentient beings—all of whom are in possession of those seeds—have not effortlessly attained liberation from the very beginning.[138]

Shakya Chokden's Reply to Question 21

Shakya Chokden's reply to question 21 addresses further details of different aspects of the dharma-sphere important for our topic. The reason for asking this question is that the *Thorough Differentiation* states that "there is no virtue or evil in the uncreated" (v. 149) and that the tathāgata-essence is uncompounded. The problem with not asking it pertains to the fact that all commentators on the text concur in interpreting uncompoundedness in the sense of permanence qua lack of momentary disintegration (*skad cig gis mi 'jig pa'i rtag pa*) and also unequivocally accept the clarity and cognition factor of experience on the universal basis (*kun gzhi'i steng gi myong ba gsal rig gi cha*) as the universal basis consciousness (*kun gzhi'i rnam shes*).

Shakya Chokden finds this approach problematic because it boils down to the following self-contradictory line of thought: Because those interpreters explain the stainless seeds on the universal basis (*kun gzhi'i steng gi zag med kyi sa bon*) as the tathāgata-essence itself, they will have to accept those seeds as uncompounded (i.e., not momentarily disintegrating) and consequently not virtues. Those seeds will then also have to be accepted as unspecified—in particular, unobscured unspecified phenomena—because they are the universal basis consciousness itself.[139]

Shakya Chokden's argument is based on his position that the stainless seeds *are* the universal basis's factor of experience. Consequently, he criticizes the above approach as unreasonable on the grounds that those stainless seeds are the antidote of the universal basis consciousness, exist at the time of the abode-transformation (*gnas gyur*) of the universal basis consciousness, become the entity of the liberation-body (*rnam par grol ba'i sku*) and the dharma-body (*chos kyi sku*), and serve as the antidotes of the causal karmas and afflictions with their resultant sufferings. Furthermore, they are not stained seeds (*zag bcas kyi sa bon*) because they are the stainless primordial mind (*zag med kyi ye shes*), as evidenced by such passages as the *Sublime Continuum*'s "The stainless knowing that the embodied ones have is like honey."[140]

In support of this position, Shakya Chokden cites the *Summary of Mahāyāna*: "What is viewed as the abode of those seeds of predispositions to listening [*thos pa'i bag chags kyi sa bon*]? The ones that have become the predispositions to listening based on buddhas' awakening enter any abode. They enter the fruitional consciousness [*rnam par smin pa'i rnam par shes pa*] in the manner of coexistence [with it], like milk and water. They are not the universal basis consciousness [itself] because of being the very seeds of its antidotes [*gnyen po'i sa bon*]."[141] Also from the same text:

> Even without the emergence of the world-transcendent mind [*'jig rten las 'das pa'i sems*], they are the antidotes of the complete entanglement of afflictions, the antidotes of going into the bad transmigrations, and the separating antidotes of everything faultily done.[142] . . . They are not the universal basis consciousness but are rather included in the dharma-body [*chos kyi sku*] and the liberation-body [*rnam par grol ba'i lus*].[143] . . . How does the universal basis consciousness's and what is not the universal basis consciousness's co-abiding like water-and-milk become decreased in all respects? This [process] is similar to a swan's drinking milk from water. Also, it is similar to the abode-transformation, with the decrease in predispositions of the ground of what is not meditative equipoise [*mnyam par gzhag pa ma yin pa'i sa'i bag chags*] and the increase in predispositions of the ground of meditative equipoise [*mnyam par gzhag pa'i sa'i bag chags*], upon separation from worldly desires.[144]

In brief, writes Shakya Chokden, it is correct to say that whatever is the fruitional part of the universal basis (*kun gzhi'i rnam smin gyi cha*) is necessarily an unspecified phenomenon. But it is not certain that even all stained seeds on the universal basis, not to mention the stainless seeds, are necessarily unspecified phenomena. To demonstrate this point, he refers to the seeds of stained virtues (*dge ba zag bcas kyi sa bon*) and the seeds of nonvirtues (*mi dge ba'i sa bon*), implying that the former are virtues and the latter nonvirtues.

One might object that were such the case, it would follow that there are nonvirtues in the upper realms of form and formlessness. (This objection is based on such statements as the *Treasury of Abhidharma*'s "All afflictions in the upper realms are unspecified phenomena.")[145] Shakya Chokden concurs, replying that according to the *Summary of Abhidharma*, inhabitants of the higher realms do have nonvirtues because they have their seeds. The implication is that the position of the higher Abhidharma overwrites that of the lower Abhidharma. He adds that Sakya Pandita himself treated the seeds of virtues and nonvirtues as the actual virtues and nonvirtues because such an interpretation fits the definitions he provided in verses 42 and 43:

> Virtue is what is well performed,
> Producing happiness as its fruition.
> Evil is what is faultily performed,
> Producing suffering as its fruition.[146]

Were it not the case, he says, the seeds of positive vows (*sdom pa*) and negative vows (*sdom min*) would not be, respectively, virtues and nonvirtues, in which case positive vows would not be virtues and negative vows would not be nonvirtues because there is no other way but to identify the vows themselves as seeds! Consequently, virtues and nonvirtues in terms of subsequent connection (*rjes su 'brel pas dge ba dang mi dge ba*)[147] also have to be posited as, respectively, actual virtues and nonvirtues because they are primarily the causes producing entities of fruitions (*rnam smin gyi ngo bo skyed byed kyi rgyu*).

Connecting this discussion with the dedication of virtues, Shakya Chokden makes an important observation: from a subtler perspective (i.e., when one takes into account the fact that all impermanent phenomena are momentary), with respect to dedicatable virtues too, what is directly (*dngos su*) dedicated is seeds because at the time of dedication the manifest virtues (*dge ba mngon gyur*) that had been previously created have already ceased to exist. He concludes that although the universal basis consciousness's own entity is unspecified, it is not certain that whatever predispositions are placed on it are exclusively unspecified. This is because the universal basis is the abode of *all* knowables.[148]

Proceeding to the actual answer, he writes that there are two types of stainless seeds: the ones obtained by nature (*chos nyid kyis thob pa*) and the ones truly appropriated anew (*gsar du yang dag par blangs pa*). The latter are the developmental lineage. The former are the naturally abiding lineage, and therefore they are uncompounded. Nevertheless, this does not mean that they do not undergo momentary disintegration. The fact that they disintegrate does not contradict their being posited as permanent because they are posited as such in the sense of there being neither the beginning nor the end of their continuity of similar type (*rigs 'dra'i rgyun*). Furthermore, those stainless seeds are virtues, because when they meet with nourishing conditions (*gsos 'debs byed kyi rkyen*) their entity turns into powers and other virtues. They are not unspecified phenomena, because it is impossible for an unspecified entity (*lung ma bstan gyi ngo bo*) to become a virtue no matter how much its defilements have been purified, much as brass will not turn into gold even if its defilements have been purified. As for the statement in the *Thorough Differentiation* that there is no virtue in the uncreated, it refers specifically to dedicatable virtues, which, Shakya Chokden argues, is clear from verse 149 itself.[149]

In their conflicting interpretations of the dharma-sphere and related categories, Shakya Chokden and Gorampa agree (for different reasons) that the ultimate cannot be dedicated, but they disagree on many important points. Gorampa persistently sides with Sakya Pandita in his claims that the ultimate is beyond virtue and nonvirtue, beyond mental phenomena, beyond momentariness, and beyond even existence. Shakya Chokden argues for the contrary: that the dynamic dharma-sphere, understood as both the stainless seeds obtained by nature and the ultimate reality, is a virtue, is a mental phenomenon qua primordial mind, is existent, and is a momentary phenomenon serving as a cause of ārya dharmas. It is the ultimate virtue.

8 | Who Owns the Highest Virtue?

Gorampa vs. Shakya Chokden on the Buddha-Essence

This chapter addresses Gorampa's and Shakya Chokden's replies to questions that deal with details of the buddha-essence. Questions 12 and 22 address the nature of the ultimate in connection with the buddha-essence. Question 23 explores the pervasiveness of the buddha-essence, dealing with who and what do or do not have it. Question 24 prompts the discussion of which approaches to the buddha-essence should be taken as interpretive or definitive.

*

12. If emptiness with the essence of compassion
 Is not the sugata-essence,
 Then what about the developmental lineage
 Being taught as the sugata-essence?

22. If whatever was taught as the sugata-essence
 Were uncompounded,
 Then what about the nine essences
 Taught in the *Sublime Continuum of Mahāyāna?*

Question 12 targets verse 72 of the *Thorough Differentiation:*

> Some assert the term *sugata-essence*
> As emptiness with the essence of compassion.
> [No.] This is what purifies the element of the sugata-essence.
> It is not the actual element.

Question 22 targets verse 125 of the *Thorough Differentiation:*

> Since all eight collections of consciousness are compounded,
> They are not feasible as the sugata-essence,
> Because it is taught in sūtras
> That the sugata-essence is uncompounded.

In his reply to question 12, Gorampa writes that because of not differentiating between establishing the existence of something and establishing being something, Shakya Chokden misunderstood the *Sublime Continuum*'s passages implied in his question. As for his own position, Gorampa sides with that of Drakpa Gyeltsen, which he briefly outlines. Answering question 22, Gorampa refers to the argument he has just made in the previous question and mocks Shakya Chokden.

Answering questions 12 and 22 together, Shakya Chokden argues against accepting literally the statements made in verses 72 and 125 of the *Thorough Differentiation.* Invoking authoritative texts and logical arguments, he also argues against what he sees as misinterpretations of Sakya Pandita's text. Regarding Shakya Chokden's question 12, he writes that it was not intended to express his own position. Answering question 22, he reconciles the meaning of uncompoundedness in the *Thorough Differentiation*'s verse 125 and his interpretation of the buddha-essence as momentary and compounded. He also specifies that his questions were targeting not Sakya Pandita's own position but the positions of those who misinterpreted it. His aim is to demonstrate that despite what he wrote in the *Thorough Differentiation,* Sakya Pandita did accept the dharma-sphere as primordial mind and not just freedom from proliferations that transcends even knowing.

Gorampa's Reply to Question 12

Gorampa presumes that when mentioning that the developmental lineage was taught as the sugata-essence, Shakya Chokden was referring to the *Sublime Continuum*'s passage establishing the existence of the sugata-essence in embodied beings on the basis of the perfect buddha-bodies' emanating, the suchness's being indivisible, and the lineage's existing, followed later by the passage on the fivefold division concerning the lineage, which addresses the two lineages—the naturally abiding and the developmental—through which the three buddha-bodies are obtained. The first passage reads:

> Because the perfect buddha-body emanates,
> Because suchness is indifferentiable,

> And because of having the lineage, all embodied beings
> Are always possessors of the buddha-essence.[1]

The second reads:

> The lineage is to be known as being of two types:
> The one naturally abiding without beginning
> And the supreme one correctly taken up.
> It is asserted that from these two lineages
> The three buddha-bodies are obtained:
> The first body through the first one,
> The latter two through the second.[2]

He responds that in that case it will absurdly follow that the two form-bodies (the enjoyment and emanation bodies) of a buddha are also the sugata-essence because of being the subdivisions of the five and that the Buddha's teachings on emptiness and his teachings on the variety of conventional phenomena will also be the sugata-essence because of being subdivisions of the perfect buddha-body's emanations.

Thus, continues Gorampa, Shakya Chokden basically misunderstood those passages and made the mistake of not distinguishing between positing or establishing the existence of something (*yod 'god* and *yod sgrub*, respectively) and positing or establishing being something (*yin 'god* and *yin sgrub*, respectively). While the *Sublime Continuum* posits the existence of the lineage as a proof of the existence of the sugata-essence, Gorampa believes that Shakya Chokden reads the passage as saying that if something is the lineage, it necessarily has to be the sugata-essence. Mocking Shakya Chokden, Gorampa likens him to someone who at the time of proving the existence of fire on a smoky mountain pass on the basis of the existence of smoke claims that if something is smoke it has to be fire.

Addressing his own position on the five divisions concerning the lineage (the naturally abiding lineage, the developmental lineage, and the three buddha-bodies) existing in the embodied beings, Gorampa writes that he shares the position of Drakpa Gyeltsen (*grags pa rgyal mtshan*, 1147–1216, one of the five founding masters of Sakya) that the naturally abiding lineage exists as characteristics (*mtshan nyid*), the developmental lineage exists as positive qualities (*yon tan*), and the three buddha-bodies exist as potentiality-powers (*nus mthu*).[3]

Gorampa's Reply to Question 22

Gorampa writes that he has already provided a clear explanation of the issue raised in question 22 (implying that the explanation has already been provided in his answer to question 12). Mocking Shakya Chokden's reasoning, he writes that it is similar to the following consequence:

> If whatever was taught as fire
> Were hot and burning,
> Then what about fire being explained as smoke
> When fire on a mountain pass is proved by smoke?[4]

In other words, in Gorampa's opinion, in this question regarding the nine essences[5] Shakya Chokden again confused existential and predicative statements, similar to someone who mistakenly takes the reasoning establishing the presence of fire by the presence of smoke as proving that fire is smoke.

Shakya Chokden's Reply to Questions 12 and 22

Shakya Chokden provides together answers to two questions that, as he explains, address similar issues, although they refer to different passages in Sakya Pandita's text. First, he explains the reasons for asking these questions: According to the explicit teachings of the *Thorough Differentiation,* the sugata-essence is necessarily uncompounded, and the knowledge of the union of emptiness and compassion (*stong nyid dang snying rje zung du 'jug pa'i mkhyen pa*) is not the actual element of the sugata-essence (*khams bde bar gshegs pa'i snying po*). Also, later Tibetan interpreters unanimously claim that in the *Sublime Continuum* all sentient beings' having the actual buddha-essence was posited as the probandum, and the three factors (*don rnam pa gsum*) were posited as its proof.[6] Because that reason cannot be a reason of result (*'bras bu'i rtags*), it has to be a reason of nature (*rang bzhin gyi rtags*). Thus the *Sublime Continuum* arguably proves, on the basis of the existence of the three recognizable buddha-essences, with the help of nine examples,[7] that all sentient beings have the actual buddha-essence. If what is exemplified by those nine were not posited as the actual buddha-essences, there would be no connection between the reasons and what is being proven. If they were posited as the actual buddha-essences, then one would have to face the fact of there being many compounded phenomena included in the reasons, such as the developmental lineage (*rgyas 'gyur gyi rigs*), its ability to produce the two buddha-bodies for others' benefit (*gzhan don gyi sku gnyis*), and the profound and extensive primordial-mind dharma-bodies (*zab pa dang rgya che ba'i ye shes chos sku*) in the buddha-ground (*sangs rgyas kyi sa*).[8]

Regarding the problem with not asking these questions, Shakya Chokden writes that apparently, all commentators on the *Thorough Differentiation* claim that all sentient beings' being possessors of the buddha-essence is the intent (*dgongs pa*) of this treatise and that it is also its intent to interpret the presence of the buddha-bodies ornamented with clear and perfect major and minor signs (*mtshan dpe gsal rdzogs*) in the mental continua of all sentient beings as nonliteral and having a special intent (*sgra ji bzhin pa ma yin pa'i dgongs pa can*). He sees several problems with this approach, claiming that it contradicts the following authoritative texts: the *Sublime Continuum* with its commentary by Asaṅga, Sakya Pandita's own writings, and the writings of Drakpa Gyeltsen.

Shakya Chokden explains that the *Sublime Continuum* presents the teachings on the buddha-essence present in sentient beings as having interpretive meaning by outlining their basis of intent, purpose, and damage to the explicit meaning. The basis of intent is the three factors, and the purpose is the elimination of the five faults.[9] As for the damage to the explicit meaning, the *Sublime Continuum* posits the buddha-essence primarily in terms of the positive qualities' inseparability (*yon gtan dbyer med pa*) from it, which is possible only in the state of buddhahood. That inseparability—the last of the ten presentations through which the buddha-essence is taught in the *Sublime Continuum*—is expressed in the following verse:

> Thus, nirvāṇa will not be achieved
> Without achieving buddhahood,
> Which is similar to the inability to view the sun
> With its light and rays discarded.[10]

In the same answer, Shakya Chokden also states that "Sakya Pandita treated the buddha and its essence as the same." We should see these statements of the existence of the buddha-essence only in the state of buddhahood as expressing the *Thorough Differentiation*'s position on the *Sublime Continuum* as Shakya Chokden saw it—not Shakya Chokden's own position.[11] He likewise points out that not only in the *Thorough Differentiation* but also in several other texts, such as the *Thorough Clarification of the Sage's Intent*,[12] Sakya Pandita treated the claim that all sentient beings possess the buddha-essence as nonliteral and having a special intent. Shakya Chokden also quotes extensively from Drakpa Gyeltsen's *Purification Commentary* in order to demonstrate that even that master did not accept such a position literally despite some claims otherwise.[13]

Having addressed contradictions of the abovementioned approach with textual statements, Shakya Chokden moves to its contradictions with reasoning, focusing in particular on what he sees as its three faults. The first is the inability to identify the essence. When discussing it, he disagrees with explanations of the essence involving such categories as the naturally pure mind (*sems rang bzhin gyis rnam par dag pa*), the mind of union of clarity and emptiness (*sems gsal stong zung 'jug*), or the defiled mind empty of reality (*dri ma dang bcas pa'i sems bden stong*). In his opinion, they fail to identify the buddha-essence because they treat it as the natural purity only (*rang bzhin rnam dag rkyang pa*), while the buddha-essence has to be identified as the inseparability from the positive qualities of powers, and so on (*stobs sogs yon tan dang dbyer med pa*). For support, he cites well-known passages from the *Sublime Continuum* and its commentary by Asaṅga, such as the former's "The element is not empty of the unsurpassed dharmas / That have characteristics of inseparability [from it]."[14]

The second fault is the lack of differentiation between the actual essence and the basis of intent (*dgongs gzhi*) behind teaching it, a mistake that, in Shakya Chokden's opinion, has been committed by most later Tibetans, who have treated the basis of intent as the actual essence. By contrast, according to what he sees as the correct approach, the essence that was literally taught in the sūtra statements about all sentient beings' being possessors of the buddha-essence is the primordial mind of emptiness inseparable from the positive qualities of powers, and so on (*stobs sogs yon tan rnams dang dbyer med pa'i stong pa nyid kyi ye shes*). What was intended as the basis of intent behind teaching that all sentient beings have it is their having the suchness with defilements (*dri ma dang bcas pa'i de bzhin nyid*)—the primordial mind on the level of the basis (*gzhi dus kyi ye shes*). Referring to the *Sublime Continuum*'s passage "And because of having the lineage, all embodied beings / Are always possessors of the buddha-essence,"[15] he explains that the reason for teaching the suchness with defilements as the basis of intent is the imputation of the existence of the actual essence's cause as the actual existence of the essence.[16]

The third fault lies in not distinguishing Sakya Pandita's position on the buddha-essence from that of other thinkers, in particular Ngok Lotsawa Loden Sherap (*rngog lo tsā ba blo ldan shes rab,* 1059–1109). According to Shakya Chokden, while the *Sublime Continuum,* together with its commentary, clearly presents the basis of intent for teaching the essence as the primordial mind of emptiness (*stong pa nyid kyi ye shes*), Ngok Lotsawa termed the nonimplicative negation factor of reality (*chos nyid med dgag gi cha*) *natural sugata-essence* (*rang bzhin bde bar gshegs pa'i snying po*) and treated it as the essence that actually abides in the mental continua of sentient beings. And although most later Tibetans follow this approach, it disagrees with the *Sublime Continuum* and Asaṅga's commentary, which present both the actual essence and the basis of intent behind teaching it exclusively as the implicative negation factor (*ma yin dgag gi cha*). If the essence is interpreted as the nonimplicative negation, the meaning of its inseparability from positive qualities is incomplete. Referring to verses 130 and 131 of the *Thorough Differentiation,* regarding the dharma-sphere's lacking divisions, Shakya Chokden argues that Sakya Pandita too refuted the interpretation of the essence and the basis of intent as the nonimplicative negation. Summarizing the differences between the two thinkers' positions, he writes that Sakya Pandita treated the buddha and its essence as the same, whereas Ngok Lotsawa differentiated between the two, accepted the existence of the buddha-essence within sentient beings, and treated that essence as the actual essence of both buddhas and sentient beings.[17]

In addition, without providing his actual name, Shakya Chokden briefly addresses the position of Dölpopa Sherap Gyeltsen (*dol po pa shes rab rgyal mtshan,* 1292–1361): that all sentient beings have within them the reality-buddha (*chos nyid kyi sangs rgyas*), in which all positive qualities of powers, and so on, of the definitive meaning (*nges don*) are complete. On the causal level that buddha is unclear; on the resultant level it becomes clear. He also specifies that Dölpopa did *not* claim that on the causal level there exists the buddha ornamented with clear and perfect major and minor signs (*mtshan dpe gsal rdzogs kyis brgyan pa'i sangs rgyas*).

Rather than refuting Ngok Lotsawa's and Dölpopa's positions in favor of Sakya Pandita's, Shakya Chokden treats all three as valid (*tshad ldan*), as in fact the *only* valid interpretations of the buddha-essence that emerged in Tibet.[18] Here we should note that he refers to their interpretations of the buddha-essence per se, not their interpretations of the *Sublime Continuum*'s position on the buddha-essence.

Moving to the actual answer, Shakya Chokden first addresses question 12. He explains that when asking whether the developmental lineage was taught as the buddha-essence, he only had in mind a well-known interpretive approach (*grags tshod kyi 'chad tshul*) to the issue and wanted to see what responses his question would elicit. Other than that, the question was not intended to represent his own position. According to him, all five categories (the two lineages and their abilities [*nus pa*] to produce the three bodies) were taught as the basis of intent behind teaching the essence, since it was with the three factors (the dharma-body, suchness, and the dharma-sphere) in mind that all sentient beings were explained as possessors of the buddha-essence. For support he cites a part of Asaṅga's *Explanation of [Maitreya's] "Sublime Continuum of Mahāyāna."* The fuller passage reads: "With respect to suchness with defilements, by what factors was it taught that 'all sentient beings are possessors of the tathāgata-essence'? In brief, the Bhagavan taught that 'all sentient beings are always possessors of the tathāgata-essence' on the basis of three factors: 'Because the perfect buddha-body emanates, / Because suchness is indifferentiable, / And because of having the lineage, all embodied beings / Are always possessors of the buddha-essence.' "[19]

Moving to question 22, Shakya Chokden writes that Sakya Pandita's statement in verse 125 that according to sūtras the sugata-essence is uncompounded has to be understood as meaning that it is uncompounded by karmas, afflictions, and so on, not that it is free from production and disintegration as such. This is because neither the actual essence, the dharma-body in the buddha-ground, nor the basis of intent behind teaching it, the primordial mind of emptiness, is uncompounded in the latter sense. As we have just seen in Shakya Chokden's answer to question 12, according to him, Sakya Pandita treated the buddha and the buddha-essence as the same, a position that should not be taken as that of Shakya Chokden himself. Likewise, this statement that the actual essence is the dharma-body in the buddha-ground should not be taken as expressing Shakya Chokden's own position but as that of Sakya Pandita as Shakya Chokden understands it.

The textual source Shakya Chokden provides in support of this interpretation is the passage from the *Lion's Roar of Śrīmālādevī Sūtra* quoted in Asaṅga's commentary: "[That] very primordial mind of the tathāgata-essence [*de bzhin gshegs pa'i snying po'i ye shes*] is tathāgatas' primordial mind of emptiness [*de bzhin gshegs pa rnams kyi stong pa nyid kyi ye shes*]."[20] He treats the primordial mind here not just as a subject observing the tathāgata-essence (in which case it still could be argued that the tathāgata-essence transcends impermanence) but as constituting the very nature of the tathāgata-essence, thereby making it impermanent.

With respect to the reasoning supporting this position, Shakya Chokden explains that when the primordial mind on the level of the basis has become purified of defilements, it is born as the entity of the positive qualities of powers, and so on (*stobs sogs yon tan gyi ngo bor skye ba*), with no possibility of ever turning into the entity of defilements of attachment, and so on (*chags sogs dri ma'i ngo bor 'gyur ba*). Note that the emphasis here is not on what primordial mind can or cannot become but on the fact that it can *become* something, which makes it compounded, changeable. If, he argues, such were also applicable to the nonimplicative negation factor of emptiness (*stong nyid med dgag gi cha*), it would follow that something that is not consciousness can function as a substantial cause (*nyer len*) of consciousness.[21] In other words, he argues that emptiness understood as a nonimplicative negation cannot serve as a substantial cause of such features of buddhahood as powers and other positive qualities that in his opinion are impermanent phenomena.

Consequently, Shakya Chokden suggests that verse 125 should be read as follows: The subject, the eight collections of consciousness, is not feasible as the sugata-essence because of being compounded by causes that are karmas, afflictions, and predispositions of ignorance dualistically appearing as the apprehended and the apprehender (*gzung 'dzin gnyis su snang ba'i ma rig pa'i bag chags*). There is a pervasion, because it is taught in sūtras that the essence is not compounded by those; the actual essence is the ultimate perfection of purity (*gtsang ba dam pa'i pha rol tu phyin pa*), while its basis of intent is the natural purity (*rang bzhin gyis rnam par dag pa*). He adds that read that way, the verse refutes the following positions, which were apparently advocated by the *Single Intent:* the universal basis consciousness (*kun gzhi'i rnam par shes pa*) itself is the sugata-essence,[22] with all positive qualities spontaneously accomplished and with even those on the tenth ground not being able to see it in full completeness.[23]

At the end of the section, in verse form Shakya Chokden reiterates and further expands critical points related to the above questions. He also addresses verses 126 and 127 of the *Thorough Differentiation,* clarifies whose position his questions were actually aimed at, and absolves himself from blame for criticizing Sakya Pandita. As Shakya Chokden's verses clarify his position on the ultimate as a virtue, I quote them in their entirety:

> If that element is not a thing,
> Then what about the explanation of the lineage-element [*rigs khams*]
> As the honey-like stainless knowing [*zag pa med pa'i shes pa*]?
>
> If that element is not even a nonthing,
> Then have [you] asserted
> The sphere of mind with defilements [*dri mar bcas pa'i sems kyi dbyings*] as a thing
> Or as not even the buddha-element [*sangs rgyas kyi khams*]?

If [you] include whatever is cognition [*rig pa*]
In only the eight collections of consciousness,
Then what about that [instruction by the Buddha]
To rely on primordial mind [*ye shes*] and not trust consciousness [*rnam shes*]?

If the clarity factor [*gsal cha*] of the universal basis were the universal basis
itself,
It would contradict [that factor's being] the stainless mind [*zag med sems*].
If it is not, then where will you seek
The attestation of its being an unobscured unspecified [phenomenon]?

If [you] include the stainless mental continuum [*zag med sems rgyud*]
In the eight collections of consciousness, it will follow that
It is not the naturally abiding lineage.
In that case, what is the naturally abiding lineage
Taught in [Asaṅga's] *Bodhisattva-Grounds?*[24]

Do you also refute even in your own system [the claim] that
The element of sentient beings [*sems can khams*] is freedom from
proliferations,
Or do you assert it as the dharma-sphere?
In case it is the second,[25] do you assert
That dharma-sphere as a knowing or as permanent?

If it is a knowing, it will turn out to be a thing.
If it is asserted as permanent, [it will contradict the fact that]
Nobody among Buddhists asserts that what is not a knowing
[Can] act as a substantial cause of a knowing,
Or that [something] permanent [can] be an element of sentient beings.

It is difficult to give answers to these questions
For individuals who explain that
Not asserting the dharma-sphere as a knowing
Is the intent of Maitreya's texts.

Thus, [to those who] claim that with these questions
[I was refuting] this treatise [of Sakya Pandita, I will explain:]
This supreme [individual] who glories
Like the best bull in a herd of bulls

Eliminated others' assertions
Through examining them by these analyses
From the standpoint of the element of sentient beings
Not being the primordial mind of the dharma-sphere,
And [therefore,] these thorns [of my criticism] do not apply [to him].

Because explaining the "freedom from proliferations" as an implicative
negation
Wherein the collections of proliferations have been negated
Is the [approach of] Maitreya's texts,
It is easy to remove the thorns of criticism of
Freedom from proliferation as "permanent" or "consciousness."[26]

In this way, Shakya Chokden argues that all the main and auxiliary questions contained in this section were in fact aimed at those who claim—and attribute that claim to Sakya Pandita—that according to such texts of Maitreya as the *Sublime Continuum,* the dharma-sphere is not the primordial mind understood as an implicative negation but rather the complete freedom from proliferations that transcends even knowing. The questions were not aimed at the position of Sakya Pandita himself, who in Shakya Chokden's opinion only provisionally assumed the position that the dharma-sphere is the freedom from proliferations that transcends knowing and who did not attribute that position to the texts of Maitreya. As for those texts themselves, they presented the dharma-sphere as primordial mind. *Although* being a knowing, that type of an implicative negation is distinct from consciousness. *Because* of being a knowing, it is impermanent.

*

23. If the dharma-sphere of not only sentient beings
But matter too were the essence,
Then what about the explanation of sentient beings alone
As possessors of the buddha-essence?
If apart from [the dharma-sphere of] sentient beings,
The dharma-sphere of matter were not the essence,
Then what about tantras'
And the *Three Bodhisattva Commentaries*'s teaching
That the buddha-essence exists in everything inanimate
and animate?

This question targets verses 130 and 131 of the *Thorough Differentiation:*

One may think, "Although the dharma-sphere of inanimate matter
Is not the sugata-essence,
The dharma-sphere of sentient beings
Is the sugata-essence."

No. The Victor taught that
The dharma-sphere does not have divisions.
Reasoning also proves this.

In his reply, Gorampa argues that verses 130 and 131 do not provide any basis for this question. In his opinion, the question also contradicts Shakya Chokden's own position on the sugata-essence. In his detailed reply, Shakya Chokden explains that his question was motivated by previous misinterpretations of the *Thorough Differentiation*'s position. His position is that Sakya Pandita was refuting the claims that the dharma-sphere or the lineage is the actual buddha-essence but did accept the dharma-body as the buddha-essence. Shakya Chokden also addresses several issues related to the identification of the buddha-essence.

Gorampa's Reply to Question 23

Gorampa cites verses 130 and 131 and inquires: "To whom, about what passage, and regarding what meaning are you asking this question?" In other words, he does not agree that those verses somehow imply that Sakya Pandita accepted that the dharma-sphere of both animate and inanimate phenomena is the tathāgata-essence.

Gorampa also points out that the underlying meaning of the question contradicts Shakya Chokden's position on the sugata-essence. This is because, he says, it is well known that Shakya Chokden himself previously accepted that only buddhas have the sugata-essence, while sentient beings do not.[27] How would Shakya Chokden respond if asked his own question in paraphrase:

If apart from [the dharma-sphere of] buddhas,
The dharma-sphere of sentient beings were not the essence,
Then what about tantras'
And the *Three Bodhisattva Commentaries*'s teaching . . . ?

It is also well known, continues Gorampa, that according to Shakya Chokden's later position, the sugata-essence exists starting from the first bodhisattva-ground, because this is when it starts to be seen by bodhisattvas. It does not exist prior to that because it is not seen before then. How, then, would Shakya Chokden respond if asked:

If apart from [the dharma-sphere of Mahāyāna] āryas,
The dharma-sphere of ordinary beings were not the essence,
Then what about tantras'
And the *Three Bodhisattva Commentaries*'s teaching . . . ?

Citing one of the nine examples taught in the *Sublime Continuum*—that of a treasure under a house of a poor person who does not know about it—Gorampa adds that it will turn out that such examples and their explanation in that text do not demonstrate that the sugata-essence exists despite not being seen or that although it exists it is not seen. This is because, according to Shakya Chokden, those who do not see the sugata-essence do not have it, while those who see it do not need proof of its existence.[28]

Shakya Chokden's Reply to Question 23

Explaining the reasons for asking this question, Shakya Chokden writes that numerous commentators on verses 130 and 131 of the *Thorough Differentiation*, siding with Ngok Lotsawa, explained only the nonimplicative negation factor of reality (*chos nyid med dgag gi cha*) as the essence. Others—Pökhangpa in particular—explained the passage as meaning that with respect to being or not being a virtue, there is no difference between the reality of matter (*bems po'i chos nyid*) and the reality of sentient beings (*sems can gyi chos nyid*). Yet others, thinking that the *Thorough Differentiation* rejected the interpretation of the essence as the nonimplicative negation factor of freedom from proliferations (*spros bral med dgag gi cha*), explained as the essence exclusively the mind's union of clarity and emptiness (*sems gsal stong zung 'jug*).

Regarding the problem with not asking the question, Shakya Chokden writes that if the first approach is accepted, it will follow that not only sentient beings but all knowables in general are possessors of the tathāgata-essence, which will entail that all of them either have already become or are suitable for becoming buddhas. In his opinion, the second approach is somewhat better, but it too should be subjected to further scrutiny because according to the *Dharmas of Maitreya* and writings of their followers, the reality of sentient beings should be explained as a virtue. If Pökhangpa's position referred exclusively to the dedicatable virtue, it would be refuted by Sakya Pandita's criticisms given in verse 97.

Regarding the third position, Shakya Chokden thinks it could work *if* positing all sentient beings (and not matter, etc.) as possessors of the buddha-essence were the intent of the *Thorough Differentiation*. Yet even then, it would turn out that phenomena other than sentient beings, such as the external universe, and so on, are not pervaded by the essence, because proponents of this third position, having negated the reality of matter as the buddha-essence, have accepted that this text explains only the dharma-sphere of sentient beings as the essence. But that will be problematic because of contradicting the explanations that all knowables are pervaded by the natural dharma-body given in such tantric texts as the *Litany of the Names of Mañjuśrī*,[29] the *Three Bodhisattva Commentaries*, and the *Hevajra Tantra*.[30] The latter, for example, states:

> From me all transmigrations originate.
> From me the three places also originated.
> By me this all is pervaded.
> No other nature of transmigrations is observed.[31]

The actual answer is divided into a main and an auxiliary part. In the main part, Shakya Chokden explains that regardless of which of the two interpretations of the dharma-sphere is accepted (i.e., as the nonimplicative negation or the union of clarity and emptiness), if the above passages from the *Thorough Differentiation* are taken as presenting it as the tathāgata-essence, the consequence of all knowables' being possessors of the tathāgata-essence would be unavoidable. But the passages did not teach that. Referring to the three bases of application of the term *tathāgata-essence* taught in the *Sublime Continuum*—the dharma-sphere, the lineage, and the dharma-body—he argues that in the *Thorough Differentiation* Sakya Pandita refuted the first two's being the actual tathāgata-essence and explained only the third as being it.

Shakya Chokden explains that starting in verse 121, Sakya Pandita refuted the position that the lineage that is not subsumed under the dharma-sphere is the tathāgata-essence, arguing that this is because it is newly compounded. In verses 130 and 131 he refuted the claim that the dharma-sphere of sentient beings is the essence, arguing that because there are no divisions in the dharma-sphere, it would follow that all knowables are possessors of the essence. Then, in verse 132, he explained what was intended in the teaching that all sentient beings are possessors of the tathāgata-essence: it is sentient beings' minds' freedom from the extremes of proliferations that allows both saṃsāra and buddhahood to manifest. Thus, the dharma-sphere of sentient beings was presented as the actual element of sentient beings and the basis of intent of the tathāgata-essence. To demonstrate why the nonimplicative negation factor of the dharma-sphere (*chos dbyings med dgag gi cha*) is taken as the basis of intent behind teaching the essence, in verse 133 Sakya Pandita cited the *Wisdom;* to demonstrate why the clarity-cognition factor of the dharma-sphere (*chos dbyings gsal rig gi cha*) is taken as the basis, in verse 134 he cited the *Sublime Continuum*, providing the reasoning for the *Sublime Continuum* statement in verse 135.

Because in these verses Sakya Pandita focused predominantly on the tathāgata-essence, while also referring to the sugata-element, Shakya Chokden raises an additional question, which he answers in a verse form:

"In the *Sublime Continuum of Mahāyāna,*
Dissatisfaction with sufferings, etc., were indeed taught
As functions [*byed las*] of the essence.
From where [in that text are they] known as its proofs [*sgrub byed*]?

Were they to be explained as proofs of the actual essence,
The pervasion would involve contradiction. [Also,]
On no occasion in the *Sublime Continuum*
Is the existence of the lineage treated as what is being proved [*bsgrub bya*].

There is no explanation of the proofs of the essence [in that text]
Other than the three factors and the nine examples"—
Were such doubts to arise,
Few would know how to provide answers to them.

[My answer is that] in order to provide a proof for explaining that element
As the basis of intent behind [teaching] the buddha-essence,
Striving for nirvāṇa[, etc.,] were explained
As functions of the element.

Because similar to the nature of fire being heat
The nature of the element is the nonabiding nirvāṇa,
That element was explained as
The basis of intent behind [teaching] the essence.[32]

Shakya Chokden thereby explains the reason why in those verses (as well as in verse 136, which provides the example of heat and fire) Sakya Pandita addressed both the essence and the element. Being by nature the nonabiding nirvāṇa, the element was demonstrated through its functions, similar to fire being demonstrated through heat. The connection between that element and the essence is that the former is the basis of intent behind teaching the latter. The element's functions, then, were taught not in order to prove the essence per se (although they were indeed taught as the essence's functions too) but in order to prove the basis of intent—the element—through its functions.

In the auxiliary part of the answer, Shakya Chokden clarifies the way the abovementioned nonimplicative and implicative negations were taken as the bases of intent behind teaching the essence. Regarding the nonimplicative negation, he explains that although all knowables are pervaded by the basis of intent behind teaching the essence, they are not explained as possessors of the essence. What attests the teaching that only sentient beings are the essence-possessors is that there is no need to teach all knowables as such and that when the reality of sentient beings has been purified of defilements, they become tathāgatas, while such is not possible for matter, and so on. For support, he cites the *Ornament of Mahāyāna Sūtras:*

> Although suchness is in everything
> Without difference, purified
> It is the tathāgatahood. Therefore,
> All migrators are possessors of its essence.[33]

Regarding the implicative negation, he addresses the following statement: if the explanation of only the naturally luminous mind with defilements (*dri ma dang bcas pa'i sems rang bzhin gyis 'od gsal ba*) as the basis of intent behind teaching the buddha-essence belongs to the system of the *Sublime Continuum,* then it will contradict the passage just quoted, according to which all knowables are pervaded by the natural dharma-body (*rang bzhin chos sku*).[34] He agrees that for those who accept the apprehended and the apprehender as different substances (*gzung 'dzin rdzas gzhan*) this problem would be unavoidable. Nevertheless, here, in the context of Mahāyāna textual systems, when explanations are in agreement with the Yogācāra textual system, there is no contradiction between all knowables being pervaded by the natural dharma-body and the reality of matter not being explained as the buddha-essence. Why? Because according to the Yogācāra system, all appearances as external objects (*don du snang ba*) have the entity of the perceiver's own knowing (*snang mkhan rang gi shes pa'i ngo bo*). That entity furthermore has two "parts," or factors: the relative defilement factor (*kun rdzob dri ma'i cha*) and the ultimate primordial mind factor (*don dam ye shes kyi cha*). The former is the phenomenon of saṃsāra. The latter abides as the entity of the naturally nirvāṇic dharma-body (*rang bzhin gyis mya ngan las 'das pa'i chos kyi sku'i ngo bo*). All dualistic factors (*gnyis snang gi cha*) emerge from that primordial mind, similar to clouds emerging from the sky and waves emerging on water.[35]

In other words, he explains that according to the final view of the Yogācāra system, which does not hold the apprehended and the apprehender to be different substances, all apprehended phenomena have the nature of the apprehender, the mind perceiving them. Because the ultimate nature of the apprehender is the natural dharma-body, that nature is said to pervade both that mind and its appearances, to which all phenomena are reduced. But it does not follow that external material phenomena as such—that is to say, as different in substance from mind—have the buddha-essence. Moreover, it may be asked, how can they have it if they do not exist in the first place?

Now, Shakya Chokden's interpretation of mind's appearances as not being substantially different from mind perceiving them leads to the following question: Is it then accepted that when the perceiver achieves buddhahood, all its appearances achieve buddhahood too? Yes, it is accepted, he writes, supporting his claim with the following passage from the *Ornament of Clear Realizations:* "The purity of the result is / The very purity of form, and so on."[36] The reason he provides is that no phenomena of saṃsāra appear to the primordial mind of the buddha's reality-body (*sangs rgyas kyi chos kyi sku'i ye shes*) by way of its own appearances (*rang snang gi tshul*). Yet given that the mental continua of individual sentient beings are different, this reason does not mean that when the reality of one person's mind is purified of defilements, the same also happens with the reality of minds of all other beings.[37] As this line of reasoning makes clear, Shakya Chokden understands the achievement of buddhahood as the purification and disappearance of the dualistic thinking (the apprehender) accompanied by the disappearance of its appearances (the apprehended). Neither the former nor the latter is somehow transformed into the state of buddhahood. Rather, they vanish, and what is left in buddhahood is the aforementioned ultimate primordial mind—the naturally nirvāṇic dharma-body—which used to underlie them and now fully manifests without them.

*

24. If what is demonstrated by the example
 Of a precious image in rags had a [special] intent,
 Would it not turn out that sentient beings
 Do not have the naturally abiding lineage?

This question targets verses 138 through 140 of the *Thorough Differentiation:*

> Nevertheless, the teachings in some sūtras
> And the *Sublime Continuum of Mahāyāna*
> That the buddha-essence exists
> In sentient beings,
> Similar to a precious image in rags,
>
> Are to be known as [having a special] intent.
> It is taught that their basis of intent is emptiness,
> And the purpose is the elimination of the five faults.
>
> The valid cognition [realizing] the damage to the explicit [meaning exists]
> Because if such buddha-element existed,

> It would be equivalent to the self [taught by] non-Buddhists,
> And would turn out to be a true thing.
> This is also because it would entirely contradict
> The sūtras of definitive meaning.

Gorampa uses his reply as an occasion to present his own position on the buddha-essence: that the entity or nature of the buddha-essence, also understood as the dharma-sphere, has the definitive meaning and is the ultimate reality; the buddha-essence's existence in the mental continua of sentient beings has the interpretive meaning and is a relative reality.

In his reply, Shakya Chokden writes that this question too was motivated by several previous misinterpretations of Sakya Pandita's position on the buddha-essence. Providing detailed comments on the meaning of verses 138–40, he asserts that the *Thorough Differentiation* was explicitly refuting the lineage and the dharma-sphere as the actual buddha-essence and implicitly demonstrated that only the dharma-body is the buddha-essence.

Gorampa's Reply to Question 24

In his reply, which does not target Shakya Chokden's question alone, Gorampa outlines his position on which teachings on the sugata-essence have the definitive meaning (*nges don*) and which the interpretive meaning (*drang don*). He writes that many of his contemporaries who boast of being learned scholars appear to claim that if something is taught to have the interpretive meaning, it has to be nonexistent even on the conventional level. Criticizing that position, he points out that it is held by those same thinkers who also differentiate between the interpretive and definitive meanings on the basis of the two realities as taught in the *King of Meditative Concentration Sūtra.*[38] That sūtra presents the teachings on emptiness as having the definitive meaning and the teachings about sentient beings and other conventional phenomena as having the interpretive meaning. He criticizes those scholars' position as entailing that everything subsumed under the category of relative reality is nonexistent because of being taught as having an interpretive meaning. (In particular, he objects to the claim that because the universal basis is taught to have the interpretive meaning, it does not exist conventionally.) Yet he also disagrees with the view that if something has an interpretive meaning it necessarily has to exist conventionally. After all, according to Candrakītri, for example, the Buddha also taught, with regard to the interpretive meaning, that phenomena have nature, although in fact they do not.

Providing passages from the *Descent to Laṅka Sūtra*[39] and the *Sublime Continuum,* Gorampa summarizes what he sees as the correct approach: because the naturally abiding lineage, the sugata-essence, the ultimate reality, and the dharma-sphere are directly seen by the individually self-cognizing primordial mind of āryas (*'phags pa so so rang rang rig pa' ye shes*), their own entity is not of the interpretive meaning and is not a relative reality. Nevertheless, what do have the interpretive meaning are the teachings that they exist in the mental continua of sentient beings by way of the support and the supported (*rten dang brten pa'i tshul*), or as being accomplished (*bsgrub pa'i tshul*), as demonstrated by the examples given in the *Tathāgata-Essence Sūtra,* the *Sublime Continuum,* and so forth. This is so because other than being freedom from the proliferations of the four extremes (*mtha' bzhi spros bral*), the nature of mind does not exist at all in the way suggested by those examples. The basis of intent behind their being taught as existent in accordance with those examples is the nature of mind free from proliferations, as taught in the *Descent to Laṅka Sūtra.* The purpose is the removal of the five faults[40] as taught in the *Sublime Continuum.* The damage to the explicit meaning is that if they existed by way of the support and the supported or as being established, as illustrated by those examples, they would be similar to the substantially existent self, which, according to non-Buddhists, exists apart from the aggregates.[41]

Alternatively, Gorampa explains that the dharma-sphere, the sugata-essence, and so on, have the definitive meaning because of being the ultimate reality. Their existence in the mental continua of sentient beings has the interpretive meaning because of being a relative reality. He argues that this interpretation is based on the *Sublime Continuum* itself, which reads:

> Due to realizing migrators in terms of the reality of peace [*zhi ba'i chos nyid*],
> It is [the wisdom realizing] the mode, which is
> Because of the complete purity by nature and
> Because of the primordial extinction of afflictions.
>
> Because the mind realizing the complete [range of] knowables
> Sees the existence of the reality of omniscience
> In all sentient beings,
> It is [the wisdom realizing] the existence of multiplicity itself.[42]

Gorampa explains that the text thereby teaches that the reality of migrators' minds characterized by the thorough pacification of proliferations of the two types of self is the mode (*ji lta ba,* i.e., the ultimate reality), while that reality's existence in the mental continua of migrators is the multiplicity (*ji snyed pa,* i.e., a relative reality). He claims that if that distinction is understood, then the distinction between the ultimate and conventional realities, as well as between the definitive and interpretive meanings, will be effortlessly realized. One will also be free of doubts regarding whether the final intent of the *Sublime Continuum* lies in self- or other-emptiness and likewise will gain certainty about the ways Sakya Pandita interpreted Buddhist teachings.[43]

Shakya Chokden's Reply to Question 24

Shakya Chokden writes that question 24 was motivated by the fact that several commentators on the *Thorough Differentiation* claimed that of the three positions on the buddha-essence well known to Tibetan scholars,[44] the position of Ngok Lotsawa in general agrees with the presentation in the *Sublime Continuum*, and in particular it is accepted by Sakya Pandita. Furthermore, it is mistakenly assumed that the meaning of passages starting with verse 138 is that according to the explicit teachings (*dngos bstan*) of the *Sublime Continuum*, all sentient beings are possessors of the buddha-essence ornamented with the major and minor marks, buddha powers, and so forth.

Shakya Chokden also addresses three problems with not asking the question. One is that if Ngok Lotsawa's position accords with what was intended by the *Sublime Continuum*, then the question arises what the intended probandum of the line "Are always possessors of the buddha-essence" was.[45] Were one to reply that it was all sentient beings' having the actual buddha-essence, then it would turn out that all beings possess the naturally pure reality (*rang bzhin rnam dag gi chos nyid*). This is because one has accepted that the intended probandum of the passage was all embodied ones' being possessors of the essence and one has also asserted the naturally pure reality as the actual essence.[46] If one agrees, then the three proofs of that probandum will either be proving what has already been proved or be something not proved being used as a proof. This is because the dharma-body's emanating, and so on, were posited as proofs that all sentient beings have the naturally pure reality, while the meaning of the three is none other than their being possessors of the naturally pure reality.

According to Shakya Chokden, in general both the *Sublime Continuum* and its commentary by Asaṅga use the existence of the suchness with defilements (*dri bcas de bzhin nyid*) in the mental continua of sentient beings exclusively as a proof, not as a probandum that has to be proved. In particular, the *Thorough Differentiation* did *not* mean to interpret the intent of the *Sublime Continuum* as following: having explained the reality of sentient beings as the actual essence, to use as the probandum all sentient beings' having it and to posit the three proofs in order to prove that. Rather, as was done in verse 132, it posited the reality of mind as freedom from proliferations in order to prove the suitability of buddhahood to emerge from sentient beings. It furthermore explained that the purpose of teaching that all sentient beings are possessors of the buddha-essence is to abandon the five faults. But that fivefold purpose will not be accomplished by teaching that they are possessors of the essence qua suchness with defilements (*dri bcas de bzhin nyid kyi snying po can*). And if one thinks that the fivefold purpose is the very purpose of explaining that the buddha with all complete positive qualities is present in sentient beings, then it is correct: what should be accepted as the essence is that whose teaching as the essence has that purpose; it is incorrect to accept as the essence that which does not have that fivefold purpose.[47] Note that here Shakya Chokden argues that only that essence whose teachings have that fivefold purpose should be accepted as the essence. He does *not* argue that any teachings on the essence that have such a fivefold purpose should be accepted as teaching the actual essence.

Another problem is that it is wrong to claim that the *Thorough Differentiation* explains as nonliteral and having an interpretive meaning the *Sublime Continuum* teachings that all sentient beings have the buddha-essence with all positive qualities complete. This is because the *Sublime Continuum* teaches exclusively that sentient beings *do not* have the essence with all positive qualities of powers, and so on, complete. And while such is indeed taught in many sūtras of the last dharmacakra, the *Sublime Continuum* interprets such teachings as having a special intent. Thus, if the *Thorough Differentiation* were to explain such interpretation as having a special intent, it would be a misunderstanding of a double negation. In other words, refuting the refutation made in the *Sublime Continuum* would constitute accepting the opposite of what the *Sublime Continuum* accepts.

Yet another problem with not asking is that were one to interpret as nonliteral the *Sublime Continuum*'s using a buddha statue wrapped in rags as an example of sentient beings' having the buddha-element (*sangs rgyas kyi khams*), then its teachings about sentient beings' having the naturally abiding lineage would have to be interpreted through the basis of intent, purpose, and damage to the explicit meaning. This is because the *Sublime Continuum,* when identifying the nine meanings illustrated by the nine examples, explains that what is demonstrated by that example is the ability of the naturally abiding lineage to produce the entity-body (*ngo bo nyid kyi sku*).

Shakya Chokden adds that some might think that in those passages Sakya Pandita explained as interpretive the *Sublime Continuum*'s teaching that sentient beings have the essence with the entity of purity, bliss, permanence, and self (*gtsang bde rtag bdag*) as well as permanence, stability, peace, and eternity (*rtag brtan zhi ba g.yung drung*). He disagrees, arguing that while the *Sublime Continuum* does teach that sentient beings have the suchness with defilements (*dri bcas de bzhin nyid*), it does not teach that they have the undefiled suchness (*dri med de bzhin nyid*). And those eight qualities of permanence, stability, and so on, are explained as the features of specifically the undefiled—not the defiled—suchness.[48]

In his actual answer, Shakya Chokden argues that in the *Thorough Differentiation* Sakya Pandita was explicitly refuting the position that the lineage and the dharma-sphere are the actual essence and implicitly demonstrating that only the dharma-body is the essence. In verses 138–40, where he was referring to the teachings in the *Sublime Continuum,* and so on, on the existence in sentient beings of the buddha-essence as being like a precious image in rags, Sakya Pandita was likely answering the following question: Because the meaning of the essence's pervading all sentient beings is none other than the dharma-body's pervading all sentient beings, do you accept it literally? Alternatively, in his use of the term *sublime continuum* (*rgyud bla ma*) he might have been referring not to the *Sublime Continuum* itself but to the sūtras of the last dharmacakra (*tha ma'i mdo*), as in the reference in the *Sublime Continuum,* "Later, in this sublime continuum."[49] Otherwise, he writes, to make the passage easier to understand, the order of lines can be changed in such a way that lines 3–5 are placed first, followed by lines 1–2 and the rest. In translation, lines 1–6 would then read as follows:

> The teachings that buddha-essence exists
> In sentient beings
> Similar to a precious image in rags
> Are nevertheless, according to some sūtras
> And the *Sublime Continuum of Mahāyāna,*
> To be known as [having a special] intent.[50]

This approach is justified, he argues, by the fact that the *Sublime Continuum* and the *Nirvāṇa Sūtra* teach that the teachings that sentient beings are pervaded by the essence have an interpretive meaning.[51] Clearly, he is uncomfortable with the literal reading of the *Thorough Differentiation* passage, which suggests precisely what he is arguing against: that according to Sakya Pandita, it is the very teachings of the *Sublime Continuum* on the precious image-in-rags-like buddha-essence that have a special intent and interpretive meaning.

Next, Shakya Chokden summarizes the meaning of verses 138–40: The basis of intent behind teaching that all sentient beings are pervaded by the dharma-body with the nature of permanence, stability, peace, and eternity is the natural dharma-body (*rang bzhin chos sku*). There are two bearers of the name "dharma-body": the natural dharma-body and the resultant dharma-body (*'bras bu chos sku*). The former is not the actual dharma-body. The dharma-body is the body (*lus*) of such phenomena as the buddha-powers, and so on. The natural dharma-body is called "dharma-body" because those positive qualities can emerge inseparably from it. It is also called "element of sentient beings" (*sems can gyi khams*), but it is not called their "essence" (*snying po*) because although sentient beings emerge from it, it is impossible for that dharma-sphere to become the entity of phenomena of saṃsāra.[52]

Regarding the purpose, Shakya Chokden explains that treating all sentient beings literally as possessors of the essence of the permanent and stable dharma-body would contradict the middle dharmacakra. The purpose of teaching sentient beings as possessors of the essence in a nonliteral way is the elimination of the five faults. Damage to the explicit meaning would occur if what is called the primordial mind of the natural dharma-body (*rang bzhin chos kyi sku'i ye shes*)—the actual dharma-body[53]—existed in all sentient beings; that dharma-body would be equal to the self imputed by non-Buddhists. Not only that but the fault of accepting a true thing (*bden dngos*) would also occur as a result of accepting the buddha-essence as a common locus of the primordial mind of the dharma-body and permanence, stability, peace, and eternity. Accepting that common locus will also contradict sūtras of definitive meaning because the middle dharmacakra taught that all phenomena are empty of their entities, while that dharma-body is explained as not being empty of its entity by such words as "It is not empty of the unsurpassed [dharmas]."[54]

Summarizing in verse form his understanding of the *Sublime Continuum* and the *Thorough Differentiation* approaches, Shakya Chokden writes:

> The *Sublime Continuum* treatise clearly demonstrated
> As [having] an interpretive meaning [the teachings that] all are pervaded by
> The essence [characterized by] purity, bliss, permanence, and self;
> Permanence, stability, peace, and eternity;
>
> And inseparable from the positive qualities of powers, and so on.
> This is because it taught that the inseparable purity, and so on,
> Do not exist anywhere but
> On the very pure [level of buddhahood].[55]

In this treatise and in the *Thorough Differentiation*
There were taught two dissimilar, distinct
Modes of demonstrating damage to the explicit meaning [of the teachings]
That all are pervaded by the buddha-essence:

"All dharmas are empty of entity" and
"The inseparable positive qualities of powers, and so on, are not complete"—
Those are the explanatory ways
Of self-emptiness and other-emptiness.[56]

The last part of Shakya Chokden's answer is an auxiliary discussion that deals with, among other issues, the interpretation of the famous passage from the *Sublime Continuum* that we have encountered before:

Because the perfect buddha-body emanates,
Because suchness is indifferentiable,
And because of having the lineage, all embodied beings
Are always possessors of the buddha-essence.

According to Shakya Chokden, the passage answers the question what was intended in the *Tathāgata-Essence Sūtra*'s teachings that all sentient beings are possessors of the buddha-essence. The answer is that all embodied ones are always possessors of the buddha-essence because the perfect buddha's dharma-body always emanates. Then what is the meaning of *emanate?* It refers to the indifferentiability of suchness: the dharma-body is the combination of the two purities, one of which—the natural purity—is indifferentiable from the suchness of sentient beings. In that case, since suchness pervades all knowables, why are only the embodied beings posited as possessors of the buddha-essence? The reason is that only the embodied beings, and nothing else, have the buddha-lineage.

Shakya Chokden also demonstrates that the position that the intent of the *Sublime Continuum* is that all sentient beings are not possessors of the buddha-essence contradicts neither the position of Drakpa Gyeltsen outlined in such texts as the aforementioned *Purification Commentary* nor that of Shakya Chokden's own teacher, the influential tantric master Ngorchen Künga Zangpo (*ngor chen kun dga' bzang po*, 1382–1456). According to Shakya Chokden, Künga Zangpo, like Sakya Pandita, accepted the interpretation of the essence from the standpoint of the middle dharmacakra.[57]

Both Gorampa and Shakya Chokden agree that in the *Thorough Differentiation* Sakya Pandita interpreted the buddha-essence and the dharma-sphere as freedom from proliferations, thereby rejecting any possibility of interpreting it as a virtue. Gorampa is content with accepting this position as the actual approach of Sakya Pandita and further clarifying its details, such as which statements about the buddha-essence have the definitive or the interpretive meaning. Shakya Chokden, by contrast, insists that this position was assumed by Sakya Pandita only provisionally and that in fact he did accept the buddha-essence and the dharma-sphere as primordial mind (a buddha's primordial mind with respect to the buddha-essence), with everything it entails. That allows Shakya Chokden to present his position as actually being shared by Sakya Pandita. That position, as we know, is that primordial mind is the ultimate reality, a virtue, and thus the ultimate virtue.

Final Remarks

The Virtue of Contesting the Ultimate Virtue

The deeper we delve into the polemics about the ultimate virtue, the more complex the overall issue appears to be. Even when we focus on specific thinkers or systems of thought, the picture is far from uniform. It is tempting to claim, for example, that some thinkers treat the ultimate as a virtue because they emphasize the third dharmacakra ideas presenting ultimate reality as the buddha-essence endowed with positive characteristics. Others do not treat it as a virtue because they emphasize the second dharmacakra's interpretations of ultimate reality as transcending all characteristics. As we have seen, although these two tendencies are indeed present, the situation is much more nuanced. While this is not to say that all interpretations of the ultimate or virtue are equally valid depending on context, it is to admit that interpretations are informed by conflicting conceptual frameworks, based on dichotomous sources, and put to different ends. Some of those ends are purely philosophical, some soteriological, some practical, some educational, some defending one's own tradition and challenging rival traditions and thinkers, some forced while allegedly unearthing a deeper underlying meaning. It is not surprising, then, that eventually the diverse ideas surrounding the ultimate virtue clashed and triggered the heated polemics documented in this book.

With the exception of the *Single Intent* with its commentaries (at least as far as the passages we addressed are concerned), all Tibetan writings explored above are overtly polemical. The *Single Intent* too, as Dorjé Sherap writes, makes claims regarding such issues as the dedication of virtues that run contrary to the "mainstream" approach. Intentionally or not, the *Single Intent*'s writings were destined to provoke critical responses by articulating an unusual and hard-to-defend approach: demonstrating the single intent behind diverse teachings attributed to the Buddha by extensively quoting from and blending together ideas derived from heterogeneous sources. Given that those sources advocated conflicting worldviews about reality, virtue, and so on, the unequivocal success of that project was unlikely. It is little wonder, then, that the claims articulated in the *Single Intent* became an easy target of Sakya Pandita's sharp criticisms in the *Thorough Differentiation.* In his attacks, he used one particular position—that of Nihsvabhāvavāda Madhyamaka and the second dharmacakra—which by his time was already favored by Tibetans. In the *Good Questions,* Shakya Chokden noted the one-sidedness of that position and raised the possibility of alternative approaches that he saw as equally, if not more, valid.

By contrast, Gorampa, in his *Elimination of Mistakes,* focused on further honing and defending Sakya Pandita's position rather than providing alternative perspectives on the issues raised by Shakya Chokden. In contrast to Shakya Chokden, he mostly argued for just one approach that he saw as aligned with that of Sakya Pandita. Gorampa's responses to Shakya Chokden's questions demonstrate that he faithfully followed Sakya Pandita's text and that his interpretation utilized the Madhyamaka views based on the second dharmacakra. His explanations help clarify Sakya Pandita's approach. Some of those explanations, in particular his interpretation of the buddha-essence, go further and provide what can be taken as Gorampa's distinctive position: interpreting teachings on the buddha-essence derived from what is usually classified as the third dharmacakra with its commentaries, from the standpoint of the Madhyamaka teachings based on the second dharmcakra. Yet it is also clear that his main task in answering Shakya Chokden's questions was to defend Sakya Pandita's position outlined in the *Thorough Differentiation,* even if that meant glossing over more sensitive or weaker points of the text.

It was Shakya Chokden who, after examining those points with the *Good Questions,* burrowed deeper into them with his *Golden Lancet,* uncovering and developing creative and provocative perspectives. Using multiple sources from Kangyur and Tengyur, he compartmentalized and differentiated dichotomous approaches based on Niḥsvabhāvavāda and Yogācāra systems. He likewise attempted to clarify what he saw as different intents motivating Buddhist thinkers' addressing virtues, the ultimate, the dharma-sphere, and the buddha-essence. That said, he adopted a rather inclusive approach to the Buddhist systems, in particular the ones derived from the second and third dharmacakras. While making clear distinctions between them and showing which specific position was adopted by Sakya Pandita, he treated them as valid in their own right. To that end, he engaged in sophisticated arguments, aligning his views with those of the *Thorough Differentiation* without at the same time departing from his own unique ideas, such as the view of the ultimate reality as momentary, functional, and virtuous. In the process, he developed creative and provocative interpretations. In particular, what made his approach to the ultimate virtue unique was that he applied to the ultimate the common understanding of virtue as a phenomenon producing positive results, providing in the process intriguing perspectives on the nature of mind, the potential for awakening, and Buddhist practice. Most striking, Shakya Chokden advanced the position that only the ultimate virtue—that is, the virtue qua the dharma-sphere—exists because only the dharma-sphere exists and the dharma-sphere is a virtue. This position was informed by his interpretation of the ultimate virtue in the other-emptiness system.

Addressing Tibetan polemics on the ultimate virtue, we also note limitations, especially pertaining to texts Tibetan thinkers referred to or focused on. Despite their different approaches, all four thinkers addressed in this study were heavily reliant on Indian writings and thus limited by the ideas derived from them. Both Dorjé Sherap and Shakya Chokden referred to and literally accepted well-known influential texts presenting ultimate reality as a virtue. Following Sakya Pandita, and presenting numerous polemical arguments, Gorampa dismissed the literal acceptance of those descriptions, claiming that they had referred not to an actual but to a merely imputed virtue. Exploring the same Indian texts, Shakya Chokden argued that they did warrant the interpretation of the dharma-sphere as a virtue, at least as far as the other-emptiness standpoint was concerned. In contrast to the *Single Intent,* which mostly resorts to scriptural citations, the *Golden Lancet* provides numerous reasonings, polemical and otherwise, supporting that interpretation.

The four thinkers were also limited by the scope of the Tibetan texts they chose to deal with. While extensively fishing from the ocean of Indian texts, Dorjé Sherap's interpretations were limited by the scope of the root text of the *Single Intent.* Sakya Pandita focused on perceived problems with ideas advanced in, among other sources, the Kagyü writings. Both Shakya Chokden and Gorampa were constrained by the *Thorough Differentiation,* which they discussed and commented upon, as well as the *Good Questions,* which made inquiry into it. In other words, their discussion was mostly limited to the issues raised in the *Good Questions,* which in turn targeted the *Thorough Differentiation,* which in turn targeted the ideas advanced in the *Single Intent.* Those limitations notwithstanding, these thinkers' writings are a good example of how polemics facilitates honing, clarifying, expanding, and updating philosophical views. It is not unlikely that at least some of the claims regarding the ultimate virtue advanced by the four Tibetan thinkers were a direct outcome of the ongoing polemics. Thus, their polemics served heuristic purposes as well.

We should also note that despite the limitations and polemical nature of the Tibetan texts addressed here, their scope is not limited to polemics or to philosophical issues per se. The texts serve as a good example of polemical arguments and philosophical ideas spilling out into the realm of Buddhist practice. At different places in their writings, our authors either hinted at or explicitly pointed out important connections between the ways Buddhist ideas are understood and those ideas' structuring of Buddhist practice. These authors' belief that the way one upholds and interprets philosophical ideas affects one's practice made the polemics regarding those ideas particularly intense. One such issue is the dedication of the ultimate virtue to awakening. All four thinkers concur that whether or not one treats reality as a virtue and whether or not one understands it as subject to dedication bear not only on the philosophical but on the practical level as well. According to Sakya Pandita and Gorampa, if the dharma-sphere is treated as dedicatable because of being an actual virtue, its dedication will undermine one of the main and indispensable components of the path to awakening—wisdom realizing ultimate reality. Dorjé Sherap takes the opposite view, arguing for the positive outcomes of dedicating the virtuous ultimate reality. While accepting the ultimate as a virtue, Shakya Chokden rejects the possibility of its dedication becoming a realistic dedication—the only fully complete dedication in Buddhist practice.

The four thinkers also addressed or hinted at the relationship between one's understanding of reality qua virtue and contemplative practice. Polemics regarding that relationship became especially heated because of the emphasis placed on practical outcomes of different takes on the ultimate. For Sakya Pandita and Gorampa, the very acceptance of the ultimate virtue / the ultimate as a virtue is an obstacle to the practice of the Buddhist path and therefore should be avoided. Sakya Pandita warns us of great dangers in treating the ultimate as anything other than freedom from proliferations (not to mention the dangers of dedicating it). Gorampa concurs. For Dorjé Sherap and Shakya Chokden, by contrast, the ultimate virtue (understood by them differently) plays a very important role in contemplative practice. Dorjé Sherap treats mahāmudrā itself as the ultimate virtue incorporated into practice. Shakya Chokden argues that if one does not treat reality as a virtue, in tantric practice the two collections could not be accumulated.

The conflicting interpretations of the ultimate virtue documented in this study demonstrate how contingent and context-dependent the category of the ultimate virtue and related ideas are. It is not surprising, then, that after initial attempts to find the only true answer or solution to the issue of the ultimate virtue and perhaps transforming one's views in the process, one might realize that an unequivocal answer does not exist. Prior to arriving at that indeterminate destination, though, one has already explored the whole gamut of interpretive strategies, textual sources, and ideas. This is what makes polemics about the ultimate virtue so enriching and gratifying. Within these polemics, Shakya Chokden's approach is particularly insightful, not because he "gets it right" but because he manages to explore deeper meanings and provide heuristic explanations of the texts addressing the ultimate virtue. He also demonstrates that the way one interprets that category depends, among other things, on system, context, perspective. Ultimately, there is not one correct interpretation of the ultimate virtue. Polemics targeting it can be viewed as a continuing process wherein conflicting takes on the issue lead to the emergence of alternative perspectives, which in turn lead to clashes of ideas in defense of one's own and challenging opponent's positions, which in turn are challenged by new ideas formed in this process. The virtue of contesting the ultimate virtue lies in the very process of contesting it.

NOTES

An Introduction

1. Approaches of some Chinese Buddhist thinkers, by contrast, appear to be less straightforward. See, for example, Ziporyn, *Evil and/or/as the Good*. See also Anālayo, "Luminous Mind"; and Shih, "Concept of 'Innate Purity of Mind,'" for discussion of several early Buddhist writings and those of several Abhidharma thinkers in which the innate purity or luminosity of mind was not accepted unquestionably or without modifications and reinterpretations.
2. Buddhist thinkers commonly divide phenomena into virtuous (*dge ba, kuśala*), nonvirtuous (*mi dge ba, akuśala*), and unspecified or neutral (*lung ma bstan, avyākṛta*).
3. For the works contained in the Tibetan canon, I provide references to the Dergé (*sde dge*) version (referred to as D) of Tengyur (*bstan 'gyur*) and Kangyur (*bka' 'gyur*) and in several places to the Lhasa version (referred to as H) of Kangyur. When addressing Tibetan writings, my translations of canonical texts are usually based on the versions used by Tibetan authors I am dealing with. Whenever possible, I indicate where those passages can be found in Tengyur and Kangyur. When there are significant differences between those versions, I address them in the notes.
4. *don dam pas dge ba gang zhe na / de bzhin nyid do. Abhidharmasamuccaya, Chos mngon pa kun las btus pa,* D4049, sems tsam, ri, 61b; Skt., *paramārthataḥ kuśalaṃ katamat / tathatā,* in Gokhale, "Fragments," 23. Note that while Asaṅga writes of "virtue in terms of the ultimate," both Sakya Pandita and Shakya Chokden, whose views are discussed in the following chapters, treat it as referring to the ultimate virtue or ultimate as a virtue (*don dam dge ba*).

2. Virtual Ambivalence

1. A well-known example is *dharma,* which according to Vasubandhu's *Principles of Explanation* has at least ten meanings: (1) knowables (*shes bya, jñeya*), (2) path (*lam, marga*), (3) nirvāṇa (*mya ngan 'das*), (4) mental object (*yid kyi yul,*

manoviṣaya), (5) merit (*bsod nams, puṇya*), (6) life (*tshe, āyus*), (7) excellent words (*gsung rab, pravacana*) of the Buddha, (8) what is subject to change (*'byung 'gyur, bhautika*), (9) what is definitive (*nges pa, niścaya*), and (10) Dharma systems (*chos lugs, dharmanīti*). *Vyākhyāyukti, Rnam par bshad pa'i rigs pa*, D4061, sems tsam, shi, 36a. While some of these meanings, such as the narrower category of dharma systems, can be subsumed under the broader categories, such as knowables, others are mutually contradictory. Nirvāṇa, for example, is often treated as transcending the scope of mental objects; life and merit can neither be subsumed under each other nor overlap; and so forth.

2. While several Sanskrit and Tibetan terms can be translated as "virtue," and different Sanskrit terms can be translated into Tibetan as *dge ba*—a word that is also used for, among others, *śubha* and *punya*—here I am dealing specifically with "virtue" standing for *dge ba* or for *kuśala* translated as *dge ba;* see below, note 21. Also note that in some contexts *śubha* can be substituted for *kuśala;* see below, note 9.
3. For a detailed discussion of the range of meanings of *kuśala* and related terms, see Schmithausen, "*Kuśala* and *Akuśala*."
4. These are virtues in terms of (1) entity (*ngo bo nyid, svabhāva*), the eleven virtuous mental factors, which are faith (*dad pa, śraddhā*), shame (*ngo tsha shes pa, hrī*), decorum (*khrel yod pa, apatrāpya*), nonattachment (*ma chags pa, alobha*), nonhatred (*zhe sdang med pa, adveṣa*), nondelusion (*gti mug med pa, amoha*), effort (*brtson 'grus, vīrya*), pliancy (*shin tu sbyangs pa, praśrabdhi*), conscientiousness (*bag yod pa, apramāda*), equanimity (*btang snyoms, upekṣā*), and nonviolence (*rnam par mi 'tshe ba, avihiṃsā*); (2) connection (*'brel ba, sambandha*), phenomena that are concordant with those eleven; (3) subsequent connection (*rjes su 'brel ba, anubandha*), their imprints or predispositions; (4) motivation (*slong ba, utthāna*), karmas of body and speech motivated by the above types of virtues; (5) the ultimate (*don dam pa, paramārtha*), suchness; (6) what is obtained by birth (*skye bas 'thob pa, upapattilābha*), fruitional results of virtues; (7) application (*sbyor ba, prayoga*), cultivation of virtues based on the practice of Dharma; (8) placing in front (*mdun du bya ba, puraskāra*), activities of worshipping Dharma images, etc., placed in front of oneself; (9) bringing benefit (*phan 'dogs pa, anugraha*) to sentient beings through the four means of gathering disciples (*bsdu ba'i dngos po, saṃgrahavastu*): generosity (*sbyin pa, dāna*), kind words (*snyan par smra ba, priyavādita*), helpfulness (*don spyod pa, arthacaryā*), and consistency between words and deeds (*don mthun pa, samānārthatā*); (10) completely maintaining (*yongs su 'dzin pa, parigraha*), maintaining rebirth in the higher realms, etc.; (11) antidotes (*gnyen po, pratipakṣa*) of afflictions, etc.: (12) thorough pacification (*nye bar zhi ba, upaśama*), different types of nirvāṇa; and (13) concordant causes (*rgyu mthun pa, niṣyanda*), special positive qualities, such as mundane and supramundane clairvoyances. D4049, sems tsam, ri, 61a–62a; Skt. in Gokhale, "Fragments," 23.

5. See above, note 1.
6. *don dam pas mi dge ba gang zhe na / 'khor ba thams cad do.* D4049, sems tsam, ri, 61b; Skt., *paramārthato 'kuśalaṃ katamat / sarvasaṃsāraḥ,* in Gokhale, "Fragments," 23.
7. *don dam par lung du ma bstan pa gang zhe na / nam mkha' dang so sor brtags pa ma yin pas 'gog pa'o.* D4049, sems tsam, ri, 63a; Skt., *paramārthato 'vyākṛtaṃ katamat / ākāśamapratisaṃkhyānirodhaśca,* in Gokhale, "Fragments," 24.
8. A common Buddhist way of classifying karmas as virtuous, nonvirtuous, and unspecified is based on the identification of their motivations or intentions as, respectively, virtuous, nonvirtuous, and unspecified.
9. *Abhidharmakośabhāṣya, Chos mngon pa'i mdzod kyi bshad pa,* D4090, mngon pa, ku, 174a.; Skt. in Pradhan, *Abhidharmakośabhāṣyam of Vasubandhu,* 202. Note that while the Sanskrit text of *Explanation* treats these four as divisions of *kuśala,* the *Treasury of Abhidharma* itself explicitly uses *śubha* for the first of them, nirvāṇa (and implicitly, by extension, for the other three), thereby treating *śubha* and *kuśala* as interchangeable in that context. Both terms are translated as *dge ba* in Tibetan. Thus, *paramārthaśubha* in the root text is translated as *dam pa'i don du dge,* and *paramārthena kuśala* in the autocommentary as *don dam par dge ba.* Regarding the four types of virtues, Vasubandhu writes that nirvāṇa is the complete pacification of sufferings; being the supreme bliss (*mchog tu bde ba, paramakṣema*), it is the ultimate virtue / virtue in terms of the ultimate (*don dam par dge ba, paramārthena kuśala*). The three roots of virtues—nonattachment (*ma chags pa, alobha*), nonhatred (*zhe sdang med pa, adveṣa*), and nondelusion (*gti mug med pa, amoha*)—together with shame and decorum, not being dependent on other virtues in terms of concordance or motivation, are virtues in terms of entity (*ngo bo nyid kyis dge ba, svabhāvena kuśala,* i.e., virtues by their own nature). Phenomena concordant with those five are virtues by concordance (*mtshungs par ldan pas dge ba, saṃprayōgeṇa kuśala*). Physical and verbal karmas motivated by these latter two types of virtues, as well as such phenomena as birth, attainment, cessation, and absorption without discrimination (*'du shes med pa'i snyoms par 'jug pa, asaṃjñāsamāpatti*), are virtues by motivation (*kun nas slong bas dge ba, samutthānena kuśala*). D4090, mngon pa, ku, 174a; Pradhan, *Abhidharmakośabhāṣyam of Vasubandhu,* 202. Vasubandhu likens these four types of virtues to, respectively, the lack of illness, medicine that helps to eliminate illness, a drink mixed with that medicine, and milk from a cow that has drunk a drink mixed with that medicine. Ibid.; the discussion of these four types occurs in the chapter on karmas. (Note that Asaṅga and Vasubandhu treat the category of the ultimate virtue differently and subsume nirvāṇa under different types of virtues.)
10. After discussing the correspondent types of nonvirtues, the first of which—the nonvirtue in terms of the ultimate (*don dam par mi dge ba, paramārthena*

akuśala)—is saṃsāra, Vasubandhu addresses the following challenge: in that case, because stained (*zag bcas, sāsrava*) phenomena belong to saṃsāra, no stained phenomena could possibly be neutral or virtuous. Vasubandhu's answer is that in the ultimate sense (*don dam par, paramārthat*) it is indeed so. Nevertheless, such phenomena can be either neutral or virtuous, depending on whether their fruition (*rnam par smin pa, vipāka*) is either neutral or positive. D4090, mngon pa, ku, 174a–b; Pradhan, *Abhidharmakośabhāṣyam of Vasubandhu,* 202–3. Vasubandhu also posits two types of what is unspecified ultimately (*don dam par lung du ma bstan pa, paramāvyakṛta*): space (*nam mkha', ākāśa*) and the nonanalytical cessation (*so sor ma brtags pas 'gog pa, apratisaṃkhyānirodha*). D4090, mngon pa, ku, 174b; Pradhan, *Abhidharmakośabhāṣyam of Vasubandhu,* 203.

11. See chap. 4 for the full passage from *Thorough Differentiation,* vv. 42–43.
12. See above, note 4.
13. The absence or presence of realization of reality determines whether particular virtuous karmas merely produce good results within saṃsāra or turn into the means of its transcendence. While both good and bad worldly karmas are ultimately rooted in ignorance, which is mistaken about the way things are, the world-transcending karmas are based on and linked with the wisdom that realizes the ultimate.
14. Within the six causes, *producing causes* (*byed pa'i rgyu, kāraṇahetu*) subsume the five other types of causes, and their results within the five types are dominant results; every functional phenomenon serves as a producing cause of other impermanent phenomena in terms of allowing them to arise, thus contributing to their arising. *Coemergent causes* (*lhan cig 'byung ba'i rgyu, sahabhūhetu*) are phenomena that simultaneously condition or mutually support each other. *Concomitant causes* (*mtshungs par ldan pa'i rgyu, saṃprayuktahetu*), a subtype of coemergent causes, are co-occurring primary minds (*citta*) and mental factors, or concomitants (*caitta*). *Fruitional causes* (*rnam par smin pa'i rgyu, vipākahetu*) are usually considered to be stained virtuous karmas or nonvirtuous karmas producing fruitional results. *Omnipresent causes* (*kun tu 'gro ba'i rgyu, sarvatragahetu*) are factors that produce afflicted phenomena, making one wander in different realms of saṃsāra and preventing liberation from it. *Homogeneous causes* (*skal mnyam gyi rgyu, sabhāgahetu*) are causes whose results belong to the same class, such as virtuous karmas producing and multiplying further virtuous karmas. Within the five results, *fruitional results* (*rnam smin gyi 'bras bu, vipākaphala*) are mental and physical components of the appropriated aggregates (*nyer len gyi phung po, upādānaskandha*) that are products of fruitional causes created in previous lives. *Results concordant with causes* (*rgyu mthun gyi 'bras bu, niṣyandaphala*) are results concordant with, in particular, omnipresent causes and homogeneous causes; of their two types, the ones concordant with previous actions are *actions as results concordant with*

causes (*byed pa rgyu mthun gyi 'bras bu*), such as striving to perform acts of generosity because of acts of generosity performed in previous lives, while the ones concordant with results of previous actions are *experiences as results concordant with causes* (*myong ba rgyu mthun gyi 'bras bu*), such as enjoying wealth owing to acts of generosity performed in previous lives. *Dominant results* (*bdag po'i 'bras bu, adhipatiphala*) are general results of producing causes; they can also be identified more specifically as good or bad locales one is born into and "dominates" owing to previous good or bad karmas. *Person-made results* (*skyes bus byed pa'i 'bras bu, puruṣakāraphala*) are results of coemergent causes and concomitant causes; they are results produced by living beings, such as material products, attainments of different stages of the path, and so on. *Separative results* (*bral ba'i 'bras bu, visaṃyogaphala*), which properly speaking are not results *produced* by causes, are such states as nirvāṇa, wherein the objects of abandonment are eliminated through wisdom.

15. These thinkers include Sakya Pandita and Gorampa.
16. The other five are space (*nam mkha', ākāśa*), nonanalytical cessation (*so sor brtags pa ma yin pas 'gog pa, apratisaṃkhyānirodha*), analytical cessation (*so sor brtags pas 'gog pa, pratisaṃkhyānirodha*), motionlessness (*mi g.yo ba, āniñjya*), and cessation of discrimination and feelings (*'du shes dang tshor ba 'gog pa, saṃjñāvedayitanirodha*). *Abhidharmasamuccaya, Chos mngon pa kun las btus pa,* D4049, sems tsam, ri, 53b–54a.
17. Ibid., 54a.
18. Ibid.
19. Apte, *Practical Sanskrit-English Dictionary,* 589.
20. Edgerton, *Buddhist Sanskrit Grammar and Dictionary,* 188.
21. The narrowness of the term *dge ba* is one of the reasons why I prefer to translate it as "virtue," and not as "good(ness)," for example. After all, I am concerned with specifically *Tibetan* perspectives on the question of ultimate virtue. "Good" (which better translates such Tibetan terms as *bzang po, yag po,* or *legs pa*) would be too broad, too inclusive. (Cf. *Vajradhvaja's Dedication,* cited in the next chapter, which uses both "good" and "virtue" even in one and the same verse.) For example, some phenomena—such as a thought or mind—can be called in Tibetan both *bzang po* and *dge ba* (with related but different connotations). Yet others—such as a book—can be said to be *bzang po,* but cannot be called *dge ba,* in a nonmetaphorical sense at least. This is somewhat similar to "goodness" being a broader category than "virtue" in English. There is one advantage of translating *dge ba* or *kuśala* as "good": in contrast to "virtue," "good"—similarly to the Sanskrit and Tibetan terms—can be taken as either a noun or an adjective. But given the aforementioned reasons, I prefer to use "virtue" for *dge ba,* and whenever the latter is used in the adjectival sense to translate it as "virtuous." It is also worth mentioning that because *dge ba* can be used both in the adjectival and the nominal sense, the expression *chos dbyings*

dge ba, for example, can indicate that the dharma-sphere (*chos dbyings*) has virtue as its quality and is therefore virtuous, or that it functions or acts as a virtue and is therefore a virtue itself. Although this is an important distinction, the Tibetan polemics regarding the ultimate virtue—including the virtue of the dharma-sphere—that we will be dealing with do not address it, and this is yet another reason why, depending on context, I translate *dge ba* as either "virtue" or "virtuous."

22. Ultimate reality is a hotly debated topic in Tibet, in large part because its correct understanding is believed to be crucial for achieving the highest Buddhist objective—nirvāṇa. Tibetan thinkers commonly claim that if the ultimate is not correctly identified or understood, one will not be able to directly realize it and cultivate that realization in contemplative practice, a practice without which the doors to awakening are closed.
23. For details, see Tsering Wangchuk, *"Uttaratantra" in the Land of Snows.*
24. For details, see Komarovski, *Tibetan Buddhism and Mystical Experience.*
25. *Prajñānāmamūlamadhyamakakārikā, Dbu ma rtsa ba'i tshig le'ur byas pa shes rab ces bya ba.* Hereafter, *Wisdom.*
26. *Mahāyānottaratantraśāstra, Theg pa chen po rgyud bla ma.* Hereafter, *Sublime Continuum.*
27. It should be noted that this question concerns the dedication of virtues to one's own final awakening of buddhahood for the sake of others, not giving one's virtues to or sharing them with others either before or after that goal has been achieved. The term *dedication* translates the Tibetan (*yongs su*) *bsngo ba,* which itself is the translation of the Sanskrit *pariṇāmanā.* While some scholars working in the field of East Asian Buddhism tend to interpret *pariṇāmanā* (usually rendered *huixiang* in Chinese) as "merit transfer" or "sharing merits" and interpret it as actually giving to or sharing with others one's own positive karmas, virtues, and so on, this does not apply in the world of Tibetan Buddhism. Tibetan thinkers would argue against interpreting *bsngo ba* as transferring or sharing merits on the grounds that since buddhas have inexhaustible, limitless virtues, and since the sole purpose of becoming a buddha is to benefit others, were the sharing of virtues possible, the buddhas would have already shared them with all sentient beings, thereby alleviating all sufferings and bringing everyone to awakening. As for those who have not yet achieved buddhahood, we can recall the often repeated "axiom" regarding the "karmic law," namely, that one cannot experience results of karmas that have not been performed by oneself. This position makes it impossible for others to experience results of positive karmas dedicated to them even if such sharing were possible. And even if, hypothetically speaking, positive karmic potentials from karmas performed by one person could be possessed by another, they would cease being karmic potentials per se because no karmas can be performed, their potentials accumulated, and their results ripen in the mental continua of those who

did not have the intention to perform those karmas in first place. For further details of the usage and translation of the term *pariṇāmanā,* see also Nagao, "Usages and Meanings of Pariṇāmanā."

28. For different approaches to this issue see Jackson, *Enlightenment by a Single Means.*

3. The Ultimate Is a Virtue Worth Dedicating

1. *Dgongs gcig pa'i 'grel chen snang mdzad ye shes sgron me.* Hereafter, *Illuminating Lamp.* Passages from the root text of the *Single Intent* (*Dgongs gcig*) are contained in *Writings on the Holy Dharma of Single Intent* (*Dam chos dgongs pa gcig pa'i yig cha*). Hereafter, *Writings.* They are supplemented with commentaries and additions by several authors, of which *Illuminating Lamp* is the most extensive. The discussion in this chapter is based on *Writings,* 2:137–43, 402–3, 411–15. Several passages from that source are not found in *Snang mdzad ye shes kyi sgron ma*—the earliest extant version of the manuscript, likely produced between 1267 and 1290—whose unpublished edition by Sobisch I also utilized (regarding that version see Sobisch's foreword to the manuscript's reproduction, *Illuminator, A Light of Gnosis*). I indicate those passages in the notes as "possibly a later addition."
2. Although there is no reason to doubt that the *Single Intent's* teachings derive from Jikten Gönpo, it is difficult to clearly distinguish between the exact words of Jikten Gönpo on the one hand and their paraphrasing, interpretation, and additions by Sherap Jungné on the other. For details of the composition and authorship of the *Single Intent* and its commentaries, see the introduction in Sobisch, *Buddha's Single Intention.*
3. *'khor 'das thams cad kyi dge ba's rtsa pa bsngo ba. Illuminating Lamp,* 2:137.
4. *bdag gis sbyin sogs bgyis pa'i bsod nams 'dis // 'gro la phan phyir sangs rgyas 'grub par shog.* Atīśa, *Ritual and Vows of the Generation of the Mind [of Awakening]* [*Cittotpādasaṃvaravidhikrama, Sems bskyed pa dang sdom pa'i cho ga'i rim pa*], D3969, dbu ma, gi, 246a.
5. *Illuminating Lamp,* 2:137–38.
6. *Lus* [*sic: Lung*] *dbyen gyi gzhi.*
7. *Illuminating Lamp,* 138–39.
8. Ibid., 139–40.
9. See also Shakya Chokden's discussion of differences between dedication and aspirational resolve in his reply to question 19 from *Good Questions* in chapter 7.
10. *Madhyāntavibhāga, Dbus dang mtha' rnam par 'byed pa.*
11. *Illuminating Lamp,* 140–41. As Nagao points out, "The Tibetan bsngo ba, probably means 'to intend', 'to desire', as this root is interpreted 'yid kyis mos pa byed pa', or 'smon 'dun byed pa'." He also observes that "to change" and "to

transform" are predominant in the root pari √ṇam. "Usages and Meanings of Pariṇāmanā," 83.

12. *Āryatathāgatagarbhanāmamahāyānasūtra, 'Phags pa de bzhin gshegs pa'i snying po zhes bya ba theg pa chen po'i mdo.*
13. *Āryāṅgulimālīyanāmamahāyānasūtra, 'Phags pa sor mo'i phreng ba la phan pa zhes bya ba theg pa chen po'i mdo.*
14. *'jam dpal sangs rgyas thams cad kyis shin tu nan tan gyis btags kyang de bzhin gshegs pa'i snying po mi rtag par ma brnyes te / sems can thams cad la rtag pa'i dbyings / chos kyi dbyings / mtshan dang dpe byad bzang pos brgyan pa'i chos kyi dbyings yod do.* D213, mdo sde, tsha, 157a.
15. *gal te de bzhin gshegs pa'i snying po med par gyur na / tshul khrims dang brtul zhugs la 'bad pa yang don med par 'gyur te / dper na chu bsrubs pa la mar mi 'byung ba bzhin no.* Ibid.
16. Those extremes are mentioned, for example, at the beginning of *Wisdom*, by Nāgārjuna, who writes that the dependent origination (Skt., *pratītyasamutpāda*) is free from all extremes of cessation, production, annihilation, permanence, coming, going, multiplicity, and oneness. *Prajñānāmamūlamadhyamakakārikā, Dbu ma rtsa ba'i tshig le'ur byas pa shes rab ces bya ba,* D3824, dbu ma, tsa, 1a.
17. *yod kyang mu stegs kyi rtag pa der mi gyur. Illuminating Lamp,* 141.
18. *dper na shel dang me shel dag // dag pa yi ni mtshan nyid can // nyi ma'i zer gyis phog pa na // de dag rang gi 'od zer 'byin // de bzhin kun gzhi'i rnam shes kyang // bde gshegs snying po khams dge ba // zag med yon tan ldan pa de // bsngos na 'bras bu smin par 'gyur.* Possibly a later addition. *Āryaghanavyūhanāmamahāyānasūtra, 'Phags pa rgyan stug po bkod pa zhes bya ba theg pa chen po'i mdo,* D110, mdo sde, cha, 43b, provides a rather different wording, and does not use *bsngos* in the last line, which instead reads: *gzhan du 'gyur na rab tu 'byin.* Note that this passage can be understood as endorsing the overlap, if not equivalence, between the universal basis consciousness and (the element of) the sugata-essence.
19. *sa rnams sna tshogs kun gzhi ste // bde gshegs snying po dge ba'ang de.* Ibid., 55b. The text goes on to explain: "Tathāgata teaches that essence // With the phrase *universal basis*" (*snying po de la kun gzhi sgras // de bzhin gshegs pa ston pa mdzad*). Thus, *universal basis* and *universal basis consciousness* are used here interchangeably to designate the tathāgata-essence.
20. *'gro kun dge ba ji snyed yod pa dang. Vajradhvajapariṇāmanā, Rdo rje rgyal mtshan gyi bsngo ba,* H94, phal chen, ga, 66a; *Illuminating Lamp,* 141–42. This dedication, the last of the ten extensive Vajradhvaja's dedications of possessions, virtues, etc., starts on 31a with the question, "What is the tenth complete dedication of bodhisattva-mahasattvas, which is called 'immeasurable dharma-sphere'?" (*byang chub sems dpa' sems dpa' chen po rnams kyi yongs su bsngo ba chos kyi dbyings tshad med pa zhes bya ba bcu pa gang zhe na*). The

discussion of the dedication of virtues in that section continuously invokes the dharma-sphere and, as we will see, can be interpreted in terms of the dedication of the dharma-sphere itself. *Vajradhvaja's Dedication* forms part of the collection of Mahāyāna sūtras known as *Garland Sūtra* [*Avataṃsakasūtra, Mdo sde phal po che*]. The chapter is devotional rather than philosophical in character, which means that its contents can be interpreted differently philosophically.

21. Note that while the *Dense Array Sūtra*'s first passage is unambiguous about the dedication of the sugata-essence, less clear is the sense in which it treats it as a virtue. According to the passage above, a crystal and a sunstone emit light not on their own but when they are hit by sunlight. They are pure in terms of allowing the sun's rays to penetrate in such a way that light emerges as a result. The light is emitted due to the interaction between them and the external light. The element of the sugata-essence, which in the passage is also referred to as the "universal basis consciousness," is virtuous in a similar way. It does not just produce positive results on its own. Rather, they arise as a result of its interaction with the light-like dedication. The passage does not make clear whether the sugata-essence actively participates in this interactive process as an actual cause or is a merely static object of its dedication. The second passage is even less clear. Treating the sugata-essence as a virtue, it likens it to grounds, which it explicitly calls "bases," not "causes," of various things. While the ground or land provides space and serves as a support for multiple things, it is not the cause of them all. It can be argued, therefore, that all that this second passage indicates is that the sugata-essence is virtuous for providing support for various positive phenomena, not for being their actual cause. What the two passages do make clear is that the sugata-essence is a virtue, however understood.
22. *Āryaśrīmālādevīsiṃhanādanāmamahāyānasūtra, 'Phags pa lha mo dpal phreng gi seng ge'i sgra zhes bya ba theg pa chen po'i mdo.*
23. *Illuminating Lamp*, 142.
24. *Yum rgyas pa*, that is, *Perfection of Wisdom Sūtra in Twenty-Five Thousand Lines* (*Pañcaviṃśatisāhasrikāprajñāpāramitā, Shes rab kyi pha rol tu phyin pa stong phrag nyi shu lnga pa*). Note that this text is subsumed under the second dharmacakra, and *Lion's Roar* under the third.
25. *Illuminating Lamp*, 142.
26. *Thabs mkhas pa'i dris lan gser zhun ma.* Hereafter, *Refined Gold*. The text is no longer extant.
27. *rgya mtsho lta bu'i khams dge ba // byas bsags gnyer ma'i rlabs chen gyis.* Ibid. See chap. 7 for a more extensive quotation in Shakya Chokden's reply to questions 8, 9, and 14 from *Good Questions*.
28. *'gro kun dge ba ji snyed yod pa dang // byas dang byed 'gyur de bzhin byed pa dag // bzang po ji bzhin de 'dra'i sa dag la // kun nas kun kyang bzang por reg* [H: *red*] *gyur cig.* H94, phal chen, ga, 66a.

29. *rgyal ba'i sras kyis 'di la bslab bya ste // ji snyed gang yod mtha' dag ma lus dang // khams rnams kun kyang yongs su bsdu byas te // ci nas bde gshegs stobs la 'jug par bsngo // ji ltar bcom ldan 'das kyis ni // sngon gyi bsngo ba mdzad pa ltar // rnal 'byor las byung dge ba bsngo // byang chub sems dpa'i mthu yis ni // rang gi sems kyang bsngo bar bya // de bzhin nyid kyi rang bzhin ci 'dra dang // de bzhin nyid kyi mtshan nyid ci 'dra dang // de bzhin nyid kyi ngang tshul ci 'dra ba // de 'dra'i las rnams kun kyang yongs su bsngo.* H94, phal chen, ga, 67a; the last nine lines are possibly a later addition.
30. *Illuminating Lamp,* 142–43, possibly a later addition. *Illuminating Lamp* reads *don dam pa'i dge ba* in contrast to Asaṅga's *don dam pas dge ba.*
31. Reference to the roots of accumulated virtues, since the root of existent virtue is equated with the tathāgata-essence.
32. *Illuminating Lamp,* 143.
33. *phyag rgya chen po yon tan thams cad kyi bdag nyid yin. Illuminating Lamp,* 402.
34. *gal te sangs rgyas khams med na // sdug la'ang skyo bar mi 'gyur zhing // mya ngan 'das la 'dun pa dang // don gnyer smon pa'ang med par 'gyur.* D4024, sems tsam, phi, 56b.
35. *pha rol phyin lnga byang chub yon tan ji snyed pa // de dag kun kyang shes rab pha rol phyin las skye. Āryaprajñāpāramitāsañcayagāthā, 'Phags pa shes rab kyi pha rol tu phyin pa sdud pa tshigs su bcad pa,* H17, sna tshogs, ka, 193a. Note that both passages, and especially the second, discuss the perfections—including the perfection of wisdom—as something one develops. Furthermore, they do not explicitly indicate that the perfection of wisdom itself is the ultimate reality.
36. *'di la bsal bya ci yang med // gzhag par bya ba cung zad med // yang dag nyid la yang dag lta // yang dag mthong nas* [D: *na*] *rnam par grol.* D4024, sems tsam, phi, 61b. See chap. 8, note 14, for a more extensive quotation.
37. *'dus byas bde dang 'dus ma byas bde gang yin pa // bde ba de kun 'di las 'byung bar rig par bya.* H17, sna tshogs, ka, 193a.
38. *sangs rgyas sras dang nyan thos rang rgyal lha rnams dang // 'gro ba kun gyi bde skyid chos rnams ji snyed pa // de kun shes rab pha rol phyin pa mchog las byung.* Ibid., 210a; *Illuminating Lamp,* 402–3.
39. *stong nyid rtogs na stong nyid rgyu 'bras su 'byung. Illuminating Lamp,* 411.
40. *rten cing 'brel 'byung ma gtogs pa'i // chos 'ga' yod pa ma yin te // de phyir stong nyid ma yin pa'i // chos 'ga' yod pa ma yin no.* D3824, dbu ma, tsa, 15a; *Illuminating Lamp,* 411, 414–15.

4. The Ultimate Is Not a Virtue Unless You Do Not Mean It

1. *Sdom pa gsum gyi rab tu dbye ba.* Hereafter, *Thorough Differentiation.* It is contained in Sakya Pandita Künga Gyeltsen, *Clear Differentiation,* which provides both an alternative English translation and the Tibetan text. (*A Clear Differen-*

tiation of the Three Codes and *Thorough Differentiation of the Three Types of Vows* are different translations of *Sdom pa gsum gyi rab tu dbye ba.*) The discussion in this chapter is based on verses 42–142 of chapter 1 of *Thorough Differentiation,* following the enumeration of the translator, Jared Douglas Rhoton. Translations of the passages from the *Thorough Differentiation* are my own, based on the Tibetan text.

2. Rhoton, introduction, 4.
3. For details, see Rhoton, introduction; and Jackson, *Enlightenment by a Single Means,* 67ff.
4. Allegedly, Sakya Pandita was dissuaded from completing the text but eventually decided to finish it after a dream one night in which the Buddha image was sunk in filth. He took it up and cleaned it off, but that upset many people. He then put the image down, and it was smeared with filth again, which made the bodhisattva Mañjuśrī (the embodiment of wisdom) turn his back on him and made Nāgārjuna ill. Most likely, Sakya Pandita interpreted this dream to mean that the Buddhist teachings were sunk in the filth of wrong interpretations by his contemporaries and that it was his responsibility to purify them through polemical refutations. He realized that if he did so, it would make many people unhappy, but that if he did not, it would displease those who supported right understanding of Buddhism. Consequently, after waking up, he proceeded to complete the text. See Rhoton, introduction, 9.
5. Verses 59–62, cited below.
6. While chronologically it is difficult to establish a direct link between *Single Intent* and Sakya Pandita's text, and while it is unlikely that *Thorough Differentiation* was a direct reply to *Single Intent,* it is quite likely that Sakya Pandita was aware of Jikten Gönpo's earlier teachings on the topics, which later found their way into that text. Sobisch, "Were Sa-pan and 'Jig-rten-mgon-po 'Neo-conservatives'?," 24n5.
7. This term can be understood as referring here to the aforementioned category of unspecified or neutral phenomena—not to the mental factor of equanimity which is one of the eleven virtuous mental factors (see chap. 2, note 4). For different interpretations of "equanimity" in this passage see Gorampa's and Shakya Chokden's answers to question 2 from *Good Questions.*
8. *las la dge sdig lung ma bstan // yin zhes rgyal bas mdo las gsungs // dge ba legs par spyad pa ste // rnam smin bde ba skyed pa yin // sdig pa nyes par spyad pa ste // 'bras bu sdug bsngal skyed par byed // btang snyoms gnyis ka ma yin pas // rnam par smin pa'ang gnyis ka min.*
9. *'di dag byas pa'i las yin pas // 'dus byas yin par shes par bya // chos kyi dbyings ni 'dus ma byas // yin pa'i phyir na las ma yin // des na dge dang sdig pa min // las la thub pas rnam gnyis gsungs // sems pa dang ni bsam pa'o // sems pa yid kyi las yin te // bsam pa de ni lus ngag gi'o // chos kyi dbyings ni gnyis ka min // de phyir dge sdig las las grol.*

10. *gzhan yang las la rnam bzhi gsungs // las dkar rnam smin dkar ba dang // las gnag rnam smin gnag pa dang // las dkar rnam smin gnag pa dang // las gnag rnam smin dkar ba'o // bsam pa dag pa'i sbyin pa sogs // gnyis ka dkar bas mkhas pas bya // bza ba'i don du gsod pa sogs // gnyis ka gnag pas mkhas pas spang // mang po bskyab phyir gcig gsod sogs // las gnag rnam smin dkar na bya // gsad phyir sbyin pa gtong la sogs // las dkar rnam smin gnag pa spang.*
11. *gzhan yang las la rnam ngyis gsungs // 'phen byed las dang rdzogs byed las // de dag dbye na mu bzhi yod // 'phen byed dge bas 'phangs pa la // rdzogs byed kyang ni dge ba dang // 'phen byed sdig pas 'phangs pa la // rdzogs byed kyang nis sdig pa dang // 'phen byed dge la rdzogs byed sdig // 'phen byed sdig la rdzogs byed dge.*
12. *gzhan yang gcig tu dkar ba dang // gcig tu gnag dang 'dren ma'i las // rnam pa gsum du thub pas gsungs // gcig tu dkar bas bde ba bskyed // gcig tu gnag pas sdug bsngal bskyed // 'dren ma'i las kyi bde ba dang // sdug bsngal 'dren ma bskyed par gsungs.*
13. *mu stegs grangs can pa rnams ni // gshis la dge sdig yod ces zer // rgyu la 'bras bu gnas par 'dod // bod kyang la la de rjes 'brang // rdo rje rgyal mtshan bsngo ba las // 'gro kun dge ba ji snyed yod // byas dang byed 'gyur byed pa zhes // gsungs pa'i dgongs pa 'chad pa la // kha cig grangs can lugs bzhin du // yod pa'i dge ba zhes bya ba // rang byung du ni grub par 'dod // de la bde gshegs snying po zer // grang can lugs 'di mi 'thad pas // lung dang rigs pas dgag par bya // bde gshegs snying po zhes bya ba // chos dbyings 'gyur med nyid la gsungs.*
14. *des na chos kyi dbyings la ni // bsngo ba med ces rgyal bas bshad.*
15. *Saṃpuṭanāmamahātantra, Yang dag par sbyor ba zhes bya ba'i rgyud chen po.*
16. *Rājaparikathāratnāvali, Rgyal po la gtam bya ba rin po che'i phreng ba.*
17. *kha cig bde gshegs snying po'i sgra // stong nyid snying rje'i snying por 'dod // 'di ni bde gshegs snying po'i khams // sbyong byed yin gyi khams dngos min.* In this context, Sakya Pandita appears to treat the element of the sugata-essence and the sugata-essence as the same.
18. *Pramāṇavārttikakārikā, Tshad ma rnam 'grel gyi tshig le'ur byas pa.*
19. *Śikṣāsamuccaya, Bslab pa kun las btus pa.*
20. Note that according to Sakya Pandita, compassion itself does not necessarily have to be virtuous; it can also be nonvirtuous. When rejecting the claim that love and compassion are the "natural virtues" (*gshis kyi dge ba*), he argues that the Buddha taught that unskillful love and compassion can serve as the causes of rebirth in low transmigrations, and he treated only *skillful* love and compassion as virtues. *Thorough Differentiation*, v. 85.
21. See chap. 2, note 4.
22. *don dam dge ba zhes bshad pa // de bzhin nyid la gsungs pa yin // don dam sdig pa 'khor ba kun // nam mkha' so sor brtags min gnyis // don dam lung ma bstan zhes bshad.*
23. *de bzhin nyid la dge ba zhes // bshad pa'i dgongs pa 'di ltar yin // dper na nad dang bral ba ni // lus bde nya ngan med pa la // sems bde zhes ni 'jig rten zer // 'di dag*

sdug bsngal med pa las // gzhan pa'i bde ba med mod kyi // 'on kyang sdug bsngal med tsam la // bde ba yin zhes kun la grags // de bzhin chos kyi dbyings la yang // sdig pa med pa tsam zhig las // lhag pa'i dge ba med mod kyi // dge ba yin zhes btags par zad.

24. *de bzhin chos kyi dbyings la yang // dge ba yin zhes gsungs gyur kyang // 'bras bu bde ba bskyed pa yi // dge ba dngos ni ma yin no.*
25. *ci nas chos dbyings dge ba nyid // yin na ha cang thal 'gyur te // chos kyi dbyings las ma gtogs pa'i // chos gzhan med phyir sdig pa dang // lung ma bstan yang dge bar 'gyur // de lta yin na sems can kun // ngan 'gror 'gro ba mi srid do.*
26. *Mahāyānasūtrālaṃkāra, Theg pa chen po mdo sde'i rgyan.*
27. *chos dbyings yod pa'ang ma yin te // yod tsam mi rtag gis khyab par // chos kyi grags pas legs par gsungs.*
28. *gal te mya ngan 'das dngos na // mya ngan 'das pa 'dus byas gyur // dngos po 'dus byas ma yin pa // 'ga' yang gang na'ang yod ma yin. Prajñānāmamūlamadhyamakakārikā, Dbu ma rtsa ba'i tshig le'ur byas pa shes rab ces bya ba,* D3824, dbu ma, tsa, 16a–b.
29. *rigs pas kyang ni 'di 'grub ste // yod tsam don byed nus phyir ro // chos kyi dbyings la bya byed med // de ni spros bral yin phyir ro.*
30. *gzhan yang yod pa'i dge ba ni // chos nyid yin na 'gro kun gyi // dge ba zhes bya smos ci dgos // bems po dang ni dngos med dang // 'phags pa'i chos nyid ci mi bsngo.* Depending on context, āryas who have not yet achieved nirvāṇa can be either included in or excluded from the category of sentient beings; here it is the latter.
31. *rdo rje rgyal mtshan nyid las kyang // yod pa zhes bya bsgrub par gsungs.*
32. *bsngo bas 'gyur na 'dus byas 'gyur // mi 'gyur bsngo ba don med yin // mdo sde rnams las chos kyi dbyings // 'gyur ba med ces rgyal bas gsungs.*
33. *rang bzhin rgyu dang rkyen las ni // 'byung bar rigs pa ma yin no // rgyu dang rkyen las byung ba yi // rang bzhin byas pa can du 'gyur // rang bzhin byas pa can zhes byar // ji lta bur na rung bar 'gyur // rang bzhin dag ni bcos min dang // gzhan la ltos pa med pa yin.* D3824, dbu ma, tsa, 8b.
34. *gal te rang bzhin gyis yod na // de ni med nyid mi 'gyur ro // rang bzhin gzhan du 'gyur ba ni // nam yang 'thad par mi 'gyur ro.* Ibid., 9a.
35. *gal te chos nyid de bzhin nyid // bsngo bya'i dge ba ma yin mod // byang chub sems dpa'i blo sbyong la // bsngos kyang nyes pa med snyam na.*
36. *ma yin 'di la nyes pa yod // dmigs pa'i 'du shes yod pa'i phyir // bsngo ba dug dang bcas par 'gyur.*
37. *chos nyid bsngo rgyur byed na ni // blo sbyong du yang mi rung ngo.*
38. *yongs su bsngo ba khyad par can // de yi byed pa mchog yin no // de ni dmigs med rnam pa can // phyin ci ma log mtshan nyid do. Abhisamayālaṃkāranāmaprajñāpāramitopadeśaśāstrakārikā, Shes rab kyi pha rol tu phyin pa'i man ngag gi bstan bcos mngon par rtogs pa'i rgyan zhes bya ba'i tshig le'ur byas pa,* D3786, shes phyin, ka, 5b.

39. *la la bde gshegs snying po'i sgra // chos kyi dbyings la mi zer bar // sems can kho na'i khams la 'dod.*
40. *khams de dngos po'am dngos med dam // gnyis ka min par spros bral yin // rnam pa gsum las gzhan mi srid // dngos po yin na bems po dang // rig pa gnyis su kha tshon chod // bems po sems can khams nyid du // 'dod pa mu stegs 'ga' yi lugs // yin gyi sangs rgyas pa la med // rig pa yin na rnam shes kyi // tshogs brgyad nyid las 'da' ba med // tshogs brgyad 'dus byas yin pa'i phyir // bde gshegs snying por mi 'thad de // mdo las bde gshegs snying po ni // 'dus ma byas su gsungs phyir ro.*
41. *'ga' las zag med sems rgyud ces // gsungs pa kun gzhi'i rnam shes kyi // gsal cha nyid la dgongs pa yin // de ni ma bsgribs lung ma bstan // yin phyir dge ba'i tha snyad med // 'on te zag med sems rgyud ces // tshogs brgyad las gzhan yod na ni // de tshe rnam shes tshogs dgur 'gyur // des na tshogs brgyad las gzhan pa'i // zag med sems rgyud mi 'thad do.*
42. *dngos med yin na don byed med // de la dge sdig 'thad ma yin.*
43. *gal te sems can khams dngos dang // dngos med gnyis ka ma yin par // spros bral yin na sngar bshad pa'i // chos kyi dbyings las 'da' ba med // de lta yin na chos kyi dbyings // dge sdig med par bshad zin to.*
44. *gal te bems po'i chos kyi dbyings // bde gshegs snying po ma yin yang // sems can rnams kyi chos kyi dbyings // bde gshegs snying po yin snyam na // ma yin chos kyi dbyings la ni // dbye ba med par rgyal bas gsungs // rigs pas kyang ni 'di 'grub bo.*
45. *des na de bzhin gshegs pa yi // snying po spros bral yin pa'i phyir // sems can rnams las sangs rgyas dang // 'khor ba gnyis ka 'byung ba 'thad.*
46. *gang la stong pa nyid rung ba // de la thams cad rung ba yin // gang la stong nyid mi rung ba // de la thams cad rung ma yin.* D3824, dbu ma, tsa, 15a.
47. Sakya Pandita provides a slightly different wording of the passage that was cited by Dorjé Sherap in the previous chapter: *gal te bde gshegs khams med na // sdug la skyo bar mi 'gyur zhing // nya ngan 'das la 'dod pa dang // don gnyer smon pa'ang med par 'gyur.*
48. *nye bar len pa'i phung po lnga // sdug bsngal yin zhing mya ngan las // 'das pa bde ba yin pas na // sems ni rang gnas snyeg pa'i phyir.*
49. *me yi sgrub byed tsha ba ltar // bde gshegs khams kyi sgrub byed 'thad.*
50. The five faults are faintheartedness (*sems zhum*), despising lowly beings (*sems can dman la brnyas pa*), not upholding what is true (*yang dag mi 'dzin*), deprecation of the true Dharma (*yang dag chos la skur*), and excessive attachment to self (*bdag chags lhag pa*).
51. *'on kyang mdo sde 'ga' zhig dang // theg pa chen po rgyud bla mar // gos ngan nang na rin chen ltar // sems can rnams la sangs rgyas kyi // snying po yod par gsungs pa ni // dgongs pa yin par shes par bya // de yi dgongs gzhi stong nyid yin // dgos pa skyon lnga spang phyir gsungs // dngos la gnod byed tshad ma ni // de 'dra'i sangs rgyas khams yod na // mu stegs bdag dang mtshungs pa dang // bden pa'i dngos por 'gyur phyir dang // nges pa'i don gyi mdo sde dang // rnam pa kun tu 'gal phyir ro.*

52. *Madhyamakāvatāra, Dbu ma la 'jug pa.*
53. *bsngo ba de yang mdor bsdu na // gnas dang gnas ma yin pa gnyis // gnas kyi bsngo ba 'grub par gsungs // gnas min bsngos kyang 'grub mi 'gyur.*
54. *Display of the Positive Qualities of Noble Mañjuśrī's Buddha-Field* (*Āryamañjuśrībuddhakṣetraguṇavyūhanāmamahāyānasūtra, 'Phags pa 'jam dpal gyi sangs rgyas kyi zhing gi yon tan bkod pa zhes bya ba theg pa chen po'i mdo*), D59, dkon brtsegs, ga, 279a. This text forms part of the collection of Mahāyāna sūtras known as the *Jewel Heap Sūtra* [*Ratnakūṭasūtra, Dkon mchog brtsegs pa'i mdo*].
55. *'di dag gnyis ka mdo las gsungs // 'jam dpal sangs rgyas zhing las ni // chos rnams thams cad rkyen bzhin te // 'dun pa'i rtsa la rab tu gnas // gang gis smon lam ci btab pa // de 'dra'i 'bras bu thob par 'gyur // zhes gsungs 'di ni gnas la dgongs // dri med byin gyis zhus pa'i mdor // chos rnams chos nyid bsngo ba yis // mi 'gyur gal te gyur na ni // dang po'i sangs rgyas gcig nyid kyi // bsngo ba deng sang cis mi 'grub // ces gsungs 'di ni gnas min gyi // bsngo ba nyid la dgongs pa yin.* In the last verse of that passage, Sakya Pandita is paraphrasing in the verse form the prose passage from the *Sūtra Requested by Noble Vimaladattā* [*Āryavimaladattāparipṛcchānāmamahāyānasūtra, 'Phags pa dri ma med kyis byin pas zhus pa zhes bya ba theg pa chen po'i mdo*], D77, dkon brtsegs, ca, 250a, which is discussed in Gorampa's and Shakya Chokden's answers to Shakya Chokden's question 20. As we will see, the sūtra passage referred to aspirational resolve, not dedication. *Sūtra Requested by Noble Vimaladattā* is also a part of the *Jewel Heap Sūtra.*
56. *des na bsgno rgyu'i dge ba dang // bshags par bya ba'i sdig pa yang // byas pa'i dge sdig yin mod kyi // ma byas pa la dge sdig med.*

5. Admiring Your Virtues, I Have Questions to Ask

1. *Sdom gsum rab dbye la dri ba legs pa*, in *Collected Writings of Gser-mdog paṇ-chen Śākya-mchog-ldan*, 17:448–62. Hereafter, *Good Questions.*
2. East-central, west-central, and eastern Tibet, respectively.
3. For further details see Komarovski, *Visions of Unity*, 20 and 37–38.
4. *Sdom pa gsum gyi bstan bcos la dris shing rtsod pa'i lan sdom gsum 'khrul spong*, in *Collected Works of Kun-mkhyen Go-rams-pa Bsod-nams-seng-ge*, 9:489–619. Hereafter, *Elimination of Mistakes* or EM.
5. *Sdom gsum gyi rab tu dbye ba'i bstan bcos kyi 'bel gtam rnam par nges pa legs bshad gser gyi thur ma*, in *Collected Writings of Gser-mdog paṇ-chen Śākya-mchog-ldan*, 6:439–7:229. Hereafter, *Golden Lancet* or GL.
6. While the questions are not numbered in *Good Questions*, both *Golden Lancet* and *Elimination of Mistakes* contain numbered sections citing and providing responses to questions raised in *Good Questions.* While in *Good Questions* and *Elimination of Mistakes* the questions follow the same order, in *Golden Lancet*

the order differs in several places. It appears that the order in *Good Questions* was the original one and that Shakya Chokden slightly altered it later, when providing his answers in *Golden Lancet*. The questions translated below have numbers based on both *Good Questions* and *Elimination of Mistakes*. Because of the differing order in *Golden Lancet* and the different ways questions are counted by Shakya Chokden and Gorampa, in order to retain the order given in *Good Questions* I have added letters to some numbers. For example, *Golden Lancet* addresses as number 12 questions numbered 19, 20, and 26 in *Elimination of Mistakes*. I list those questions as 12a, 12b, and 12c, respectively. Also, while the first two questions translated here are counted by Shakya Chokden separately as 9 and 10, Gorampa counts them as one question, 13. And while Gorampa counts questions 14–18 separately, Shakya Chokden consolidates them into question 11. The translation starts with the question numbered 9 in *Golden Lancet* and included in the question numbered 13 in *Elimination of Mistakes*, and it ends with the question numbered 24 and 36, respectively. To simplify cross-referencing, I enumerate the questions progressively, starting with number 1 for the first question and ending with number 24 for the last. I omit the question numbered 15 in *Good Questions* and 23 in *Elimination of Mistakes* because it is not relevant to our topic. There are some discrepancies in the wording of the questions contained in *Good Questions*, *Golden Lancet*, and *Elimination of Mistakes*. *Golden Lancet* also provides a few additional lines in a couple of questions. Except for several insignificant differences in the wording, other differences are addressed in this chapter's footnotes. The translations are mostly based on *Good Questions*, though they also include additional questions from *Golden Lancet* not found in *Good Questions*.

7. *dge ba gang yin thams cad kyi // rnam smin bde ba bskyed na ni // zag med dge ba'i rnam smin ci. Good Questions*, 450.
8. *btang snyoms gnyis ka ma yin na // bsam gtan bzhi pa yan chad kyi // zag bcas dge ba'i rnam smin dang // btang snyoms ces pa lung ma bstan // yin na kun gzhi'i sa bon las // rnam smin 'byung ba de ci zhig*. Ibid.
9. *las dkar zhes pa dge ba la // 'chad na rnam smin gnag pa ci // las nag* [GL: *gnag*] *ces pa sdig pa la // zer na rnam smin dkar ba ci*. Ibid., 450–51.
10. *rgyu yi kun slong sdig yin na // dus kyi kun slong dge yin kyang // las de dkar por mi 'gyur zhes // mngon pa gong mar* [*sic*, GL: *'og mar*] *ma bshad dam*. Ibid., 451.
11. *dus kyi kun slong mi dge ba // dag dang mtshungs pa'i dge ba ni // mo sham bu dang 'dra'o zhes // mngon pa gong mar mi 'byung ngam*. Ibid.
12. *rgyu yi kun slong 'phen byed kyi // gtso bo yin phyir 'phen byed rgyu // dus kyi kun slong 'grub byed kyi // gtso bo yin phyir 'grub byed rgyur // gong 'og mthun par gsungs min nam*. Ibid.
13. *'dod pa'i rten la dkar nag gis* [*sic*, GL: *gi*] *// las gnyis 'dres mar 'jog pa bzhin // rnam par smin pa'ang 'dres sam ci // de lta na ni ngan song dang // mtho ris rnam smin* [EM: *gnyis ka*] *rgyud gcig la // srid par khas len mi dgos sam*. Ibid.

14. *chos dbyings dge ba ma yin na // mngon rtogs rgyan dang rgyud bla dang // theg pa chen po bsdus pa dang // dbus rnam 'byed par gsung de ci.* Ibid. The line mentioning *Summary of Mahāyāna* [*Mahāyānasaṃgraha, Theg pa chen po bsdus pa*] is found only in *Golden Lancet.*
15. *sdig pa med tsam la dgongs na // ma sgribs lung bstan min kun ci.* Ibid. These two lines are not cited in *Golden Lancet* but are addressed in its section that provides answers to questions 8, 9, and 14.
16. *yod pa nyid la mi rtag pas // khyab par chos kyi grags pas gsungs // yod pa tsam la des khyab par // rigs pa'i gzhung lugs gang gis ston.* Ibid.
17. *klu sgrub kyi ni dbu ma las // dngos med la'ang 'dus byas kyis // khyab par gsungs pa min nam* [EM: *min nam ci,* GL: *ma yin nam*] *// de lta yin na chos kyi dbyings // 'dus byas yin par mi thal lam.* Ibid.
18. *stong nyid snying rje'i snying po can // bde gshegs snying po ma yin na // rgyas 'gyur rigs la bde gshegs kyi // snying por gsungs pa de ci zhig.* Ibid.
19. *chos dbyings rdzogs pa'i byang chub rgyur // 'gyur ba med na chos kyi dbyings // rgyu yi rigs su 'jog ces dang // 'phags pa'i chos kyi rgyu yi phyir // chos dbyings rigs su 'jog go zhes // tshad ldan gzhung las gsung de ci.* Ibid., 451–52.
20. *chos dbyings dam pa'i chos dang ni // dam pa ces bya dge ba la // tshad ldan gzhung las ma gsungs sam // chos dbyings ngo bo bdag med la* [*sic,* GL: *ma*] *// bde chen sgyu ma'i sku de yang // dge ba min par bzhed lags sam // de lta na ni bstod pa las // dge ba* [*sic,* GL: *ma*] *zhes kyang ma gsungs sam.* Ibid., 452. *Elimination of Mistakes* provides a different reading and consequently addresses the question whether the dharma-sphere itself is a virtue and whether it has been praised as such. See Gorampa's reply to question 14.
21. *chos dbyings lung ma bstan yin na / chos kyi dbyings las ma gtogs pa'i / chos gzhan med phyir dge ba dang // sdig pa'ang lung ma bstan du 'gyur // snyam pa'i dogs pa mi 'byung ngam.* Ibid.
22. *chos dbyings gsum kar mi rung na // de mtshungs dogs pa'ang ci mi 'byung.* Ibid.
23. *chos dbyings yod par mi bzhed na // chos kyi dbyings las ma gtogs pa'i // dngos po med pa'i* [*sic*] *dngos po kun* [GL and EM: *dngos po med phyir dngos kun kyang*] *// yod par mi bzhed de* [*sic*] *ci zhig* [GL: *yod par mi bzhed min de ci*]. Ibid.
24. *yod pa sgrub par gsungs pa yi* [*sic,* GL: *yis,* EM: *des*] *// chos dbyings dge bar ji ltar gnod.* Ibid. As we will see in Shakya Chokden's own answer to this question, in the first line he was referring to the term *sgrub pa* provided in the copies of *Thorough Differentiation* available to him. As a verb, *sgrub pa* can be taken as the present tense of the verb *accomplish* (*bsgrubs pa* being the past and *bsgrub pa* the future), but it would not fit the context here. Taken as a noun, as here, it indicates one of the two types of phenomena, positive and negative. Both *Thorough Differentiation*'s verse 103, which is targeted by this question, and *Elimination of Mistakes*'s answer to it deal with the word *bsgrub pa,* which, taken as a noun, can be translated as "accomplishment."
25. *mi 'gyur bsngo ba don med na // tshong dpon mdza' bo'i bu mo yis* [EM: *bu mo'i*

bus] // *smon lam btab pa de ci zhig. Good Questions*, 452. See also chap. 7, note 120.

26. *chos nyid bsngo rgyur byed pa ni // blo sbyong du yang mi rung na // gnas min bsngo ba* [EM: *bar*] *gsungs de ci. Good Questions*, 452.
27. *ma byas pa yi* [GL: *la*] *dge med na // theg pa chen po bsdus pa las // thog med dus nas ma byas pa'i* [GL: *ma byas chos nyid kyis thob pa*] *// kun gzhi steng gi zag med kyi // sa bon dge bar bshad de ci // de 'dra med na kun gzhi yi // gnyen por bshad pa de gang yin.* Ibid. On the basis of the wording provided in *Golden Lancet,* the first line reads, "If there are no virtues among the uncreated"; and the fifth line reads, "Uncreated, obtained by reality." On "the universal basis" in the sixth line, see chap. 6, note 6.
28. *bde gshegs snying po gang yin pa // de dag 'dus ma byas yin na // theg pa chen po rgyud bla mar // snying po dgur gsungs pa de ci. Good Questions*, 452.
29. *Three Bodhisattva Commentaries* (*sems 'grel skor gsum*) are three commentaries attributed to ārya bodhisattvas: Puṇḍarīka's *Stainless Light* [*Vimalaprabhā, Dri ma med pa'i 'od*], Vajragarbha's *Extensive Commentary on the "Condensed Meaning of the Hevajra Tantra"* [*Hevajrapiṇḍārthaṭīkā, Kye'i rdo rje bsdus pa'i don gyi rgya cher 'grel pa*], and Vajrapāṇi's *Meaning Commentary on the Cakrasaṃvara Tantra* [*Lakṣābhidhānāduddhṛitalaghutantrapiṇḍārthavivaraṇa, Mngon par brjod pa 'bum pa las phyung ba nyung ngu'i rgyud kyi bsdus pa'i don rnam par bshad pa*].
30. *sems can ma gtogs bems po'i yang // snying po chos dbyings yin na ni // sems can kho na sangs rgyas kyi // snying po can du 'chad pa ci // sems can ma gtogs bem po yi // chos dbyings snying po ma yin na // rgyud dang sems 'grel bskor gsum las // brtan g.yo kun la sangs rgyas kyi // snying po yod par gsung de ci. Good Questions*, 452. The first four lines are found only in *Golden Lancet.* Although *Elimination of Mistakes* does not cite them, it does provide a reply to them.
31. *gos hrul nang na rin chen gyis* [*sic*] *// dpe bstan dgongs pa can yin na // sems can rnams la rang bzhin gyi // gnas rigs med par mi 'gyur ram.* Ibid.

6. What Colors Are Virtues?

1. In discussing Shakya Chokden's and Gorampa's replies, I follow the order provided in *Golden Lancet,* with the exception of replies to questions 12 and 22. While Shakya Chokden's simultaneous reply to them in *Golden Lancet* follows his reply to question 11, I place it and Gorampa's replies to questions 12 and 22 at the beginning of chapter 8 because they focus predominantly on issues related to the buddha-essence. The overall order of Gorampa's (G) and Shakya Chokden's (S) replies in chapters 6–8 is as follows: G1, S1, G2, S2, G3, G4, G,5 G6, G7, S3–7 together, G8, G9, G14, S8–9 and 14 together, G10, S10, G11, S11, G13, S13, G15, G16, G17, S15–17 together, G18, S18, G19, S19, G20, S20, G21, S21, G12, G22, S12 and 22 together, G23, S23, G24, S24.

2. Gorampa did not have a high opinion of *Good Questions.* He writes in *Elimination of Mistakes* that only a few of the questions raise serious doubts and that there are some intelligent questions that need to be answered by those capable of analysis. Other than that, most questions are merely about the wording of Sakya Pandita's text. Some are scornful, some raise doubts about others' understanding due to Shakya Chokden's own lack of understanding, and some are simply pointless. Clearly, Gorampa does not see much good or virtue in Shakya Chokden's *Good Questions.* He writes that he initially left them unanswered but that he later decided to respond in order to refute those who, provoked by those questions, would attempt to denigrate Sakya Pandita and his teachings; in order to help those who believe in those teachings but cannot understand them on their own; and in order to show to followers that those questions indeed can be answered. *Elimination of Mistakes,* 492–93.
3. *de mtha' de yi rnam smin ni.* D3786, shes phyin, ka, 13a.
4. *'di ni rnam par bzhag pa gzhan kho na yin te / de'i phyir theg pa gzhan la brten nas ni gang du'ang sun 'byin pa brjod par mi bya'o. Sputhārtha, Don gsal,* D3793, shes phyin, ja, 86b; *Elimination of Mistakes,* 508.
5. *Golden Lancet,* 475–76.
6. Note that Shakya Chokden himself distinguishes between the universal basis and the universal basis consciousness. For details, see Komarovski, *Radiant Emptiness,* 191–93; and Komarovski, "There Are No Dharmas Apart from the Dharma-Sphere," 178–79.
7. *tshig rkang pa snyoms pa'i ched du.* An obvious twist on the word *equanimity,* referring here to making that line contain the same number of syllables as the other lines in the passage.
8. A well-known claim regarding the universal basis consciousness made by Yogācāra thinkers and those who adopt that category is that both the universal basis consciousness and the seeds of virtuous and nonvirtuous karmas stored in it are unspecified phenomena and thus concordant in terms of their entities.
9. *Elimination of Mistakes,* 508–10.
10. *rnam par rtog pa med pa yi // dge ba'i las kyi rnam smin ni // sems kyi tshor ba kho nar 'dod // mi dge ba'i ni lus kyi yin.* D4089, mngon pa, ku, 13a.
11. *mi dge'i las kyi rnam smin ni // lus kyi tshor ba sdug bsngal te // dge ba'i las la rtog bcas dang // rtog pa med pa gnyis yod la // rtog bcas dge ba'i rnam smin ni // lus kyi tshor ba bde bar nges // rtog med dge la bde ba dang // bcas dang btang snyoms kho na ba // gnyis ka'i rnam smin sems tshor yin // bde dang bcas pa'i rnam smin ni // sems kyi tshor ba bde ba ste // btang snyoms kho na dang bcas pa'i // rnam smin sems tshor btang snyoms so. Golden Lancet,* 477.
12. *bsam gtan gsum pa'i bar dge ba // bde ba myong 'gyur de yan chad // sdug min bde min myong 'gyur ba.* D4089, mngon pa, ku, 12b; *Golden Lancet,* 477.
13. See also Shakya Chokden's reply to question 13.

14. *btang snyoms bde sdug gnyis min pas // rnam smin gnyis min btang snyoms so.* *Golden Lancet,* 477–78.
15. *Elimination of Mistakes,* 510–11.
16. Ibid., 511.
17. Ibid., 511–12.
18. *kun slong rnam gnyis rgyu dang ni // de yi dus kyi slong zhes bya // gnyis las dang po rab 'jug byed // gnyis pa rjes su 'jug byed yin.* D4089, mngon pa, ku, 11a.
19. *rgyu'i kun nas slong ba ni 'phen par byed pa yin pa'i phyir rab tu 'jug par byed pa yin no // de'i dus kyi kun nas slong ba ni bya ba'i dus su mthun par 'jug par yin pa'i phyir rjes su 'jug par byed pa yin no // da ni bya ba de la de'i nus pa ci zhig yod / 'phangs su zin kyang de med na shi ba'i* [*sic,* D: *shi ba*] *bzhin du de yod par mi 'gyur ro.* D4090, mngon pa, ku, 174b.
20. *Elimination of Mistakes,* 512–13.
21. Ibid., 513–14.
22. Ibid., 514–15.
23. Neither the intermediate existence nor physical or verbal karmas can occur in the formless realm.
24. For details, see *Explanation of the "Treasury of Abhidharma,"* D4090, mngon pa, ku, 197b–198a.
25. For details, see Asaṅga, *Summary of Abhidharma,* D4049, sems tsam, ri, 88b.
26. *Elimination of Mistakes,* 515–16.
27. See the translation of *Explanation of the "Treasury of Abhidharma"* passages Gorampa is referring to in Shakya Chokden's answer to this question.
28. *Elimination of Mistakes,* 516–17.
29. Ibid., 517–18.
30. *Golden Lancet* uses interchangeably *nag* and *gnag,* both of which I translate as "black."
31. *'dod par gtogs pa'i dge ba ni mi dge ba dang 'dres pa'i phyir dkar nag yin la / rnam par smin pa 'dres pa'i phyir / rnam par smin pa yang dkar nag yin no // 'di ni rgyud kyi sgo nas rnam par gzhag gi / ngo bo nyid kyi sgo nas ma yin te / las sam rnam par smin pa gcig la dkar po yang yin / nag po yang yin pa de lta bu med de / phan tshun 'gal ba'i phyir ro.* D4090, mngon pa, ku, 197b.
32. *de lta na / mi dge ba yang dge ba dang 'dres pa'i phyir / dkar nag tu 'gyur ba ma yin nam zhe na / 'dod pa'i khams ni mi dge ba gdon mi za bar dge ba dang 'dre ba ni ma yin te / de stobs dan ldan pa'i phyir ro // dge ba ni stobs chung ba'i phyir 'dre bar 'gyur ro.* Ibid. These two passages are paraphrased by Gorampa in his answer to question 7.
33. *Golden Lancet,* 478–81.
34. The passage is cited by Gorampa in his answer to question 6.
35. *gzhan ni mthong bas spang bya gnag // 'dod pa las skyes gzhan dkar gnag.* D4089, mngon pa, ku, 13a.
36. *Golden Lancet,* 481–83.

37. *las la rnam bzhi dkar nag 'dres // de zad byed pa'o las nag pa // rnam smin dkar po'i 'grub byed dang // dkar po'ang rnam smin nag po yi // 'grub byed dbye bas gnyis su bshad // 'di dang 'og tu 'dren ma'i las // bshad pa'i mi zlos khyad par ni // dngon pa gong 'og lugs yin te // las de gzugs can yin min no. Golden Lancet,* 483–84.
38. Ibid., 484–86.

7. Is the Ultimate an Actual Virtue?

1. Here Gorampa refers to the passage from *Ornament of Clear Realizations* that lists eleven objects of observation. The first three are virtues, nonvirtues, and unspecified phenomena, and the latter eight include the compounded and uncompounded phenomena, etc. For the translation and discussion, see Shakya Chokden's answer to question 8. It is clear that he did not imply in his question that all the eight latter objects of observation are virtues.
2. See references in Shakya Chokden's answer to question 8.
3. He thus refers to verse 79 of *Thorough Differentiation,* where Sakya Pandita argues that it is designated "virtue" merely in terms of the absence of evil.
4. *Elimination of Mistakes,* 518.
5. Ibid., 519.
6. *chos dbyings ngo bo dge min na // bde chen sgyu ma'i sku de yang // dge ba min par bzhed lags sam // de lta na ni bstod pa las // dge ba ces kyang ma gsungs sam.* Note that the word "praise" can refer specifically to Nāgārjuna's *Praise of the Dharma-Sphere* that addresses the dharma-sphere as "Virtue throughout beginning, middle, and end" (*thog ma bar dang mthar dge ba*), *Dharmadhātustotra, Chos kyi dbyings su bstod pa,* D1118, bstod tshogs, ka, 65a.
7. *Elimination of Mistakes,* 524.
8. *dmigs pa chos rnams thams cad de // de yang dge la sogs pa yin // 'jig rten pa yi rtogs pa dang // gang dag 'jig rten 'das 'dod dang // zag bcas zag pa med chos dang // gang dag 'dus byas 'dus ma byas // slob ma thun mong chos rnams dang // gang dag thub pa'i thun mong min.* D3786, shes phyin, ka, 3b.
9. *Sputhārtha, Don gsal,* D3793, shes phyin, ja, 90a.
10. *Golden Lancet,* 486–87.
11. *dge dang rnam par dag pa'i phyir.* D4024, sems tsam, phi, 61b.
12. *Golden Lancet,* 486–87.
13. *ci'i phyir yongs su grub pa zhes bya zhe na / gzhan du mi 'gyur ba'i phyir yongs su grub bo / / rnam par dag pa'i dmigs pa yin pa dang / dge ba'i chos thams cad kyi mchog yin pa'i phyir / mchog gi don gyis yongs su grub pa zhes bya'o.* D4048, sems tsam, ri, 16a–b.
14. *dge gnyis thob par bya ba'i phyir.* D4021, sems tsam, phi, 41a; *Golden Lancet,* 487. The other virtue is the compounded virtue (*'dus byas kyi dge ba*).
15. The uncompounded and compounded virtues are, respectively, nirvāṇa and the path or nirvāṇa and the virtues of saṃsāra.

16. *rnam dag chos kyi dbyings // sgrub pa'i 'phags lam brgyad // ston pa'i dam chos la // gus pas phyag 'tshal lo. Triratnastotra, Dkon mchog gsum gyi bstod pa,* D1146, bstod tshogs, ka, 110a.
17. *dam pa'i chos ni thog mar dge ba // tha mar dge ba // bar du dge ba.*
18. *dam pa dam min 'jug mi 'jug. Abhidharmakośakārikā, Chos mngon pa'i mdzod kyi tshig le'ur byas pa,* D4089, mngon pa, ku, 20a.
19. *dam pa dge ba kho na la 'jug cing / dam pa ma yin pa mi dge ba la mi 'jug pas na / skyes bu dam pa zhes bya'o. Golden Lancet,* 488. *Explanation of the "Treasury of Abhidharma"* is more specific, referring in particular to karmas: "They engage exclusively in what is holy—virtuous karmas—and do not engage in what is not holy—nonvirtuous ones" (*de dag ni las dam pa dge ba kho na la 'jug cing dam pa ma yin pa mi dge ba la mi 'jug pa*). D4090, mngon pa, khu, 24a. That said, it does not preclude some ultimates, as they are understood in the Sarvāstivāda system articulated in the *Treasury of Abhidharma,* from being a virtue or virtuous; the list of the seventy-five ultimately real phenomena, or dharmas, according to that system includes volition/intention (*sems pa, cetanā*), which is what defines karmas.
20. *'das dang ma byon da ltar gyi // rgyal ba gang lags de kun gyi // yum ni dge ma khyod lags te // khyod ni lha mo rgyal ba'i sras // rang bzhin med pa'i rang bzhin can // sangs rgyas yum gyur de yi mtshan // dge ba* [D: *dge ma*] *bdag gis brjod par bgyi. Āryaprajñāpāramitānāmāṣṭaśataka, 'Phags pa shes rab kyi pha rol tu phyin pa'i mtshan brgya rtsa brgyad pa zhes bya ba,* D25, shes rab sna tshogs, ka, 174a; *Golden Lancet,* 488.
21. Although it is clear that here Shakya Chokden is referring to the *Summary of Abhidharma,* he does seem to treat the two Abhidharma texts as subtypes of one system, as the discussion below demonstrates. See also note 22 below.
22. *Golden Lancet,* 488–89. This is specifically articulated in the *Explanation of the "Treasury of Abhidharma"* (see chap. 2, note 10). As we saw in chapter 2, the *Summary of Abhidharma* also treats the unspecified in terms of the ultimate as space and the nonanalytical cessation. It treats different types of nirvāṇa—which are analytical cessations—as virtues in terms of thorough pacification and suchness as the virtue in terms of the ultimate.
23. *Bstan bcos ye shes la 'jug pa.* The *Explanation of the "Treasury of Abhidharma"* simply refers to *Treatise* (*bstan bcos*).
24. *chos dkar po rnams gang zhe na / dge ba'i chos rnams dang / ma sgribs* [*sic,* D: *bsgribs*] *la lung du ma bstan pa rnams yin no.* D4090, mngon pa, ku, 198a; *Golden Lancet,* 489.
25. The three factors are basis of intent (*dgongs gzhi*), purpose (*dgos pa*), and damage to the explicit meaning (*dngos la gnod byed*).
26. *Golden Lancet,* 488–89.
27. Contaminated virtues *do* serve as the causes of the suffering of change and the all-pervasive suffering.

28. *Golden Lancet*, 489.
29. *Abhidharmasamuccaya, Chos mngon pa kun las btus pa*, D4049, sems tsam, ri, 63a.
30. Ibid., 61b.
31. Ibid., 62a.
32. *Golden Lancet*, 490.
33. Explaining what suffering in terms of ultimate reality (*don dam pa'i bden par sdug bsngal ba*) is, the *Summary of Abhidharma* states, "'In brief, the five appropriated aggregates are suffering'—these words taught suffering in terms of ultimate reality" (*mdor na nye bar len pa'i phung po lnga sdug bsngal lo zhes gsungs pa ni don dam pa'i bden par sdug bsngal ba'o*). *Abhidharmasamuccaya, Chos mngon pa kun las btus pa*, D4049, sems tsam, ri, 75a. The same text refers to nirvāṇa as the "basis of ultimate happiness" (*don dam pa'i bde ba'i gzhi*). 92a.
34. *oṃ svabhāvaśuddhāḥ sarvadharmāḥ svabhāvaśuddho 'haṃ* (oṃ, all things are pure by nature, I am pure by nature).
35. *oṃ śūnyatā jñāna vajra svabhāvātmako 'haṃ* (oṃ, I am the self whose nature is the vajra of primordial mind of emptiness).
36. *Golden Lancet*, 490.
37. For further details, see Komarovski, *Visions of Unity*, chap. 5.
38. *Maitreyaparipṛcchā, Byams zhus kyi le'u.*
39. These three correspond to the three natures (*ngo bo nyid gsum, trisvabhāva*) of the Yogācāra tradition: the imaginary (*kun btags, parikalpita*), the dependent (*gzhan dbang, paratantra*), and the perfect (*yongs grub, parinispanna*).
40. *Golden Lancet*, 490–91.
41. As we will see below, according to Shakya Chokden it is permanent with respect to its continuity, but it is also momentary.
42. Further details are provided in Shakya Chokden's answer to question 10.
43. *Golden Lancet*, 491–92.
44. Here and below, Shakya Chokden treats *Single Intent* and *Writings* as a single unit.
45. See chap. 3, note 1.
46. *rgya mtsho lta bu'i khams dge ba // bya* [sic] *bsags gnyer ma'i rlabs chen gyis // spud pa lta bu'i dge ba 'di // bla na med pa'i byang chub bsngo. Golden Lancet*, 493.
47. Ibid., 492–93.
48. Shakya Chokden himself does not limit the category of Madhyamaka to that of Niḥsvabhāvavāda (*ngo bo nyid med par smra ba*, Proponents of Entitylessness). See below, note 71.
49. *Golden Lancet*, 493.
50. For details of his interpretation of reality as impermanent, see Komarovski, *Visions of Unity*, chap. 5, sec. 2.
51. He adds that likewise there are two ways of positing something as compounded and uncompounded.

52. This is a reference to such works as Asaṅga's *Bodhisattva-Grounds* (*Bodhisattvabhūmi, Byang chub sems dpa'i sa*), D4037, sems tsam, wi, 47b, which describes the state of awakening as characterized by two types of abandonments (*spangs pa*)—of afflictive obscurations and obscurations of knowables—and two types of primordial mind that are free from those obscurations.
53. Drakpa Gyeltsen clearly demonstrates that even in several Madhyamaka systems, primordial mind—including primordial mind on the level of buddhahood—is accepted. See his *Precious Tree: Clear Realizations of Tantras* (*Rgyud kyi mngon par rtogs pa rin po che'i ljon shing*), in *Excellent Words of Glorious Sakyapas* [*Dpal ldan sa skya pa'i gsung rab*], 18:290–94.
54. *Golden Lancet*, 494.
55. *rang bzhin yod tsam dang // 'brel pa can gyi ngo bo yang. Pramāṇavārttikakārikā, Tshad ma rnam 'grel gyi tshig le'ur byas pa,* D4210, tshad ma, ce, 94b; *Elimination of Mistakes,* 519.
56. *'jig pa yod tsam 'brel ba can // nyid phyir sgra ni mi rtag nyid.* D4210, tshad ma, ce, 104b; *Elimination of Mistakes*, 520.
57. *'jigs* [*sic*] *pa dngos po tsam dang ni // rjes 'brel phyir na rtag nyid min.* D4210, tshad ma, ce, 120a; *Elimination of Mistakes*, 520. Gorampa further clarifies the meaning of *Thorough Differentiation*'s verse 89 in his *Lotus Blossom: Answers to Questions* [*Dris lan pad mo bzhad pa*], in *Collected Works of Kun-mkhyen Go-rams-pa Bsod-nams-seng-ge*, 10:63–65, where he writes that the five passages from *Commentary on Valid Cognition*—including the ones cited above—that demonstrate that the mere existence is pervaded by impermanence were written from the standpoint of the Sautrāntika approach to the ultimate truth. But verse 89 was written from the standpoint of Madhyamaka, which is *Thorough Differentiation*'s own tradition. The meaning of the passage then is that if the dharma-sphere is a virtue explained in the context of "as many virtues of migrators as there exist," then which of the three is it—a thing posited as existent, a nonthing posited as existent, or the freedom from proliferations, which is neither of the two, posited as existent? If it is the first, then the dharma-sphere in that context is not existent, because Dharmakīrti's argument on the level of Sautrāntika that existence is pervaded by impermanence applies to the Madhyamka system as well. Because in that context existence is what is able to function (literally, "able to produce effects," *don byed nus pa*), Mādhyamikas also accept the reasoning that if a permanent thing can produce effects, it will follow that it produces all effects simultaneously. In verse 89, Sakya Pandita addressed only the first option, explaining the second and the third options in verses 128 and 129, respectively.
58. *'jig la 'bras dang yod nyid bzhin.* D4210, tshad ma, ce, 101b.
59. *Tshad ma rigs pa'i gter.*
60. *Elimination of Mistakes*, 520–21.

61. *nyid* is often translated as "-ness" or "-hood." "Existence-ness" or "existence-hood" would be a more precise, albeit awkward, translation of *yod pa nyid.*
62. *Golden Lancet,* 494–96.
63. *Treasure of the Science of Valid Cognition: The Root Text and the Commentary* (*Tshad ma rigs pa'i gter gyi rtsa ba dang 'grel pa;* Bod ljongs mi dmangs dpe skrun khang, 1989), 9.
64. *Pramāṇaviniścaya, Tshad ma rnam par nges pa.*
65. Thus, *mere existence* can refer to conceptually conceived phenomena that either do or do not at all exist on a conventional level.
66. *Golden Lancet,* 496–98.
67. They are the last four of *Five Dharmas of Maitreya:* (1) *Ornament of Clear Realizations* [*Abhisamayālaṃkāranāmaprajñāpāramitopadeśaśāstrakārikā, Shes rab kyi pha rol tu phyin pa'i man ngag gi bstan bcos mngon par rtogs pa'i rgyan zhes bya ba'i tshig le'ur byas pa*]; (2) *Ornament of Mahāyāna Sūtras* [*Mahāyānasūtrālaṃkāra, Theg pa chen po mdo sde'i rgyan*]; (3) *Differentiation of the Middle and Extremes* [*Madhyāntavibhāga, Dbus dang mtha' rnam par 'byed pa*]; (4) *Differentiation of Phenomena and the Nature of Phenomena* [*Dharmatadharmatāvibhaṅga, Chos dang chos nyid rnam par 'byed pa*]; and (5) *Sublime Continuum of Mahāyāna* [*Mahāyānottaratantraśāstra, Theg pa chen po rgyud bla ma*].
68. *de nyid zad pa med pa'i phyir // rtag pa zhes kyang brjod pa yin.* D3786, shes phyin, ka, 11b. According to Haribhadra's *Clear Meaning,* the passage refers specifically to one of the four buddha-bodies—the dharma-body. He describes it as "the dharma-body with the selfness of primordial mind that exists on the basis of individually ascertaining yogis' mental continua, emerging each moment" (*ye shes kyi bdag nyid kyi chos kyi sku rnal 'byor pa so sor nges pa'i rgyud kyi rten la yod pa skad cig re re la 'byung ba*). D3793, shes phyin, ja, 134a. On this interpretation, the dharma-body can be understood as impermanent with respect to its momentariness and permanent with respect to its continuity.
69. *las dang nyon mongs pas mngon par 'dus ma byas pa nyid kyi phyir / 'dus byas ma yin no. Abhidharmasamuccaya, Chos mngon pa kun las btus pa,* D4049, sems tsam, ri, 59a.
70. The full line, most of which Shakya Chokden omits (with the exception of the last part), reads: "Because of being actual things in the sense of following one's wishes, turning toward [nirvāṇa] and away from [saṃsāra], they are not uncompounded either" (*'dod ba bzhin du byed pas mngon du phyogs pa dang / rgyab kyi lta bas dngos po nyid kyi phyir 'dus ma byas kyang ma yin no*). Ibid. In his *Garlands of Waves of the Ocean of Yogācāras' Scriptures: Explanation of the Holy Dharma of [Asaṅga's] "Summary of Higher Knowledge"* [*Dam pa'i chos mngon pa kun las btus pa'i rnam par bshad pa rnal 'byor spyod gzhung rgya mtsho'i rlabs kyi phreng ba*], in *Collected Writings of Gser-mdog paṇ-chen Śākya-mchog-ldan,*

14:95, Shakya Chokden relates the "turning toward" and "away from" to nirvāṇa and saṃsāra, respectively.

71. *dngos por smra ba,* Proponents of Phenomenal Existence. This category subsumes three of the four Buddhist tenets, not Madhyamaka. It should be noted that Shakya Chokden includes in it one of the two types of Yogācāra—Satyākāravāda (*rnam bden pa,* True Aspectarians), which he treats as synonymous with Cittamātra—but not the other type—Alīkākāravāda (*rnam rdzun pa,* False Aspectarians), which he includes in the category of Madhyamaka alongside Niḥsvabhāvavāda. Thus, for him, not all Buddhist tenet systems belong either to Vastusatpadārthavāda or Niḥsvabhāvavāda; Alīkākāravāda is neither. When Shakya Chokden treats the Buddhist tantric systems as subdivisions of Madhyamaka, they too do not fall into either of the two categories. For details, see Komarovski, *Visions of Unity,* chaps. 2–4.
72. *chos dbyings yod pa'ang ma yin te // yod la mi rtag gis khyab par // chos kyi grags pas legs par gsungs. Golden Lancet,* 498–99.
73. *chos dbyings yod pa ma yin na // chos dbyings ye shes ji ltar yod.* Ibid., 500.
74. Note that the primordial mind of the dharma-sphere is also one of the five primordial minds of a buddha.
75. *Golden Lancet,* 499–500.
76. For the actual passage, see below, note 79.
77. *Elimination of Mistakes,* 521–22.
78. This does not apply to all "later Tibetans," because such thinkers as Gorampa would not accept it in the context of the Niḥsvabhāvavāda Madhyamaka reasoning. But it does apply to Geluk thinkers even in that context.
79. *dngos dang dngos med 'dus byas yin.* D3824, dbu ma, tsa, 16b. The implication is that such cannot be accepted because it will contradict Sakya Pandita as well as Nāgārjuna, who in the same verse says: "How can nirvāṇa be [either of] / The two—things and nonthings? / Nirvāṇa is uncompounded; / Things and nonthings are compounded" (*ji ltar mya ngan 'das pa ni // dngos dang dngos med gnyis yin te // mya ngan 'das pa 'dus ma byas // dngos dang dngos med 'dus byas yin*). Ibid.
80. *Golden Lancet,* 500–501.
81. Ibid., 501–2.
82. *Elimination of Mistakes,* 524.
83. *Golden Lancet,* 515–16.
84. *gnyis dngos ped pa'i* [*sic,* D: *dang*] *dngos med pa'i // dngos po.* D4021, sems tsam, phi, 41a.
85. *Golden Lancet,* 517.
86. Cf. the discussion at the end of Shakya Chokden's reply to question 2.
87. For further details, see Shakya Chokden's answer to question 21.
88. *de phyir gnyis stong gang yin pa // de ni de yi'ang de nyid yin.* D4210, tshad ma, ce, 126b. According to Shakya Chokden's *Enjoyment Ocean of the Entirely Good*

Dharma: Explanation of the Extensive Treatise "Commentary on Valid Cognition" [*Rgyas pa'i bstan bcos tshad ma rnam 'grel gyi rnam bshad kun bzang chos kyi rol mtsho*], in *Collected Writings of Gser-mdog paṇ-chen Śākya-mchog-ldan,* 18:492, the meaning of the passage is that the thatness empty of the two, the apprehended and the apprehender, is the thatness of that mind that appears as the two, the apprehended and the apprehender.

89. *Golden Lancet,* 516–17.
90. *rang bzhin dang ni rgyas pa dang // de ni rten dang brten pa dang // yod med nyid* [D: *gnyis*] *dang yon tan ni // sgrol ba'i don du shes par bya.* D4020, sems tsam, phi, 4a. Shakya Chokden omits the first line. In his *Explanation of the Ornament of Sūtras* [*Sūtrālaṃkārabhāṣya, Mdo sde'i rgyan gyi bshad pa*], D4026, sems tsam, phi, 137b, Vasubandhu explains regarding the lineage of *both* types: "It exists as a causal entity and does not exist as a resultant entity. The lineage should be understood as also [having] the meaning of releasing positive qualities, because positive qualities are released and emerge from it" (*de ni rgyu'i dngos por yod do // 'bras bu'i dngos por med do // rigs ni yon tan sgrol ba'i don du yang rig par bya ste // 'di las yon tan sgrol zhing 'byung ba'i phyir ro*). This further supports Shakya Chokden's take on the lineage, and by extension on the dharma-sphere, as a causal phenomenon.
91. *Golden Lancet,* 517–18. *Illumination of the "Twenty Thousand"* [*Nyi khri snang ba;* full title: *Āryapañcaviṃśatisāhasrikāprajñāpāramitopadeśaśāstrābhisamayālaṃkāravṛtti, 'Phags pa shes rab kyi pha rol tu phyin pa stong phrag nyi shu lnga pa'i man ngag gi bstan bcos mngon par rtogs pa'i rgyan gyi 'grel pa*], D3787, shes phyin, ka, 60a: "It is the lineage with respect to releasing positive qualities. This means that 'such and such positive qualities are born and emerge from it' " (*yon tan sgrol ba'i don gyis na rigs te / de las yon tan de dang de dag skye zhing 'byung ba zhes bya ba'i don to*).
92. *Golden Lancet,* 518. Note that earlier in this answer Shakya Chokden stated that the stainless seeds persist all the way into the buddha-ground. Consequently, according to him, their producing sprouts of awakening and eventually awakening itself does not cancel their existence: as stainless knowing, they exist forever.
93. Counting the dharma-sphere as 1 here simply indicates that if it is treated as the ultimate virtue, no other virtue can exceed it. The dharma-sphere itself should exceed any other virtue because of its unique ultimate status.
94. *Elimination of Mistakes,* 525.
95. Ibid., 525–26.
96. Sakya scholars, including Shakya Chokden himself, typically have a low opinion of this type of literature, which is studied by beginner students in the rival Geluk (*dge lugs*) tradition. Interestingly, what students of Collected Topics learn about the positive pervasion is that although an existent or a knowable itself is permanent, not all existents or knowables are permanent; although a

knowable itself is an unspecified phenomenon, not all knowables are unspecified; and although a knowable itself is a conceptual construct, not all knowables are conceptual constructs.

97. *Elimination of Mistakes,* 526.
98. In *Thorough Differentiation* Sakya Pandita clearly stated that the dharma-sphere "is not even existent." But we have seen that according to Shakya Chokden, such was done only with regard to finally dispelling all proliferations.
99. This statement is made from the standpoint of those who do not accept the dharma-sphere as a virtue.
100. *de lta yin na sems can rnams // bden 'gror 'gro ba mi srid cing // ngan 'gror 'gro ba'ang mi srid 'gyur. Golden Lancet,* 519.
101. Ibid., 519–20.
102. See above, note 67.
103. Note that in contexts such as this, Shakya Chokden uses *reality* (*chos nyid*) and *the dharma-sphere* (*chos dbyings*) interchangeably.
104. *Golden Lancet,* 521–22.
105. Ibid., 522–23.
106. *chos kyi dbyings ni ma gtogs pa* [D: *par*] *// 'di ltar chos yod ma yin te.* D4021, sems tsam, phi, 44b.
107. *chos kyi dbyings las ma gtogs pa // gang phyir chos med de yi phyir.* D4020, sems tsam, phi, 18a.
108. According to Shakya Chokden's interpretation of the three natures, the dependent *does* have the entity of the dharma-sphere because it has the entity of the perfect. The dependent's entity is not the dependent itself. But that does not make the dependent the actual perfect, because ultimately the dependent does not exist. For details, see Komarovski, "From the Three Natures to the Two Natures."
109. *blo dang ldan pas gnyis po med rig nas // de mi ldan pa'i chos kyi dbyings la gnas.* D4020, sems tsam, phi, 6b.
110. *dmigs pa la ni brten nas su // mi dmigs pa ni rab tu skye // mi dmigs pa la brten nas su // mi dmigs pa ni rab tu skye //* [*de yi phyir na dmigs pa ni // mi dmigs ngo bo nyid du grub //*] *de lta bas na dmigs pa dang // mi dmigs mnyam par shes par bya.* D4021, sems tsam, phi, 40b. Shakya Chokden skips lines 5 and 6. On the basis of Vasubandhu's *Commentary on* [*Maitreya's*] *"Differentiation of the Middle and Extremes"* (*Madhyāntavibhāgaṭīkā, Dbus dang mtha' rnam par 'byed pa'i 'grel pa*), D4027, sems tsam, bi, 3a, the first verse of the passage is unpacked as follows: on the basis of the observation of the mere cognizance, the nonobservation of external objects is thoroughly produced; and on the basis of the nonobservation of external objects, the nonobservation of the mere cognizance is thoroughly produced. Vasubandhu further matches the mere cognizance (*rnam par rig pa tsam*) with the apprehender (*'dzin pa*), and ob-

jects (*don*) with the apprehended (*gzung ba*). This supports Shakya Chokden's claim of the nonexistence of both the apprehended and the apprehender.

111. *Golden Lancet,* 523–24.
112. Ibid., 524. See also Komarovski, "There are no Dharmas Apart from the Dharma-Sphere."
113. *ci nas chos dbyings dge ba nyid // yin na ha cang thal 'gyur te // sdig dang lung ma bstan gyi yang // ngo bo dge bar 'gyur ba dang // chos kyi dbyings las ma gtogs pa'i // chos gzhan med phyir sdig pa dang // lung ma bstan yang med par 'gyur // de lta yin na sems can 'ga' // ngan 'gror 'gro ba mi srid do. Golden Lancet,* 525–26.
114. *yod pa bsgrub par gsungs pa des // chos dbyings dge la ji ltar gnod. Elimination of Mistakes,* 526.
115. *phyogs bcu'i 'jig rten khams na yod pa yi* [H: *kun na gang yod pa'i*] // *dge ba de dag yang dag bsgrub pas na* [H: *sgrub pa na*] // *'gro ba kun la phan dang bde sems kyis // ye shes mkhas pa* [H: *la*] *de dag yongs su bsngo.* H94, phal chen, kha, 184a.
116. *Elimination of Mistakes,* 526–27. See chap. 5, note 24, for different readings of Shakya Chokden's question to which Gorampa replies here.
117. Depending on the context, the pair can also be translated as "establishment" and "negation."
118. *phyogs bcu'i 'jig rten khams na gang yod pa'i // dge ba de dag yang dag bsgrubs pas na // 'gro ba kun la phan dang bde sems kyis // ye shes mkhas la de dag yongs su bsngo.* Shakya Chokden uses the past tense *bsgrubs pa* here, unlike Gorampa, who uses *bsgrub pa.*
119. *Golden Lancet,* 526.
120. *Elimination of Mistakes,* 527. The version of *Good Questions* available to Gorampa reads *tshong dpon mdza' bo'i bu mo'i bus* (By the merchant chief Maitrakanyaka's son) in the second line. He criticizes this wording, arguing that it is not found in what he sees as the scriptural source for the Maitrakanyaka story, *Repaying Kindness Sūtra* (*Mdo sde drin lan bsab pa*). Explaining why Maitrakanyaka was called so, Gorampa writes that according to that sūtra, there was a merchant in Varanasi named Mitra (*mdza' bo*), all of whose sons died. Later, when yet another son was born, he named him Maitrakanyaka (*mdza' bo'i bu mo,* i.e., "Mitra's Daughter," apparently in order to avoid misfortune). The wording "Maitrakanyaka's son" does not appear anywhere in that text, he writes. Ibid.
121. For details, see Brough, "Some Notes on Maitrakanyaka."
122. When briefly addressing Maitrakanyaka's story, Gorampa himself uses the word "aspirational resolve" (*smon lam*), writing that Maitrakanyaka "made the aspirational resolve: 'Let the brain illness of all sentient beings ripen on me'" (*sems can gyi klad nad bdag la smin par gyur cig ces pa'i smon lam btab*). *Elimination of Mistakes,* 527.
123. See chap. 2, note 14.

124. See ibid.
125. The dharma-sphere does become partially free from adventitious obscurations starting from the first bodhisattva-ground, that freedom increasing as one approaches buddhahood.
126. *de la 'jig rten mthun 'jug la // dgongs nas phyi rol don du gsungs // tha snyad spyod pa'i rigs pa la // dgongs nas chos rnams sems su gsungs.*
127. *Golden Lancet,* 529–30.
128. Ibid., 530–31. Of the three types of bodhicitta—the shepherd-like bodhicitta (wherein one resolves to achieve buddhahood only after all other beings have achieved it), the boatman-like bodhicitta (wherein one resolves to achieve buddhahood together with all other beings), and the king-like bodhicitta (wherein one resolves to achieve buddhahood before others)—the first one is believed to be the strongest, thereby bringing one to buddhahood faster than the other two and thus before all other beings have achieved it.
129. *gnas min bsngo bar gsungs de ci. Elimination of Mistakes,* 527.
130. More specifically, one of its parts, *Sūtra Requested by Vimaladattā.* See chap. 4, note 55.
131. *bsgyur* can be translated as "change" or as "transform."
132. *bu mos smras pa / rigs kyi bu chos rnams kyi chos nyid ni smon lam gyi dbang gis bsgyur bar mi nus so // gal te nus par gyur na /* [D adds: *sems can thams cad yongs su mya ngan las bzla'o zhes*] *de bzhin gshegs pa re re'i dgongs pa de smon lam gyi dbang gis ji ltar mi 'grub ste / rnam grangs 'dis ni smon lam gyi dbang gis bsgyur bar mi nus par rigs* [*sic,* D: *rig*] *par bya'o.* D77, dkon brtsegs, ca, 250a.
133. *Elimination of Mistakes,* 528.
134. *Golden Lancet,* 531.
135. Shakya Chokden cites the passage in almost the same form as in Gorampa's answer: "The girl said: 'Son of good family. The reality of dharmas cannot be transformed by the power of aspirational resolve. If it could, then why have each tathāgata's intents, "let all sentient beings achieve complete nirvāṇa," not been accomplished by the power of aspirational resolve? Thus, it is to be known that the reality of dharmas cannot be transformed by the power of aspirational resolve'" (*bu mos smras pa / rigs kyi bu chos rnams kyi chos nyid ni smon lam gyi dbang gis sgyur* [D: *bsgyur du*] *mi nus lags so // gal te nus par gyur na sems can thams cad yongs su mya ngan las 'da'o* [D: *bzla'o*] *zhes de bshin gshegs pa re re'i dgongs pa de smon lam gyi dbang gyis ji ltar mi 'grub* [D: adds *ste*] *// rnam grangs 'dis na chos rnams kyi chos nyid ni smon lam gyi dbang gis sgyur mi nus par rig par bya'o*) [D: *rnam grangs 'dis na smon lam gyi dbang gis bsgyur bar mi nus par rig par bgyi'o*]. D77, dkon brtsegs, ca, 250a.
136. *smon lam de yang mdor bsdu na // gnas dang gnas ma yin pa gnyis // gnas kyi smon lam 'grub par gsungs // gnas min smon yang 'grub mi 'gyur. Golden Lancet,* 531–32.
137. Gorampa appears to refer to questions 1 and 2.

138. *Elimination of Mistakes*, 528–29.
139. *Golden Lancet*, 533.
140. *lus can la yod zag pa med pa'i shes pa sbrang ma'i rtsi dang 'dra.* D4024, sems tsam, phi, 59a.
141. *thos pa'i bag chags kyi sa bon de'i gnas ci zhig yin par lta zhe na / sangs rgyas rnams kyi byang chub la brten nas thos pa'i bag chags su gyur pa gang yin pa gnas gang la yang 'jug pa de / lhan cig 'dug pa'i tshul gyis rnam par smin pa'i rnam par shes pa la 'jug ste / 'o ma dang chu bzhin no // de ni kun gzhi'i rnam par shes pa ma yin te / de'i gnyen po'i sa bon nyid yin pa'i phyir ro.* D4048, sems tsam, ri, 10b.
142. *de ni 'jig rten las 'das pa'i sems ma byung du zin kyang / nyon mongs pa'i kun nas dkris pa'i gnyen po dang / ngan song du 'gro ba'i gnyen po dang / nyes par byas pa thams cad de nges par byed* [*sic*] *pa'i gnyen po yin no.* Ibid., 11a.
143. *de ni kun gzhi'i rnam par shes pa ma yin gyi / chos kyi sku dang rnam par grol pa'i lus su bsdus pa yin te.* Ibid. On the same page Asaṅga specifies that those seeds of predispositions to listening of even the beginner bodhisattvas are subsumed under the dharma-body, and those of śrāvakas and pratyekabuddhas are subsumed under the liberation-body.
144. *ji ltar kun gzhi'i rnam par shes pa dang / kun gzhi'i rnam par shes pa ma yin pa chu dang 'o ma bzhin du / lhan cig gnas pa rnam pa thams cad du 'grib par ji ltar 'gyur zhe na / ngang pas chu las 'o ma 'thungs pa lta bu dang / 'jig rten pa'i 'dod chags dang bral ba na / mnyam par gzhag pa ma yin pa'i sa'i bag chags 'gribs te / mnyam par gzhag pa'i sa'i bag chags 'phel nas gnas gyur pa bzhin no.* Ibid.; *Golden Lancet*, 534–35.
145. *gong ma thams cad lung ma bstan.* D4089, mngon pa, ku, 16b.
146. We should note that the first two lines of the passage cited there at least on the surface limit the context of the discussion of virtues, and so on, to the discussion of karmas.
147. See chap. 2, note 4.
148. *Golden Lancet*, 535–36. "Own entity" here does not refer to the ultimate or the perfect nature, but to the aforementioned fruitional part of the universal basis consciousness.
149. Ibid., 536.

8. Who Owns the Highest Virtue?

1. *rdzogs sangs sku ni 'phro phyir dang // de bzhin nyid dbyer med phyir dang // rigs yod phyir na lus can kun // rtag tu sangs rgyas snying po can.* D4024, sems tsam, phi, 56a.
2. *rigs de rnam gnyis shes bya ste // thog med rang bzhin gnas pa dang // yang dag blangs pa mchog nyid do // rigs 'di gnyis las sangs rgyas kyi // sku gsum thob par 'dod pa ste // dang pos sku ni dang po ste // gnyis pa yis ni phyi ma gnyis.* Ibid., 61b.
3. *Elimination of Mistakes*, 522–23.

4. Ibid., 529.
5. This is a reference to the tathāgata-essence illustrated by the nine examples, such as a precious image wrapped in filthy rags, honey amid bees, a treasure under a poor person's house, and so forth.
6. This is a reference to the first verse cited in Gorampa's answer to question 12.
7. See above, note 5.
8. *Golden Lancet,* 503–4.
9. See chap. 4, note 50.
10. *des na sangs rgyas ma thob par // mya ngan 'das pa mi 'thob ste // 'od dang 'od zer spangs nas ni // nyi ma lta bar mi nus bzhin.* D4024, sems tsam, phi, 58b. The ten presentations (*rnam bzhag rnam pa bcu*) refer to the essence (*ngo bo*), cause (*rgyu*), result (*'bras bu*), function (*las*), endowment (*ldan pa*), engaging (*'jug pa*), phases (*gnas skabs*), all-pervasiveness (*kun tu 'gro ba*), permanent unchangeability (*rtag tu mi 'gyur ba*), and inseparability of the positive qualities (*yon gtan dbyer med pa*).
11. For details of and changes in Shakya Chokden's interpretations of the buddha-essence, see Komarovski, "Reburying the Treasure." See also below, note 27.
12. *Thub pa'i dgongs pa rab tu gsal ba.*
13. Shakya Chokden calls Drakpa Gyeltsen's work *Purification Explanation* [*Rnam bshad dag ldan*]. The full title is *Purification Commentary Destroying Impurities: Explanation of "[Hevajra in] Two Chapters"* [*Brtag pa gnyis pa'i rnam par bshad pa ma dag pa rnams 'joms par byed pa'i rnam 'grel dag ldan*]. Hereafter, *Purification Commentary. Golden Lancet,* 504–9.
14. *rnam dbye med pa'i mtshan nyid can // bla med chos kyis stong ma yin. Golden Lancet,* 509–10. This is part of the seminal passage from the *Sublime Continuum* "There is nothing to eliminate here, / Nothing at all to establish. / Reality is to be viewed as reality. / Having seen [it], one is liberated. / The element is empty of the adventitious [defilements] / Which have the character of being separable [from it]. / It is not empty of the unsurpassed dharmas / Which have the character of not being separable [from it]" (*'di la bsal bya ci yang med // gzhag par bya ba cung zad med // yang dag nyid la yang dag lta // yang dag mthong na rnam par grol // rnam dbye bcas pa'i mtshan nyid can // glo bur dag gis khams stong gi // rnam dbye med pa'i mtshan nyid can // bla med chos kyis stong ma yin*). D4024, sems tsam, phi, 61b.
15. For a more extensive quotation, see Asaṅga, *Explanation of [Maitreya's] "Sublime Continuum of Mahāyāna,"* cited below.
16. *Golden Lancet,* 510.
17. Ibid., 510–11.
18. Ibid., 511–12. For details of these thinkers' approaches to the buddha-essence, see Tsering Wangchuk, *"Uttaratantra" in the Land of Snows.*
19. *de la dri ma dang bcas pa'i de bzhin nyid kyi dbang du mdzad nas sems can thams cad ni de bzhin gshegs pa'i snying po can no zhes gsungs pa gang yin pa de don gang*

gi yin zhe na / rdzogs sangs sku ni 'phro phyir dang // de bzhin nyid dbyer med phyir dang // rigs yod phyir na lus can kun // rtag tu sangs rgyas snying po can // mdor bsdu na don rnam pa gsum gyis sems can thams cad ni rtag tu de bzhin gshegs pa'i snying po can no zhes bcom ldan 'das kyis gsungs. Mahāyānottaratantraśāstravyākhyā, Theg pa chen po'i rgyud bla ma'i bstan bcos kyi rnam par bshad pa, D4025, sems tsam, phi, 88a.

20. *de bzhin gshegs pa'i snying po'i ye shes nyid ni / de bzhin gshegs pa rnams kyi stong pa nyid kyi ye shes yin.* Ibid., 114a.
21. *Golden Lancet,* 512–13. Note that in general Shakya Chokden clearly distinguishes between two types of knowing (*shes pa*)—consciousness (*rnam shes*) and primordial mind (*ye shes*)—with no overlap possible. See Komarovski, *Visions of Unity,* 158ff. and 239ff., for details. Thus, this reference to consciousness can be taken in a metaphorical sense: in the same way that only consciousness can serve as a substantial cause of consciousness, only primordial mind can serve as a substantial cause of primordial mind. It is also possible that he refers to primordial mind as consciousness here in the same way that some Indian works he comments on do. See ibid., 147; see also verses at the end of this section, where Shakya Chokden refers specifically to knowing.
22. Cf. chap. 3, notes 18–19.
23. *Golden Lancet,* 513–14.
24. As Asaṅga explains in that text, the naturally abiding lineage exists since beginningless times and is obtained by nature/reality (*thog ma med pa'i dus can chos nyid kyis thob pa*). D4037, sems tsam, wi, 2b. Those qualities do not necessarily apply to the eight collections.
25. Because the first is clearly not an option, it is not discussed.
26. *khams de dngos po ma yin na // rigs khams sbrang rtsi dang 'dra ba // zag med shes par bshad de ci // khams de dngos med kyang min na // dri mar bcas pa'i sems kyi dbyings // dngos por 'dod dam sangs rgyas kyi // khams kyang min par 'dod gyur tam // rig pa gang yin rnam shes kyi // tshogs brgyad nyid du sdud byed na // ye shes la rton rnam shes la // yid rton min pa de ci zhig / kun gzhi gsal cha kun gzhi nyid // yin na zag med sems su 'gal // min na ma sgribs lung ma stan* [sic] *// yin pa'i shes byed gang nas btsal // zag med sems rgyud tshogs brgyad du // sdud par byed na rang bzhin gyi // gnas rigs min par thal bar 'gyur // de lta na ni byang sa las // gsungs pa'i rang bzhin gnas rigs gang // rang lugs la yang sems can khams // spros bral yin pa 'gog byed dam // yang na chos kyi dbyings su 'dod // gnyis pa ltar na chos dbyings de // shes par 'dod dam rtag par 'dod // shes pa yin na dngos por 'gyur // rtag par 'dod na shes min pas // shes pa'i nyer len byed pa'am // rtag pa sems can khams nyid du // 'dod pa sangs rgyas pa la med // ces pa'i dri ba 'di dag la // chos dbyings shes par mi 'dod pa // byams pa'i gzhung gi dgongs pa zhes // 'chad po rnams kyis lan ldon dka' // des na dri ba 'di dag gis // bstan bcos 'di ni dkag go ces // ba lang khyu yi tshogs dag tu // khyu mchog lta bur rlom pa mchog // chos dbyings ye shes ma yin pa'i // sems can khams kyi dbang byas nas // brtag*

pa 'di dag gis brtags pas // gzhan gyi 'dod pa sun phyung zhing // tsher ma 'di dag 'jug pa med // spros bral zhes pa spros pa'i tshogs // bkag pa'i ma yin dgag pa la // 'chad pa byams pa'i gzhung yin pas // spros bral rtag pa'am rnam shes shes // brtags pa'i tsher ma 'byin par sla. Golden Lancet, 514–15.

27. I did not find this statement in Shakya Chokden's early writings. In fact, already in *Essence of Sūtras and Tantras: Explanation of the Buddha-Essence* [*Sangs rgyas kyi snying po'i rnam bshad mdo rgyud snying po*], written in 1474, he explained that according to the unsurpassed yoga tantras, the buddha-essence pervades all phenomena; that according to the nontantric teachings of the third dharmacakra, only Mahāyāna āryas have it; and that the buddha-essence as the nonimplicative negation of all extremes of proliferations taught in the second dharmacakra is not the actual buddha-essence. For details, see Komarovski, "Reburying the Treasure."
28. *Elimination of Mistakes,* 529–30.
29. *Mañjuśrījñānasattvasyaparamārthanāmasaṃgīti, 'Jam dpal ye shes sems dpa'i don dam pa'i mtshan yang dag par brjod pa.*
30. *Golden Lancet,* 536–38.
31. *nga las 'gro ba thams cad 'byung // nga las gnas gsum po yang byung // nga yis 'gro kun khyab pa ste // 'gro ba'i rang bzhin gzhan ma mthong. Hevajratantrarājanāma, Kye'i rdo rje zhes bya ba rgyud kyi rgyal po,* D417, rgyud, nga, 10a. The three places are the places below, on, and above the earth.
32. *theg pa chen po rgyud bla mar // sdug la skyo sogs snying po yi // byed las yin par bshad mod kyi // sgrub byed yin par gang las shes // snying po dngos kyi sgrub byed du // bshad na khyab pa 'gal bar 'gyur // rigs yod pa ni rgyu* [*sic*] *bla mar // bsgrub byar mdzad pa'i skabs yod min // snying po'i sgrub byed don gsum dang // dpe dgu las gzhan bshad pa med // ces pa'i dogs pa byung gyur na // de yi lan ldon shes pa nyung // khams de sangs rgyas snying po yi // dgongs gzhir 'chad pa'i sgrub byed du // myang ngan 'das pa don gnyer ba // khams kyi byed las yin par bshad // me yi rang bzhin tsha ba ltar // khams kyi rang bzhin mi gnas pa'i // myang ngan 'das pa yin pas na // khams de snying po'i dgongs gzhir bshad. Golden Lancet,* 538–40.
33. *de bzhin nyid ni thams cad la // khyad par med kyang dag gyur pa // de bzhin gshegs nyid de yi phyir // 'gro kun de yi snying po can.* D4020, sems tsam, phi, 10a.
34. Although that passage is from the *Ornament of Mahāyāna Sūtras,* it is quoted (with slightly different wording in the first two lines) in Asaṅga's *Explanation of* [*Maitreya's*] *"Sublime Continuum of Mahāyāna,"* D4025, sems tsam, phi, 111b.
35. *Golden Lancet,* 540–42.
36. *'bras bu dag pa gzugs la sogs // dag pa nyid de gang gi phyir.* The passage continues: "Therefore, because they are not different / And not splittable, the two are described as pure" (*de gnyis tha dad ma yin zhing // bcad du med pas dag par brjod*). D3786, shes phyin, ka, 6a.

37. *Golden Lancet*, 542.
38. *Āryasarvadharmasvabhāvasamatāvipañcitasamādhirājanāmamahāyānasūtra, 'Phags pa chos thams cad kyi rang bzhin mnyam pa nyid rnam par spros pa ting nge 'dzin gyi rgyal po zhes bya ba theg pa chen po'i mdo.* D127, mdo sde, da, 1b–170b.
39. *Āryalaṅkāvatāramahāyānasūtra, 'Phags pa lang kar gshegs pa'i theg pa chen po'i mdo.* D107, mdo sde, ca, 56a–191b.
40. See chap. 4, note 50.
41. *Elimination of Mistakes*, 531–34.
42. *'gro ba zhi ba'i chos nyid du // rtogs phyir ji lta nyid de yang // rang bzhin gyis ni yongs dag phyir // nyon mongs gdod nas zad phyir ro // shes bya mthar thug rtogs pa'i blos // thams cad mkhyen pa'i chos nyid ni // sems can thams cad la yod par // mthong phyir ji snyed yod pa nyid.* D4024, sems tsam, phi, 55b. Gorampa follows the same reasoning in his *Appearance of Light of Good Explanations Illuminating the Three—the Basis, the Path, and the Result: Supplement to the Thorough Differentiation of the Three Types of Vows* [*Sdom pa gsum gyi rab tu dbye ba'i kha skong gzhi lam 'bras gsum gsal bar byed pa'i legs bshad 'od kyi snang ba*], in *Collected Works of Kun-mkhyen Go-rams-pa Bsod-nams-seng-ge*, 9:650–51.
43. *Elimination of Mistakes*, 534–35. Interestingly, Gorampa claims that in his contemporary Tibet only he has unmistakenly realized these points (535). For further details of his interpretation of the buddha-essence, see Ngawang Jorden, "Buddha-Nature."
44. Those of Sakya Pandita, Ngok Lotsawa, and Dölpopa addressed in Shakya Chokden's reply to questions 12 and 22.
45. This is a reference to the passage cited before and at the end of this chapter: "Because the perfect buddha-body emanates, / Because suchness is indifferentiable, / And because of having lineage, All embodied beings / Are always possessors of the buddha-essence."
46. This is a reference to Ngok Lotsawa's position.
47. *Golden Lancet*, 542–44.
48. Ibid., 545–47.
49. *slar yang bla ma'i rgyud 'dir ni.* This line is a part of the passage that first refers to the teachings on phenomena's being illusory, dream-like, and so on, and then states: "Having previously been presented in that way, / Later, in this sublime continuum, / In order to abandon the five faults / It was taught: 'the element does exist'" (*sngar ni de ltar rnam bzhag nas // slar yang bla ma'i rgyud 'dir ni // nyes pa lnga dag spang ba'i phyir // khams yod nyid ces bstan pa yin*). D4024, sems tsam, phi, 62a.
50. *gos ngan nang na rin chen ltar // sems can rnams la sangs rgyas kyi // snying po yod par gsungs pa ni // 'on kyang mdo sde 'ga' zhig dang // theg pa chen po rgyud bla mar // dgongs pa yin par shes par bya.*
51. *Golden Lancet*, 548–49.

52. Here too Shakya Chokden clearly treats the natural dharma-body as the dharma-sphere and emphasizes its causal nature.
53. Note that within the twofold division into the natural dharma-body and the resultant dharma-body, the primordial mind of the natural dharma-body corresponds to the latter.
54. See above, note 14, for the fuller passage. Note that Shakya Chokden refers specifically to the second dharmcakra as the sūtras of definitive meaning because this is the position of *Thorough Differentiation* that he is interpreting here.
55. This is a reference to the three levels taught in *Sublime Continuum*, D4024, sems tsam, phi, 56b: impure (*ma dag*), impure-pure (*ma dag dag pa*), and very pure (*shin tu rnam dag*), corresponding respectively to the levels of sentient beings, bodhisattvas, and buddhas.
56. *snying po gtsang bde rtag bdag dang // rtag brtan zhi ba g.yung drung dang // stobs sogs yon tan dbyer med pas // kun la khyab pa drang don du // rgyud bla'i gzhung gis gsal bar bstan // dbyer med gtsang sogs sangs rgyas kyi // shin tu rnam dag las gzhan du // med ces gsungs pa yin phyir ro // bstan bcos 'di dang rgyud bla mar // snying pos kun la khyab pa la // dngos la gnod byed ston pa'i tshul // mi 'dra'i khyad par gnyis gsungs pa // chos kun ngo bos stong pa dang // stobs sogs yon tan dbyer med pa // ma tshang zhes de rang stong dang // gzhan stong 'chad pa'i lugs yin no. Golden Lancet*, 549–51.
57. Ibid., 551–55.

BIBLIOGRAPHY

Abbreviated Perfection of Wisdom Sūtra [Āryaprajñāpāramitāsañcayagāthā, 'Phags pa shes rab kyi pha rol tu phyin pa sdud pa tshigs su bcad pa]. H17, sna tshogs, ka, 189a–215a.

Anālayo. "The Luminous Mind in Theravāda and Dharmaguptaka Discourses." *Journal of the Oxford Centre for Buddhist Studies* 13 (2017): 10–51.

Apte, Vaman Shrivaram. *The Practical Sanskrit-English Dictionary*. Rev. and enl. ed. Poona, India: Prasad Prakashan, 1957.

Āryavimuktisena. *Illumination of the "Twenty Thousand"* [*Nyi khri snang ba;* full title: *Āryapañcaviṃśatisāhasrikāprajñāpāramitopadeśaśāstrābhisamayālaṃkāravṛtti, 'Phags pa shes rab kyi pha rol tu phyin pa stong phrag nyi shu lnga pa'i man ngag gi bstan bcos mngon par rtogs pa'i rgyan gyi 'grel pa*]. D3787, shes phyin, ka, 14b–212a.

Asaṅga. *Bodhisattva-Grounds* [*Bodhisattvabhūmi, Byang chub sems dpa'i sa*]. D4037, sems tsam, wi, 1b–213a.

———. *Explanation of [Maitreya's] "Sublime Continuum of Mahāyāna"* [*Mahāyānottaratantraśāstravyākhyā, Theg pa chen po'i rgyud bla ma'i bstan bcos kyi rnam par bshad pa*]. D4025, sems tsam, phi, 74b–129a.

———. *Summary of Abhidharma* [*Abhidharmasamuccaya, Chos mngon pa kun las btus pa*]. D4049, sems tsam, ri, 43b–120a.

———. *Summary of Mahāyāna* [*Mahāyānasaṃgraha, Theg pa chen po bsdus pa*]. D4048, sems tsam, ri, 1a–43a.

Atīśa Dīpaṃkaraśrījñāna. *Ritual and Vows of the Generation of the Mind [of Awakening]* [*Cittotpādasaṃvaravidhikrama, Sems bskyed pa dang sdom pa'i cho ga'i rim pa*]. D3969, dbu ma, gi, 245a–248b.

Brough, John. "Some Notes on Maitrakanyaka: Divyāvadāna XXXVIII." *Bulletin of the School of Oriental and African Studies, University of London* 20, no. 1/3 (1957): 111–32.

Candrakīrti. *Engaging in Madhyamaka* [*Madhyamakāvatāra, Dbu ma la 'jug pa*]. D3861, dbu ma, 'a, 201b–219a.

Dense Array Sūtra [*Āryaghanavyūhanāmamahāyānasūtra, 'Phags pa rgyan stug po bkod pa zhes bya ba theg pa chen po'i mdo*]. D110, mdo sde, cha, 1b–55b.

Descent to Laṅka Sūtra [*Āryalaṅkāvatāramahāyānasūtra, 'Phags pa lang kar gshegs pa'i theg pa chen po'i mdo*]. D107, mdo sde, ca, 56a–191b.

Dharmakīrti. *Ascertainment of Valid Cognition* [*Pramāṇaviniścaya, Tshad ma rnam par nges pa*]. D4211, tshad ma, ce, 152b–230a.

———. *Commentary on Valid Cognition* [*Pramāṇavārttikakārikā, Tshad ma rnam 'grel gyi tshig le'ur byas pa*]. D4210, tshad ma, ce, 94b–151a.

Display of the Positive Qualities of Noble Mañjuśrī's Buddha-Field [*Āryamañjuśrībuddhakṣetraguṇavyūhanāmamahāyānasūtra, 'Phags pa 'jam dpal gyi sangs rgyas kyi zhing gi yon tan bkod pa zhes bya ba theg pa chen po'i mdo*]. D59, dkon brtsegs, ga, 248b–297a.

Dorjé Sherap (*rdo rje shes rab*). *Illuminating Lamp of Primordial Mind: Great Commentary on the Single Intent* [*Dgongs gcig pa'i 'grel chen snang mdzad ye shes sgron me*]. In *Writings on the Holy Dharma of Single Intent* [*Dam chos dgongs pa gcig pa'i yig cha*]. 2 vols. Thimphu, Bhutan: Kunsang Topgey, 1976.

Drakpa Gyeltsen (*grags pa rgyal mtshan*). *Precious Tree: Clear Realizations of Tantras* [*Rgyud kyi mngon par rtogs pa rin po che'i ljon shing*]. In *Excellent Words of Glorious Sakyapas* [*Dpal ldan sa skya pa'i gsung rab*], 18:240–496. N.p.: Mtsho sngon mi rigs dpe skrun khang, 2004.

———. *Purification Commentary Destroying Impurities: Explanation of "[Hevajra in] Two Chapters"* [*Brtag pa gnyis pa'i rnam par bshad pa ma dag pa rnams 'joms par byed pa'i rnam 'grel dag ldan*]. In *Collected Works of Sakya [Masters]* [*Sa skya bka' 'bum*], vol. 6 (*cha*), 387–651. 25 vols. Khams: Sde edge, 1736.

Edgerton, Franklin. *Buddhist Sanskrit Grammar and Dictionary*. New Haven, CT: Yale University Press, 1953.

Gokhale, V. V. "Fragments from the Abhidharmasamuccaya of Asaṃga." *Journal of the Bombay Branch of the Royal Asiatic Society*, n.s., 23 (1947): 13–38.

Gorampa Sönam Senggé (*go rams pa bsod nams seng ge*). *Appearance of Light of Good Explanations Illuminating the Three—the Basis, the Path, and the Result: Supplement to the Thorough Differentiation of the Three Types of Vows* [*Sdom pa gsum gyi rab tu dbye ba'i kha skong gzhi lam 'bras gsum gsal bar byed pa'i legs bshad 'od kyi snang ba*]. In *Collected Works of Kun-mkhyen Go-rams-pa Bsod-nams-seng-ge*, 9:645–705. 13 vols. Bir, India: Yashodhara Publications, 1995.

———. *Elimination of Mistakes about the Three Types of Vows: Answers to the Polemics and Questions Regarding the "[Thorough Differentiation of the] Three Types of Vows" Treatise* [*Sdom pa gsum gyi bstan bcos la dris shing rtsod pa'i lan sdom gsum 'khrul spong*]. In *Collected Works of Kun-mkhyen Go-rams-pa Bsod-nams-seng-ge*, 9:489–619. 13 vols. Bir, India: Yashodhara Publications, 1995.

———. *Lotus Blossom: Answers to Questions* [*Dris lan pad mo bzhad pa*]. In *Collected Works of Kun-mkhyen Go-rams-pa Bsod-nams-seng-ge*, 10:55–65. 13 vols. Bir, India: Yashodhara Publications, 1995.

Haribhadra. *Clear Meaning* [*Sputhārtha, Don gsal*; full title: *Abhisamayālaṃkāranāmaprajñāpāramitopadeśaśāstravṛtti, Shes rab kyi pha rol tu phyin pa'i man ngag gi bstan bcos mngon par rtogs pa'i rgyan ces bya ba'i 'grel pa*]. D3793, shes phyin, ja, 78b–140a.

Hevajra Tantra [*Hevajratantrarājanāma, Kye'i rdo rje zhes bya ba rgyud kyi rgyal po*]. D417, rgyud, nga, 1a–30a.

Hundred and Eight Names of the Perfection of Wisdom [*Āryaprajñāpāramitānāmāṣṭaśataka, 'Phags pa shes rab kyi pha rol tu phyin pa'i mtshan brgya rtsa brgyad pa zhes bya ba*]. D25, shes rab sna tshogs, ka, 174a–175b.

Jackson, David. *Enlightenment by a Single Means: Tibetan Controversies on the "Self-Sufficient White Remedy"* (dkar po chig thub). Vienna: Der Österreichischen Akademie der Wissenschaften, 1994.

Jikten Gönpo (*'jig rten mgon po*). *Single Intent* [*Dgongs gcig*]. In *Writings on the Holy Dharma of Single Intent* [*Dam chos dgongs pa gcig pa'i yig cha*]. 2 vols. Thimphu, Bhutan: Kunsang Topgey, 1976.

King of Meditative Concentration Sūtra [*Āryasarvadharmasvabhāvasamatāvipañcitasamādhirājanāmamahāyānasūtra, 'Phags pa chos thams cad kyi rang bzhin mnyam pa nyid rnam par spros pa ting nge 'dzin gyi rgyal po zhes bya ba theg pa chen po'i mdo*]. D127, mdo sde, da, 1b–170b.

Komarovski, Yaroslav. "From the Three Natures to the Two Natures: On a Fluid Approach to the Two Versions of Other-Emptiness from 15th Century Tibet." *Journal of Buddhist Philosophy* 2 (2016): 78–113.

———. *Radiant Emptiness: Three Seminal Works by the Golden Paṇḍita Shakya Chokden*. Oxford: Oxford University Press, 2020.

———. "Reburying the Treasure—Maintaining the Continuity: Two Texts by Shakya Chokden on the Buddha-Essence." *Journal of Indian Philosophy* 34, no. 6 (2006): 521–70.

———. "'There Are No Dharmas Apart from the Dharma-Sphere': Shakya Chokden's Interpretation of the Dharma-Sphere." In *The Other Emptiness: Rethinking the Zhentong Buddhist Discourse in Tibet*, ed. Klaus-Dieter Mathes and Michael R. Sheehy, 171–96. Albany: State University of New York Press, 2019.

———. *Tibetan Buddhism and Mystical Experience*. Oxford: Oxford University Press, 2015.

———. *Visions of Unity: The Golden Paṇḍita Shakya Chokden's New Interpretation of Yogācāra and Madhyamaka*. Albany: State University of New York Press, 2011.

Lion's Roar of Śrīmālādevī [*Āryaśrīmālādevīsiṃhanādanāmamahāyānasūtra, 'Phags pa lha mo dpal phreng gi seng ge'i sgra zhes bya ba theg pa chen po'i mdo*]. D92, dkon brtsegs, cha, 255a–277b.

Litany of the Ultimate Names of Mañjuśrī the Primordial Mind Being [*Mañjuśrījñānasattvasyaparamārthanāmasaṃgīti, 'Jam dpal ye shes sems dpa'i don dam pa'i mtshan yang dag par brjod pa*]. D360, rgyud, ka, 1b–13b.

Maitreya. *Differentiation of Phenomena and the Nature of Phenomena* [*Dharmadharmatāvibhāga, Chos dang chos nyid rnam par 'byed pa*]. D4022, sems tsam, phi, 46b–49a.

———. *Differentiation of the Middle and Extremes* [*Madhyāntavibhāga, Dbus dang mtha' rnam par 'byed pa*]. D4021, sems tsam, phi, 40b–45a.

———. *Ornament of Clear Realizations* [*Abhisamayālaṃkāranāmaprajñāpāramitopadeśaśāstrakārikā, Shes rab kyi pha rol tu phyin pa'i man ngag gi bstan bcos mngon par rtogs pa'i rgyan zhes bya ba'i tshig le'ur byas pa*]. D3786, shes phyin, ka, 1a–13a.

———. *Ornament of Mahāyāna Sūtras* [*Mahāyānasūtrālaṃkāra, Theg pa chen po mdo sde'i rgyan*]. D4020, sems tsam, phi, 1a–39a.

———. *Sublime Continuum of Mahāyāna* [*Mahāyānottaratantraśāstra, Theg pa chen po rgyud bla ma*]. D4024, sems tsam, phi, 54b–73a.

Nagao, Gadjin. "Usages and Meanings of Pariṇāmanā." In *Mādhyamika and Yogācāra: A Study of Mahāyāna Philosophies,* trans. and ed. Leslie Kawamura, 83–90. Albany: State University of New York Press, 1991.

Nāgārjuna. *Praise of the Dharma-Sphere* [*Dharmadhātustotra, Chos kyi dbyings su bstod pa*]. D1118, bstod tshogs, ka, 63b–67b.

———. *Precious Garland of Advice for the King* [*Rājaparikathāratnāvali, Rgyal po la gtam bya ba rin po che'i phreng ba*]. D4158, spring yig, ge, 107a–126a.

———. *Wisdom: Root Stanzas on Madhyamaka* [*Prajñānāmamūlamadhyamakakārikā, Dbu ma rtsa ba'i tshig le'ur byas pa shes rab ces bya ba*]. D3824, dbu ma, tsa, 1a–19a.

Ngawang Jorden. "Buddha-Nature through the Eyes of Go rams pa Bsod nams seng ge in Fifteenth-Century Tibet." PhD diss., Harvard University, 2003.

Perfection of Wisdom Sūtra in Twenty-Five Thousand Lines [*Pañcaviṃśatisāhasrikāprajñāpāramitā, Shes rab kyi pha rol tu phyin pa stong phrag nyi shu lnga pa*]. D9, nyi khri, ka, 1b–ga, 381a.

Pradhan, Prahlad, ed. *Abhidharmakośabhāṣyam of Vasubandhu.* Patna, India: K. P. Jayaswal Research Institute, 1975.

Puṇḍarīka. *Stainless Light* [*Vimalaprabhā, Dri ma med pa'i 'od;* full title: *Vimalaprabhānāmamūlatantrānusāriṇīdvādaśasāhasrikālaghukālacakratantrarājaṭīkā, Bsdus pa'i rgyud kyi rgyal po dus kyi 'khor lo'i 'grel bshad rtsa ba'i rgyud kyi rjes su 'jug pa stong phrag bcu gnyis pa dri ma med pa'i 'od ces bya ba*]. D1347, rgyud, tha, 107b–da, 297a.

Rhoton, Jared Douglas. Introduction to *A Clear Differentiation of the Three Codes: Essential Distinctions among the Individual Liberation, Mahāyāna, and Tantric Systems,* by Sakya Pandita Künga Gyeltsen, 3–35. Trans. Jared Douglas Rhoton. Albany: State University of New York Press, 2002.

Sakya Pandita Künga Gyeltsen (*sa skya paṇḍita kun dga' rgyal mtshan*). *A Clear Differentiation of the Three Codes: Essential Distinctions among the Individual Liberation, Mahāyāna, and Tantric Systems.* Trans. Jared Douglas Rhoton. Albany: State University of New York Press, 2002.

———. *Thorough Clarification of the Sage's Intent* [*Thub pa'i dgongs pa rab tu gsal ba*]. In *Collected Works of Sakya [Masters]* [*Sa skya bka' 'bum*], vol. 10 (*tha*), 1–198. 25 vols. Khams: Sde edge, 1736.

———. *Thorough Differentiation of the Three Types of Vows* [*Sdom pa gsum gyi rab tu dbye ba*]. In *A Clear Differentiation of the Three Codes: Essential Distinctions among the Individual Liberation, Mahāyāna, and Tantric Systems*, trans. Jared Douglas Rhoton. Albany: State University of New York Press, 2002.

———. *Treasure of the Science of Valid Cognition: The Root Text and the Commentary* [*Tshad ma rigs pa'i gter gyi rtsa ba dang 'grel pa*]. N.p.: Bod ljongs mi dmangs dpe skrun khang, 1989.

Śāntideva. *Compendium of Training* [*Śikṣāsamuccaya, Bslab pa kun las btus pa*]. D3940, dbu ma, khi, 3a–194b.

Schmithausen, Lambert. "*Kuśala* and *Akuśala*: Reconsidering the Original Meaning of a Basic Pair of Terms of Buddhist Spirituality and Ethics and Its Development up to Early Yogācāra." In *The Foundation for Yoga Practitioners: The Buddhist "Yogācārabhūmi" Treatise and Its Adaptation in India, East Asia, and Tibet*, ed. Ulrich Timme Kragh, 440–95. Cambridge, MA: Harvard University Press, 2013.

Shakya Chokden (*shākya mchog ldan*). *Enjoyment Ocean of the Entirely Good Dharma: Explanation of the Extensive Treatise "Commentary on Valid Cognition"* [*Rgyas pa'i bstan bcos tshad ma rnam 'grel gyi rnam bshad kun bzang chos kyi rol mtsho*]. In *Collected Writings of Gser-mdog paṇ-chen Śākya-mchog-ldan*, 18:189–693. 24 vols. Thimphu, Bhutan: Kunzang Tobgey, 1975.

———. *Essence of Sūtras and Tantras: Explanation of the Buddha-Essence* [*Sangs rgyas kyi snying po'i rnam bshad mdo rgyud snying po*]. In *Collected Writings of Gser-mdog paṇ-chen Śākya-mchog-ldan*, 13:124–36. 24 vols. Thimphu, Bhutan: Kunzang Tobgey, 1975. Translated in Yaroslav Komarovski, "Reburying the Treasure—Maintaining the Continuity: Two Texts by Shakya Chokden on the Buddha-Essence," *Journal of Indian Philosophy* 34, no. 6 (2006): 521–70.

———. *Garlands of Waves of the Ocean of Yogācāras' Scriptures: Explanation of the Holy Dharma of [Asaṅga's] "Summary of Higher Knowledge"* [*Dam pa'i chos mngon pa kun las btus pa'i rnam par bshad pa rnal 'byor spyod gzhung rgya mtsho'i rlabs kyi phreng ba*]. In *Collected Writings of Gser-mdog paṇ-chen Śākya-mchog-ldan*, 14:1–339. 24 vols. Thimphu, Bhutan: Kunzang Tobgey, 1975.

———. *Golden Lancet: Resolved Abundant Discourse on the "Thorough Differentiation of the Three Types of Vows" Treatise* [*Sdom gsum gyi rab tu dbye ba'i bstan bcos kyi 'bel gtam rnam par nges pa legs bshad gser gyi thur ma*]. In *Collected Writings of Gser-mdog paṇ-chen Śākya-mchog-ldan*, 6:439–7:229. 24 vols. Thimphu, Bhutan: Kunzang Tobgey, 1975.

———. *Good Questions about the "Thorough Differentiation of the Three Types of Vows"* [*Sdom gsum rab dbye la dri ba legs pa*]. In *Collected Writings of Gser-mdog paṇ-chen Śākya-mchog-ldan*, 17:448–62. 24 vols. Thimphu, Bhutan: Kunzang Tobgey, 1975.

Shih, Ru-nien. "The Concept of 'Innate Purity of Mind' in the Agamas and Nikayas." *Journal of World Religions* 13 (2009): 117–76.

Sobisch, Jan-Ulrich. *The Buddha's Single Intention: Drigung Kyobpa Jikten Sumgön's*

Vajra Statements of the Early Kagyü Tradition. Somerville, MA: Wisdom Publications, 2020.

———. Foreword to *Illuminator, A Light of Gnosis: The Great Commentary on the Single Intention,* by Dorje Sherab. Ed. Jan-Ulrich Sobisch. Munich: Garchen Stiftung, 2015.

———. "Were Sa-pan and 'Jig-rten-mgon-po 'Neoconservatives'? Utility and Futility of Source-Culture Alien Categories." *Indo-Iranian Journal* 53, no. 1 (2010): 23–33.

Sūtra Benefiting Aṅgulimāla [*Āryāṅgulimālīyanāmamahāyānasūtra, 'Phags pa sor mo'i phreng ba la phan pa zhes bya ba theg pa chen po'i mdo*]. D213, mdo sde, tsha, 126a–206b.

Sūtra Requested by Noble Vimaladattā [*Āryavimaladattāparipṛcchānāmamahāyānasūtra, 'Phags pa dri ma med kyis byin pas zhus pa zhes bya ba theg pa chen po'i mdo*]. D77, dkon brtsegs, ca, 241a–261b.

Tathāgata-Essence Sūtra [*Āryatathāgatagarbhanāmamahāyānasūtra, 'Phags pa de bzhin gshegs pa'i snying po zhes bya ba theg pa chen po'i mdo*]. D258, mdo sde, za, 245b–259b.

Tsering Wangchuk. *The "Uttaratantra" in the Land of Snows: Tibetan Thinkers Debate the Centrality of the Buddha-Nature Treatise.* Albany: State University of New York Press, 2017.

Union Tantra [*Saṃpuṭanāmamahātantra, Yang dag par sbyor ba zhes bya ba'i rgyud chen po*]. D0381, rgyud, ga, 73b–158b.

Vajradhvaja's Dedication [*Vajradhvajapariṇāmanā, Rdo rje rgyal mtshan gyi bsngo ba*]. H94, phal chen, kha, 169b–ga, 67a.

Vajragarbha. *Extensive Commentary on the "Condensed Meaning of the Hevajra Tantra"* [*Hevajrapiṇḍārthaṭīkā, Kye'i rdo rje bsdus pa'i don gyi rgya cher 'grel pa*]. D1180, rgyud, ka, 1–126a.

Vajrapāṇi. *Meaning Commentary on the Cakrasaṃvara Tantra* [*Lakṣābhidhānāduddhṛitalaghutantrapiṇḍārthavivaraṇa, Mngon par brjod pa 'bum pa las phyung ba nyung ngu'i rgyud kyi bsdus pa'i don rnam par bshad pa*]. D1402, rgyud, ba, 78b–141a.

Vasubandhu. *Commentary on [Maitreya's] "Differentiation of the Middle and Extremes"* [*Madhyāntavibhāgaṭīkā, Dbus dang mtha' rnam par 'byed pa'i 'grel pa*]. D4027, sems tsam, bi, 1a–27a.

———. *Explanation of the Ornament of Sūtras* [*Sūtrālaṃkārabhāṣya, Mdo sde'i rgyan gyi bshad pa*]. D4026, sems tsam, phi, 129b–260a.

———. *Explanation of the "Treasury of Abhidharma"* [*Abhidharmakośabhāṣya, Chos mngon pa'i mdzod kyi bshad pa*]. D4090, mngon pa, ku, 26a–khu, 95a.

———. *Praise to the Three Buddha-Bodies* [*Triratnastotra, Dkon mchog gsum gyi bstod pa*]. D1146, bstod tshogs, ka, 109b–110a.

———. *Principles of Explanation* [*Vyākhyāyukti, Rnam par bshad pa'i rigs pa*]. D4061, sems tsam, shi, 29a–134b.

———. *Treasury of Abhidharma* [*Abhidharmakośakārikā, Chos mngon pa'i mdzod kyi tshig le'ur byas pa*]. D4089, mngon pa, ku, 1a–25a.

Ziporyn, Brook. *Evil and/or/as the Good: Omnicentrism, Intersubjectivity, and Value Paradox in Tiantai Buddhist Thought.* Harvard-Yenching Institute Monograph Series, 51. Cambridge, MA: Harvard University Asia Center, 2000.

INDEX

Abbreviated Perfection of Wisdom Sūtra, 28, 29
Abhidharma, 54. *See also* higher Abhidharma; lower Abhidharma
abode-transformation, 121, 122
accomplishers, 48, 60, 62, 64–66, 70, 72
accomplishing causes, 48, 60, 62, 66, 71
accomplishing karmas, 65–66
actual existence, 49, 89–90, 91, 130, 181n61
adventitious defilements, 8, 97, 115–16, 188n14
adventitious obscurations, 2, 114–15, 186n125
aggregates, 44, 83, 143, 179n33
Alīkākārvāda, 12
analogies and examples: brass turning to gold, 123; cataracts, 106; churning butter from water, 24; crystal/sunstone, 25, 165n21; fire and heat, 44, 139; fire and smoke, 127, 128; food mixed with poison, 41; gold present in earth, 99; head of statue and its maker, 57; interest on contract, 57; milk and water, 121, 122; ocean and waves, 5; precious image in rags, 44, 51, 87, 141, 145, 146; rabbit horns, 95; seeds and sprouts, 100; sky with clouds, 100, 140; sons of barren woman, 48, 60, 63; son using father's wealth, 22, 23; sun, light, and rays, 129; swans drinking milk from water, 122; treasure under poor person's house, 137; water and waves, 140
analytical cessations, 81, 82, 95, 161n16, 178n22
applied thought, 58
apprehended and apprehender, 10, 83, 85, 92, 106, 108, 109, 133, 140–41, 182–83n88, 184n110
āryas, 30, 106, 169n30; dedicating virtues of, 23; dharmas of, 8, 9, 50, 97, 98, 99–100; direct perception by, 9; individually self-cognizing primordial mind of, 143; Mahāyāna, 136, 190n27; meditative equipoise of, 10, 106; positive qualities of, 29
Āryavimuktisena; *Illumination of the "Twenty Thousand,"* 100, 183n91
Asaṅga, 18; *Bodhisattva-Grounds,* 88, 134, 180n52; *Explanation of "Sublime Continuum of Mahāyāna,"* 129, 130, 131, 132; *Summary of Mahāyāna,* 49, 51, 59, 74, 79, 119, 121–22, 187n143. See also *Summary of Abhidharma*
aspirational resolve: dedication and, 8, 10–11, 45, 50, 112, 113, 115–16, 171n55; transformation by, 117–18, 186n135; two types, 11, 116, 118–19
Atiśa, 21
awakening: sprouts of, 10, 100, 183n92; three types, 16

black karmas, 61; black fruitions, 33, 60; Gorampa's views, 63, 66–68; white fruitions, 33, 48, 60, 61, 62
blended karmas and fruitions, 49, 60, 62, 63, 66–68, 69, 71–73
bodhicitta: shepherd-like, 116, 186n128; vajra of, 93
bodhisattva ground, first, 136, 186n125
buddha-element, 28, 41–44, 133–34, 139, 141–42, 145
buddha-essence, 1, 3; dedicating, 23, 25, 32, 86, 87, 165n21; direct perception of, 9; Dorjé Sherap's three characteristics, 24; Gorampa's and Shakya Chokden's views, compared, 148–49, 152–53; Gorampa's views, 9, 126–27, 142–44; Indian texts on, 19; as interpretive or definite, 45, 141–48; as naturally pure element, 5, 86; nine essences (examples) and, 51, 125, 128, 188n5; pervasiveness of, 135–41; questions on, 49; Sakya Pandita's views, 11, 34, 41–45, 125–26; Shakya Chokden's views, 79, 87, 126, 136, 190n27; in Tibet, polemicization of, 18; ultimate and, 125–35; as uncompounded, 121; as virtue, 25, 27, 32, 165n21
buddha-ground, 86, 88, 99, 129, 132, 183n92
buddhahood: buddha-essence and, 5, 129, 132; dedication and, 20, 115–16; dharma-sphere and, 10, 26; as permanent, 92; Shakya Chokden's view of, 141, 147, 192n55; suitability for, 145; as virtue, 15
buddha-lineage, 100, 148
buddha-nature. *See* buddha-essence
buddha-powers, 84, 147
buddhas: body, speech, mind of, 28; five primordial minds of, 182n74; reality-body of, 141; tantric visualization of, 116
Buddhist practice, 7, 9, 13, 20, 21, 83–84, 107, 153, 154
Candrakīrti, 45, 142
causal conditions, 9, 99
causal lineage, 49, 96–97
causative condition, 77
causes: and results, interdependence of, 29–30; types, 8, 15, 59, 160n14. *See also individual causes*
cessation of discrimination and feelings, 161n16
"Chapter Requested by Maitreya," 84
Chinese Buddhism, 157n1
Cittamātra, 57, 182n71
coemergent causes, 160n14
cognition, 42, 114–15, 121, 134. *See also* valid cognition
Collected Topics, 104, 183n96
Commentary on Valid Cognition (Dharmakīrti), 35, 38, 49, 89–90, 91, 99, 180n57, 182–83n88
compassion, 15, 20, 35, 113, 128, 168n20. *See also* emptiness with essence of compassion
completing evils, 33, 61
completing karmas, 33, 61, 64
completing virtues, 33, 61
compositional factors, 65–66
concomitant causes, 160n14
concordant causes, 62, 66, 158n4
consciousness, 10, 65, 106; freedom from proliferation as, 135; fruitional, 121; impure, 84; and primordial mind, distinguishing, 106, 133, 134, 189n21; two approaches to, 2–3. *See also* eight collections of consciousness; universal basis consciousness
conventionalities, correct and wrong, 108
conventional reality, 9, 41, 84, 96, 107, 108–9, 142, 143–44
correct view, 69–70

dedicatable cause, 41, 50, 112, 114, 115, 116–18
dedication, 23, 86, 123; Buddhist emphasis on, 20, 21, 27; to high state and

definite goodness, 114; meaningless, two types, 8, 112–13, 185n120; purpose of, 115; realistic and unrealistic, distinctions between, 6–7, 11, 45, 50, 116, 117, 118; results of, 117–18; transformation as essential to, 10, 39–40, 50, 112; translating term, 162n27. *See also under* aspirational resolve; buddha-essence
dedication of dharma-sphere: Gorampa's view, 117–18; as harmful, 8, 40–41, 113, 154; questions on, 50, 173n20; refutations of, 23, 32–35, 39–40; Shakya's Chokden's view, 85–86, 100, 114, 116–17; as suitable, 164n20. See also *Vajradhvaja's Dedication*
definitive meaning, 9, 26, 44, 131, 142, 143, 147, 192n54
Dense Array Sūtra, 25, 165n21
dependent origination, 8, 30, 116, 117, 164n16
Descent to Laṅka Sūtra, 143
desire realm: blended karmas and fruitions in, 49, 60, 68, 71, 72–73; mental states of, 58–59; virtues of, 66–67, 68, 73; virtuous and nonvirtuous karmas in, 69–70
developmental lineage, 100, 126–27; form-bodies and, 128–29; as positive qualities, 127; stainless seeds and, 10, 123; as sugata-essence, 49, 125, 131–32
dharma-body, 187n143; as both impermanent and permanent, 181n68; buddha-essence and, 11, 24, 136, 142, 146–48; Gorampa's views, 54–55; mahāmudrā and, 6, 28; natural, 138, 140, 147, 192nn52–53; naturally nirvāṇic, 140, 141; as naturally pure element, 5; resultant, 147, 192n53; Shakya Chokden's views, 93, 121, 122, 132
Dharmakīrti, 88, 92, 93. See also *Commentary on Valid Cognition*
dharma-possessors, 106, 109
dharmas, 16; ārya's, causes of, 8, 9, 50, 97, 98, 99–100; dharma-sphere and, 102, 103, 105, 106–9; emptiness of, 148; pure, 84; three types, 78–79; Vasubandhu's ten meanings, 157n1
Dharmas of Maitreya, 84, 92, 93, 97, 98, 99, 134, 137, 181n67. See also *Differentiation of the Middle and Extremes; Ornament of Clear Realizations; Ornament of Mahāyāna Sūtras; Sublime Continuum of Mahāyāna*
dharma-sphere, 9, 49, 50; aspirational resolve and, 11; as cause of dharmas (Asaṅga), 16; Dorjé Sherap's views, 5, 26; Gorampa's and Shakya Chokden's views, compared, 123–24, 148–49; Gorampa's views, 7–8, 94–95, 97, 143; Sakya Pandita's views, 6–7, 32–35, 38–39, 46, 93, 94, 96, 101, 184n98; Shakya Chokden's views, 9–11, 84, 88–89, 92–93, 96, 97, 98–100, 119–20, 138, 179n41, 183n90
dharma-sphere as virtue, 17, 23–24, 153; Dorjé Sherap's views, 5–6; Gorampa's views, 7–9, 76–78, 101, 102–3, 180n57; questions on, 49–50, 74–76; Sakya Pandita's views, 6–7, 36–37, 40–41, 75, 105; Shakya Chokden's textual statements on, 78–83; Shakya Chokden's views, 9–10, 83–86, 101–2, 109, 110. *See also* dedication of dharma-sphere
Differentiation of the Middle and Extremes (Maitreya), 106; on dharma-sphere, 23, 37, 49, 74, 76, 99, 107, 111; on nonobservation, 108; Shakya Chokden's interpretations, 107–8; on virtue, uncompounded, 79
Dölpopa Sherap Gyeltsen, 131, 191n44
dominant conditions, 99
dominant results, 68, 160–61n14
Dorjé Sherap, 3, 4, 151, 153; approach of, 30; Sakya Pandita and, 32, 34, 46; and Shakya Chokden, comparisons of, 12; on ultimate virtue, 5–6, 11–12, 154. See also *Illuminating Lamp of Primordial Mind*

Drakpa Gyeltsen, 88, 126, 127, 129, 180n53. See also *Purification Commentary Destroying Impurities*
Drigung Kyoppa Jiketen Gönpo. *See* Jikten Gönpo

eight collections of consciousness, 1, 7, 42, 126, 133, 134, 189n24
eight extremes of proliferations, 5, 24, 164n16
Elimination of Mistakes about the Three Types of Vows (Gorampa), 47; on dharma-sphere as virtue, 173n20; focus of, 152; on *Good Questions*, 175n2; order of questions, 171n6
emptiness, 16, 90, 99; as causes and results, 29–30; as definitive meaning, 142; as nonimplicative negation, 133; sugata-essence and, 35, 43–44, 141–42, 168n17; with supreme of all aspects, 93; synonyms of, 23; as virtue, 17. *See also* primordial mind of emptiness
emptiness with essence of compassion, 35, 49, 125
equanimity, 32, 55, 158n4, 167n7; as feeling, 56, 57, 59–60, 68; as unspecified phenomena, 48, 56–57, 59; usages of term, 56–58
ethics, 2, 20, 24
existent virtue, 5, 21–22, 23, 26, 27, 86, 88; as accomplished, 111–12; Sakya Pandita's views, 32, 34, 38–39, 41
Explanation of the "Treasury of Abhidharma" (Vasubandhu), 178n19; on black and white karmas, 66–67; on blended karmas, 69, 72–73; on lineage, 183n90; on motivation, 64–65; on ultimate unspecified phenomena, 159–60n10, 178n22; on virtues, usage of, 14, 80
explicit meaning, damage to, 44, 129, 141, 143, 145, 147, 148, 178n25
extinguishing karmas, 67

feelings, mental and bodily, 58–59
five faults, 44, 129, 141, 143, 145, 147, 170n50
form-bodies, 127, 128–29
formless realm, 59, 66, 122, 176n23
form realms, 58–59, 66, 122
freedom from extremes, 5, 28, 96, 105
freedom from proliferations, 116, 117; dedication and, 8, 154; dharma-sphere as, 38, 43, 46, 78, 94, 97, 105, 126, 135, 149, 180n57; of four extremes, 143; as implicative negation, 135; nature of mind as, 9, 145; nonimplicative negation factor of, 137; sugata-essence as, 7, 41, 134
fruitional causes, 55, 56, 59, 66, 68, 70, 160n14
fruitional results, 55, 68, 70, 72, 82, 83, 160n14
functioning capacity, 1, 15–17, 42, 91, 139, 153; dedication and, 30, 39; of dharma-sphere, 6, 7, 8, 9, 38, 85, 97–99; of primordial mind, 20; of virtue, 6, 14, 15, 25, 26, 37, 47

Garland Sūtra, 164–65n20
Geluk tradition, 182n78, 183n96
general characteristics, two types, 90–91
generosity, 17, 33, 63, 158n4, 160–61n14
Golden Lancet (Shakya Chokden), 47, 102; approach of, 53–54, 152–53; order of questions in, 171n6
Good Questions about the "Thorough differentiation of the Three Types of Vows" (Shakya Chokden), 153; on dharma-sphere, dedication of, 50–51; on dharma-sphere, virtue of, 49–50, 74–76, 173n20; Gorampa's opinion of, 175n2; intention and effect of, 47; order of questions, 171n6; second dharmacakra in, 152; three key challenges posed by, 51–52; on virtues and results, 48–49

Gorampa (Gowo Rapjampa Sönam Senggé), 3, 153; *Lotus Blossom*, 180n57; on question 1, 54–55; on question 2, 56–57; on question 3, 61, 62–63; on questions 4 and 5, 61, 63; on question 6, 61–62, 64–66; on question 7, 62, 66–68; on question 8, 76; on question 9, 77; on question 10, 89–90, 180n57; on question 11, 94–95, 182n78; on question 12, 126–28; on question 13, 97–98; on question 14, 77–78; on question 15, 102–3; on question 16, 103–4; on question 17, 104; on question 18, 110–11; on question 19, 112–13; on question 20, 117–18; on question 21, 120; on question 22, 128; on question 23, 136–37; on question 24, 142–44; on Sakya Pandita, 12, 31, 52, 61, 81; on Shakya Chokden, 53, 75, 126–27, 175n2; on ultimate virtue, overview, 7–8, 11–12. See also *Elimination of Mistakes about the Three Types of Vows*

happiness, 58; as fruition, 68; karmas and, 33; of liberation and fruitional, distinctions, 55; mahāmudrā and, 29; physical and mental, 75; ultimate, 83; and virtue, relationship of, 6, 14, 17, 32, 54
Haribhadra; *Clear Meaning*, 55, 78–79, 99, 181n68
Hevajra Tantra, 138
higher Abhidharma, 63, 71; Gorampa on, 64–65; karma types, 67, 68; on motivation, 48, 60, 62, 65, 70; on ultimate happiness and suffering, 83, 179n33. See also *Summary of Abhidharma* (Asaṅga)
homogeneous causes, 160n14
Hundred and Eight Names of the Perfection of Wisdom, 80–81

ignorance, 14–15, 65, 92, 103, 106, 160n13
Illuminating Lamp of Primordial Mind (Dorjé Sherap), 21, 22–23, 31–32, 163n2
illusory body of great bliss, 50, 75, 77, 78
impermanence, 91, 135; of buddha-essence, 132–33; of dharma-sphere, 88, 98; pervasion of, 38, 49, 89, 180n57; reasonings on, 90
implicative negation, 131, 135, 140
Indian Buddhism, 18–19, 153
intermediate existence, 66, 176n23
interpretive meaning, 45, 81, 93, 129, 142, 146, 147. *See also* special intent
introduction, 28

Jewel Heap Sūtra, 8, 117
Jikten Gönpo, 3, 4; distinctive approach of, 21–22; *Writings on the Holy Dharma of the Single Intent*, 87, 163n1, 179n44. See also *Single Intent*

Kagyü traditions, 31, 153
karmas: intention and application, 67; intention and intended, 32; in lower and higher Abhidharmas, distinctions in, 71–72; paths of, 70, 71; results of, experiencers, 162n27; types, 32, 60–61, 62, 72, 159n8; unspecified phenomena and, 102–3; as virtuous, criteria for, 14–15; worldly and world-transcending, 160n13. *See also* black karmas; blended karmas and fruitions; compositional factors; mixed karmas; stainless karmas; white karmas
karmic causality, 61–62
King of Meditative Concentration Sūtra, 142
knowables, 90–91, 100, 183n96; Gorampa on, 103; mode of being of, 10, 106; natural dharma-body in, 138; Shakya Chokden on, 123, 137, 139–40, 148

liberation-body, 121, 122, 187n143
lineage, 148; dharma-sphere as, 50, 97; fivefold division, 100, 126, 127, 132,

lineage (*continued*)
183n90. *See also* developmental lineage; naturally abiding lineage
lineage-element, 133
Lion's Roar of Śrīmālādevī Sūtra, 25, 132, 165n24
Litany of the Names of Mañjuśrī, 138
lower Abhidharma: blended karmas in, 62, 69; Gorampa on, 64–65; karmas in, three types, 71; on motivation, 48, 60; on results, separative and fruitional, 83; Shakya Chokden's interpretations, 70. See also *Treasury of Abhidharma* (Vasubandhu)
luminosity, 3, 5

Madhyamaka, 87, 109, 179n48, 180n53, 180n57. *See also* Niḥsvabhāvavāda Madhyamaka
mahāmudrā, 5–6, 27–29, 86, 87, 88, 154
Mahāyāna, 2, 16, 18–19, 22
Maitrakanyaka, 8, 50, 112, 113, 185n120, 185n122
Maitreya. See *Dharmas of Maitreya*
Mañjuśrī, 167n4
Mañjuśrī's Buddha-Field, 45, 118
mantras: śūnyatā, 83, 179n35; svabhāva, 83, 179n34
Mantrayāna. *See* Tantra
matter, inanimate, 7, 39, 42, 43, 51, 135–36, 137, 140
meditation, 20, 83–84, 107, 116. *See also* Buddhist practice
meditative equipoise, 85. *See also under* āryas
mere cognizance, 184n110
mere existence, 49, 89; and actual existence, differentiating, 90–93, 181n61, 181n65; function and, 6, 38, 97; impermanence of, 93, 180n57
mind, 29–30, 137, 138; subliminal, 3. *See also* nature of mind; primordial mind
mind training, 40–41, 50, 116, 186n128
mixed karmas, 34, 61, 72
mode of appearance, 10, 106–7
mode of being, 10, 27, 106–7
momentariness, 153; of buddha-essence, 126; of dharma-sphere, 88, 89, 92, 97, 119–20, 179n41
momentary impermanence, 88
moral conduct. *See* ethics
motionlessness, 161n16
motivations: causal and concurrent, 48, 60, 62, 63, 64–66, 67, 69; in dedication, 41; in lower Abhidharma, 14, 70, 158n4

Nāgārjuna, 30; *Praise of the Dharma-Sphere*, 177n6; *Precious Garland of Advice for the King*, 35; in Sakya Pandita's dream, 167n4. See also *Wisdom*
Nairātmyā, 50, 75, 83–84
naming, 77, 78
naturally abiding lineage, 51; Gorampa's views, 9, 126, 127, 143; Shakya Chokden's views, 9–10, 99, 100, 123, 134, 145
naturally pure element, 5–6, 23, 28, 86
natural purity, 3, 114–15, 130, 133, 148
nature-causes, 8, 97
nature of mind, 2–3, 4, 9, 143, 153
Ngok Lotsawa Loden Sherap, 130–31, 137
Ngorchen Künga Zangpo, 148
Niḥsvabhāvavāda Madhyamaka, 1, 19, 22, 182n78; Sakya Pandita's assumption of, 10, 87, 110, 152; Shakya Chokden on, 12, 152, 179n48, 182n71
nirvāṇa, 114–15, 157–58n1, 162n22; as compounded, 94–96, 182n79; as happiness, 44; nonabiding, 139; as uncompounded, 38, 79, 177n15; as virtue, 17, 82, 178n22
Nirvāṇa Sūtra, 146
nonanalytical cessation, 14, 36, 75, 81, 82, 159–60n10, 161n16, 178n22
nonimplicative negation, 85, 93, 131, 133, 137, 138, 139–40, 190n27

nonobservation, 41, 108, 184n110
nonrevelatory materiality, 70
nonvirtue in terms of ultimate, 14, 36, 159n10
nonvirtues, 2, 13, 177n1; causes and results, 15, 55, 57–59; as concept, 18; dharma-sphere and, 6, 10, 34, 38, 46; of element, 42–43; as projecting causes, 59; seeds as, 56; subsequently connected, 82–83, 123; types of, 14, 159n10; virtues concordant with, 63. *See also* ultimate nonvirtues
nonvirtuous karmas, 37–38, 58, 69–70, 178n19. *See also* black karmas

objects of abandonment, 71, 95, 160–61n14
objects of observation, 40, 41, 76, 78–79, 108, 177n1
omnipresent causes, 160n14
Ornament of Clear Realizations (Maitreya): on dedication, 41; on dharma-sphere as virtue, 49, 74; Gorampa's interpretations, 54, 76; on objects of observation, 177n1; on permanence, 92; refuting, 55; Shakya Chokden's interpretations, 78, 141, 190n36
Ornament of Mahāyāna Sūtras (Maitreya), 37, 100, 106, 107, 108, 111, 140
other-eliminations, 91
other-emptiness, 76, 107, 148; of dharma-sphere, 85, 88; nirvāṇa in, 114–15; Sakya Pandita's use of, 86; Shakya Chokden's view, 9, 12, 93, 108, 153

paths of meditation and seeing, 71
perfect, 79
perfect buddha-body, 126, 127, 132, 148, 191n45
perfection of wisdom, 77; mahāmudrā and, 5, 28, 29, 166n35; natural (*rang bzhin shes phyin*), 80
Perfection of Wisdom Sūtra in Twenty-Five Thousand Lines, 25, 165n24
Perfection of Wisdom sūtras, 30, 34–35, 77, 84, 106
permanence, 121, 135, 164n16; of dharma-body, 147; of dharma-sphere, 24, 26, 96, 98; *Sublime Continuum* on, 79, 146
permanence of continuity, 88, 92
person-made results, 160–61n14
pervasions, two types, 101, 103–4
phenomena: as changeless, 25–26; compounded, three types, 92–93; as dharma-sphere, 102, 103, 105, 109; as mental appearances, 22; in *Perfection of Wisdom*/Maitreya tradition, 84, 179n39; positive, 50, 110, 173n24; positive and negative, readings of, 111, 185n117; relative, 10, 107; three types, 78–79, 104, 157n2; uncompounded, 15–16, 45, 92–93, 161n16
Pökhangpa Rinchen Gyeltshen, 55, 58, 137
polemics: Gorampa's techniques, 53; Indian texts used for, 19; purposes served by, 153, 155; terminology's role in, 17–18; in Tibetan treaties, 31–35, 151–52, 154; on ultimate virtue, 3–4, 13–16, 151–52, 153, 154
Prāsaṅgika Madhyamaka, 109
predispositions/propensities, 59, 82–83, 99, 108, 121, 122, 187n143
primordial mind, 3, 88, 99, 140, 180nn52–53; of āryas, 143; buddhahood and, 141; as compounded, 132–33; conflicting views on, 12, 20; and consciousness, distinguishing, 134, 189n21; dharma-body as, 93, 147, 192n53; dharma-sphere as, 92, 93, 126, 135, 149, 182n74; exclusive existence of, 108; mode of seeing, 106; in tantric practice, 9, 83–84, 107
primordial-mind dharma-bodies, 129
primordial mind of emptiness, 130, 131, 132
producing causes, 59, 99, 160n14

productive causes, 6, 8, 26, 37, 97, 98
projecting causes, 9, 48, 59, 60, 71, 99
projecting evils, 33, 61
projecting karmas, 33, 61, 64, 65
projecting virtues, 33, 61
projectors, 48, 60, 62, 64–66, 70
provisional interpretations. *See* interpretive meaning
Purification Commentary Destroying Impurities (Drakpa Gyeltsen), 130, 148, 188n13
purity: innate, 157n1; of result, 141, 190n36; three levels of, 192n55; two types, 148; ultimate perfection of, 133. *See also* natural purity

reality-buddha, 131
reality-limit, 16, 23
reasonings, 30; on aspirational resolve, 118–19; on buddha-essence, 130, 132–33; on dharma-sphere, 38, 43, 96, 97; on dharma-sphere as virtue, 83–84; existence and product in, 90; on impermanence, 90; of result and of nature, distinctions in, 128; on stainless seeds, 120; on ultimate reality as changeless, 87
rebirth, 57, 138; blended fruitions and, 37–38, 49, 60, 68, 72; karmas and, 14–15, 33; in lower realms as impossible, 6, 8, 101, 102, 105, 109, 110
rebirth existence, 66
rejoicing, 114
relative reality. *See* conventional reality
Repaying Kindness Sūtra, 185n120. *See also* Maitrakanyaka
results: within causes, 31, 34, 87; concordant with causes, 68, 70, 114, 160n14; five types, 15, 114, 160n14. *See also individual results*
revelatory materiality, 70
root of existent virtue. *See* existent virtue
roots of virtues, 117; conventional, 5; creating, 6, 23; dedicating, 8, 21, 22, 27, 100, 112–13, 166n31; mahāmudrā and, 28; severing, 120; three types, 159n9

Sakya Pandita Künga Gyeltsen, 3, 23, 129, 149, 191n44; dream of, 167n4; and Ngok Lotsawa, comparison, 131; Shakya Chokden on, 9–10, 12, 55, 93, 133, 134–35; *Thorough Clarification of the Sage's Intent*, 129; *Treasure of the Science of Valid Cognition*, 90, 91; on ultimate virtue, 6–7, 11–12, 157n4; on virtue, fruition of, 14. See also *Thorough Differentiation of the Three Types of Vows*
Sakya tradition, 4, 183n96
Sāṃkhya school, 34, 91
Śāntideva; *Compendium of Training*, 35
Sarvāstivāda school, 178n19
Sautrāntika school, 180n57
second dharmacakra, 19, 76, 151; buddha-essence in, 81, 148, 190n27; dharma-body in, 147; dharma-sphere in, 46; in *Thorough Differentiation*, 152, 192n54
self: buddha-element as, 44; of non-Buddhists, 142, 147; substantially existent, 143; two types, 143–44
self-emptiness, 148; ārya dharmas in, 100; of dharma-sphere, 85; Sakya Pandita's assumption of, 9, 76, 81, 86, 87, 88, 93, 98; Shakya Chokden on, 12, 106–7
selflessness, two types, 16
sentient beings: buddha-essence/element of, Sakya Pandita's view, 7, 41–45, 135–36, 138–39, 141–42; buddha-essence of, Gorampa's view, 5, 136, 142–43, 148–49; buddha-essence of, later Tibetan interpretations, 128–29; buddha-essence of, Shakya Chokden's views, 86, 129–31, 132, 134, 137–40, 144–47, 148–49; dharma-sphere of, 26, 51, 100, 135, 138; element of, 41–43, 134, 147; motherly, 22; naturally abiding lineage of, 51, 141

separative results, 55, 83, 114, 160–61n14
Serdok Penchen Shakya Chokden. *See* Shakya Chokden
Shakya Chokden, 3, 4; on dedication, 154; *Essence of Sūtras and Tantras,* 190n27; Gorampa and, 52, 53, 73, 75, 175n2; inclusive approach of, 152–53, 155; on question 1, 55; on question 2, 57–60; on questions 8, 9, and 14, 85–89; on question 10, 90–93; on question 11, 95–96, 182n79; on questions 12 and 22, 128–35; on question 13, 98–100; on questions 15 through 17, 104–10; on question 18, 111–12; on question 19, 113–16; on question 20, 118–19; on question 21, 121–23; on question 23, 137–41; on question 24, 144–48; on ultimate virtue, overview, 9–10, 11–12, 157n4. See also *Golden Lancet; Good Questions about the "Thorough Differentiation of the Three Types of Vows"*
Sherap Jungné, 21, 26, 87
signlessness, 16, 23
Single Intent (Jikten Gönpo), 21, 153, 163n2; on emptiness, 29; as provocative, 151–52; refutations of, 86–87, 133; self-emptiness in, 76; and *Thorough Differentiation,* relationship of, 31–32, 167n6
six perfections, 20, 28, 166n35
space, 14, 34, 36, 75, 159–60n10, 161n16, 178n22
special intent, 11, 44, 51, 87, 129–30, 141, 145, 146. *See also* interpretive meaning
śrāvakas, 35, 108
stained seeds, 120, 121, 122
stainless karmas, 63, 67
stainless knowing, 9, 99, 121, 133, 183n92
stainless mental continuum, 7, 42, 134
stainless seeds, 8–10, 99, 100, 119, 120, 121–23, 183n92
Sublime Continuum of Mahāyāna (Maitreya), 19, 87; on buddha-element, 28, 44; on dharma-sphere, 8, 49, 74, 76; Gorampa's interpretations, 9, 126–27, 143, 144; later Tibetan interpretations of, 128–29; on nine essences, 51, 125, 188n5; on nothing to eliminate or establish, 29, 188n14; Sakya Pandita's interpretations, 11, 34–35; Shakya Chokden's interpretations, 79, 80, 121, 129, 130–31, 135, 139, 140, 147–48; on tathāgata-essence, three bases of application, 138; ten presentations on buddha-essence in, 129, 188n10; on three buddha-bodies, 88
subsequent attainment, 85, 106
substantial causes, 133, 134, 189n21
suchness, 79, 90; Asaṅga's use of, 16; dedicating, 23, 27; with defilements, 130, 132, 146; as indifferentiable, 126, 132, 148; as primordial mind, 99; undefiled, 146; as virtue, 36–37, 75, 76, 81
suffering, 83; of aggregates, 44, 83, 179n33; bodily feelings of, 58; completing evils and, 33; as fruition, 68; happiness and, 37; of others, 41; three types, contaminated virtues and, 82, 178n27
sugata-essence. *See* buddha-essence
Summary of Abhidharma (Asaṅga), 13–14, 19; on nonvirtue in higher realms, 122; self-emptiness in, 81, 187n21; Shakya Chokden's interpretations, 92, 181n70; on suffering, 179n33; on ultimate reality as uncompounded, 15; on virtue in terms of ultimate, 2, 6, 27, 36, 86, 157n4; on virtues in terms of entity, 35
Sūtra Benefiting Aṅgulimāla, 24
Sūtra Requested by Noble Vimaladattā, 117, 118, 171n55, 186n135
Svātantrika Madhyamaka, 109

Tantra, 116, 154, 182n71; buddha-essence in, 51, 135, 136; natural dharma-body in, 138; other-emptiness in, 12; primordial mind in, 9, 83–84, 93, 107

tathāgata-essence. *See* buddha-essence
Tathāgata-Essence Sūtra, 9, 24, 27, 143, 148
textual statements, 30
third dharmacakra, 19, 76, 146; buddha-essence in, 81, 145, 190n27; Dorjé Sherap and, 30; emphasis on, 151; Gorampa and, 152
Thorough Differentiation of the Three Types of Vows (Sakya Pandita), 31, 60, 92, 152, 153, 167n4; commentators' views, 58, 59, 69, 95, 104, 105–6, 113, 121, 129, 137; on dedication, 45, 112, 116–17, 119, 123; on dharma-sphere, 75, 76, 78, 89, 97, 101, 112, 135–36, 184n98; on equanimity, 56, 59–60; Gorampa's interpretations, 61, 62, 63, 67, 73, 89, 94–95, 102–4, 116–17; on karmas, 32–34, 60–61, 62–63, 67; self-emptiness in, 93, 98; on sentient beings' buddha-essence, 44–45, 141–42; Shakya Chokden's intentions, 47, 51–52, 149; Shakya Chokden's interpretations, 59–60, 62, 69, 71, 73, 78–79, 81, 82, 85–86, 88–89, 92, 98, 109, 110, 119–20, 126, 131, 138–39, 142, 144–46, 147–48, 192n54; and *Single Intent,* relationship of, 31–32, 167n6; strength of positions in, 45–46; on sugata-essence, 34–35, 125, 126, 128, 135–36, 141–42, 188n5; textual sources, 34–35, 94; *Vajradhvaja's Dedication* in, 34, 38, 39, 110; on virtue, defining, 54; Yogācāra in, 115
Three Bodhisattva Commentaries, 51, 135, 136, 138, 174n29
three buddha-bodies, 88, 126, 127
three natures, 107–8, 179n39, 184n108
three ultimate Jewels, 80
Tibetan texts, limitations of, 153–54
Treasury of Abhidharma (Vasubandhu), 19, 178n19; on afflictions of upper realms, 122; on blended karmas, 69; Gorampa's interpretations, 67; on motivation, 64, 70; on objects of abandonment, 71; Shakya Chokden's interpretations, 58; *virtues,* usage of, 80, 159n9. See also *Explanation of the "Treasury of Abhidharma"* (Vasubandhu)
Treatise on Engaging in Primordial Mind, 81–82
truth of path, 9, 114, 119, 120
twelve links of dependent origination, 64, 65–66
two abandonments, 180n52. *See also* objects of abandonment
two collections, 9, 15, 83–84, 154
two realities, 142

ultimate, 14, 16, 23, 36, 80, 106, 158n4
ultimate evil, 6, 36, 75
ultimate nature, 1, 2, 157n1
ultimate nonvirtues, 14, 55, 80, 82–83
ultimate reality, 29, 142–44; as changeless, 26; conventional reality and, 143–44; dedicating, 20, 31, 162n27; direct perception of, 9; diversity of views on, 3, 4; Mahāyāna use of term, 16; predispositions and, 99–100; in second and third dharmacakras, compared, 151; as sheer negation, 20; suffering and, 179n33; in Tibetan tradition, 14–16, 18, 161n15, 162n22; use of conceptuality to approach, 18–19; virtue and, 30, 32–33, 36
ultimate unspecified phenomena, 6, 14, 36, 75, 81, 159–60n10, 178n22
ultimate virtue, 2, 157n4; Asaṅga and Vasubandhu on, 13–14, 16, 159n9; contemplative practice and, 83–84; as contingent and context-dependent, 154–55; epistemological and ontological focus on, 19–20; five contested points on, 11–12; mahāmudrā and, 5–6; polemics of, 3–4, 13–16, 151–52, 153, 154; Sakya Pandita's views, 8, 34, 36; Shakya Chokden's views, 82–83, 97, 98, 133–35, 149, 153

Union Tantra, 35
universal basis consciousness, 3, 68, 121, 142; antidotes of, 9, 51, 99, 119, 120, 121; in Cittamātra, 57, 175n8; clarity and cognition factors on, 121; clarity in, 42, 134; equanimity in, 68; fruitional part, 122, 187n148; knowables in, 123; and primordial mind, relationship of, 9–10; and seeds, variant views on, 8–9, 48, 51, 56, 59, 99, 119; and sugata-essence, relationship of, 7, 25, 133, 164nn18–19, 165n21; usages of term, 56
universal principle, 91
unreal ideation, 10, 84, 106
unspecified phenomena, 8–9, 15, 120, 122; Asaṅga on, 13–14; dharma-sphere as, 50, 100–101, 102–3, 104–5; equanimity as, 48, 56–57, 59; rebirth and, 103; subsequently connected, 82; unobscured, 49, 74, 77, 81, 82, 121, 134; virtue of, 102. *See also* ultimate unspecified phenomena

Vaibhāṣika school, 66, 94, 95
Vajradhvaja's Dedication, 34; Gorampa's use of, 110–11; Sakya Pandita's interpretations, 31, 38, 39; Shakya Chokden's use of, 111–12, 113–14; tenth dedication in, 25, 26–27, 164n20
valid cognition, 44, 84, 96, 104, 108, 141
Vastusatpadārthavāda school, 93, 95, 96, 182n71
Vasubandhu: *Commentary on "Differentiation of the Middle and Extremes,"* 184n110; *Praise to the Three Buddha-Bodies*, 80. See also *Explanation of the "Treasury of Abhidharma"*; *Treasury of Abhidharma*
Vehicle of Characteristics, 88
virtue in terms of ultimate, 2, 27, 157n4, 159n9, 178n22
virtues, 15, 59, 137; as absence of evil, 6, 8, 36, 37, 49, 74, 75, 77, 81–82, 86, 98, 177n3; accumulated and existent, 26–27; Asaṅga's thirteen types, 13, 158n4; common feature of, 14, 15, 17; compounded and uncompounded, distinguishing, 79–80, 177nn14–15; as concepts, 18; concordant with nonvirtues, 63; contaminated, 82, 178n27; created, 113, 119; dedication and, 6–7, 10, 137; defining, 14, 32, 54, 122–23; imputed, 7–8, 76, 81, 153, 177n3; *kuśala* translated as, 17–18, 161n21; natural, 168n20; of oneself and others, 22–23, 113–14; of partial concordance with liberation, 86, 114; of partial concordance with merits, 114; and reality, variant approaches to, 16–17; relative, 109; scope of, 37, 43; stained and stainless, 48, 54–55, 59, 122; subsequently connected, 82–83, 123; in terms of entity, 35; three factors in naming, 82, 178n25; translation and usage, 13, 158n2; uncreated, 45, 51, 119, 123, 174n27; Vasubandhu's four types, 14, 159n9. *See also* dharma-sphere as virtue; existent virtue; roots of virtues; ultimate virtue
virtuous karmas, 1, 14, 160n14, 178n19; fruitions of, 58, 59, 69, 160n13; rebirth and, 33, 37–38. *See also* white karmas
vows, 72, 122–23

white dharmas, 82
white karmas, 61; black fruitions, 33, 48, 60, 61, 62; Gorampa's view, 62–63, 66–68; white fruitions, 33, 60
wisdom: realizing mode and multiplicity, 143; sugata-essence as factor of, 25; ultimate reality and, 15, 17, 154, 160n13; unafflicted, 5. *See also* perfection of wisdom; two collections
Wisdom (Nāgārjuna), 19; on eight extremes, 164n16; on interdependent origination and emptiness, 30; on

Wisdom (Nāgārjuna) (*continued*)
nonthings as compounded, 49; in question 11, 94–96, 182n79; Sakya Pandita's interpretations of, 34–35, 38, 40, 43–44, 138
worldly relative reality serving as method, 107
wrong view, 70, 73, 120

Yogācāra tradition, 19, 115, 152; external appearances in, 140–41; on phenomena, 22; Sakya Pandita's refutations of, 10, 109; two traditions, 182n71; universal basis consciousness in, 175n8. *See also* three natures
yogic relativity, 107

TRADITIONS AND TRANSFORMATIONS IN TIBETAN BUDDHISM

The Cosmos, the Person, and the Sādhana*: A Treatise on Tibetan Tantric Meditation*
Yael Bentor

Longing to Awaken: Buddhist Devotion in Tibetan Poetry and Song
Holly Gayley and Dominique Townsend, editors

Singer of the Land of Snows: Tibet as a Buddhist Imagined Community
Rachel H. Pang

Buddha in the Marketplace: The Commodification of Buddhist Objects in Tibet
Alex John Catanese

Milton Keynes UK
Ingram Content Group UK Ltd.
UKHW021919021224
3319UKWH00036B/728

9 780813 952161